THIS BOOK IS THE PROPERTY OF:

STATE _____
PROVINCE _____
COUNTY _____
PARISH _____
SCHOOL DISTRICT _____
OTHER _____

Book No. _____
Enter information
in spaces
to the left as
instructed

ISSUED TO	Year Used	CONDITION	
		ISSUED	RETURNED

PUPILS to whom this textbook is issued must not write on any page or mark any part of it in any way, consumable textbooks excepted.

1. Teachers should see that the pupil's name is clearly written in ink in the spaces above in every book issued.
2. The following terms should be used in recording the condition of the book: New; Good; Fair; Poor; Bad.

ISBN-13: 978-05386-7700-4
ISBN-10: 05386-7700-7

17 18 19 20 XXX 11 10 09 08

Printed in the United States of America

SOUTH-WESTERN
CENGAGE Learning

BA20GD1

TO THE STUDENT

These *Working Papers* are to be used in the study of Chapters 1-17 of CENTURY 21 ACCOUNTING. Forms are provided for:

(1) Work Together exercises
(2) On Your Own exercises
(3) Application Problems
(4) Mastery Problems
(5) Challenge Problems
(6) Reinforcement Activities 1 and 2

Printed on each page is the number of the problem in the textbook for which the form is to be used. Also shown is a specific instruction number for which the form is to be used.

You may not be required to use every form that is provided. Your teacher will tell you whether to retain or dispose of the unused pages.

The pages are perforated so they may be removed as the work required in each assignment is completed. The pages will be more easily detached if you crease the sheet along the line of perforations and then remove the sheet by pulling sideways rather than upward.

SOUTH-WESTERN

CENTURY 21

ACCOUNTING

MULTICOLUMN JOURNAL
WORKING PAPERS
CHAPTERS 1-17

CENTURY 21 ACCOUNTING

95 YEARS OF EXCELLENCE

Ross · Gilbertson · Lehman · Hanson

SEVENTH EDITION

1-1 WORK TOGETHER, p. 8

Completing the accounting equation

Assets	=	Liabilities	+	Owner's Equity
		3,000		8,000
10,000				6,000
63,000		35,000		

Extra form

Assets	=	Liabilities	+	Owner's Equity

Completing the accounting equation

Assets	=	Liabilities	+	Owner's Equity
23,000				13,000
		70,000		30,000
48,000		25,000		

Extra form

Assets	=	Liabilities	+	Owner's Equity

1-2 WORK TOGETHER, p. 12

Determining how transactions change an accounting equation

Trans. No.	Assets	=	Liabilities	+	Owner's Equity
1.					
2.					
3.					
4.					

Extra form

Trans. No.	Assets	=	Liabilities	+	Owner's Equity
1.					
2.					
3.					
4.					
5.					
6.					

Determining how transactions change an accounting equation

Trans. No.	Assets	=	Liabilities	+	Owner's Equity
1.					
2.					
3.					
4.					
5.					

Extra form

Trans. No.	Assets	=	Liabilities	+	Owner's Equity
1.					
2.					
3.					
4.					
5.					
6.					

1-3 WORK TOGETHER, p. 15

Preparing a balance sheet from information in an accounting equation

Extra form

Preparing a balance sheet from information in an accounting equation

Extra form

1-1 APPLICATION PROBLEM, p. 17

Completing the accounting equation

Assets	=	Liabilities	+	Owner's Equity
90,000		49,000		
		68,000		30,000
3,000				2,000
108,000		60,000		
19,000				11,000
		4,000		12,000
25,000		13,000		
		113,000		49,000
4,000				2,000
86,000		48,000		
12,000				7,000
		5,000		14,000
47,000		24,000		
		29,000		13,000
38,000				21,000
125,000		69,000		
11,000				6,000
		1,000		3,000

Extra form

Assets	=	Liabilities	+	Owner's Equity

1-2 APPLICATION PROBLEM, p. 17

Determining how transactions change an accounting equation

Trans. No.	Assets			=	Liabilities		+	Owner's Equity
	Cash	+	Supplies +	Prepaid Insurance =	Accts. Pay.— Swan's Supply	+	Accts. Pay.— York Co. +	Frank Mori, Capital
Beg. Bal. 1.	0 +2,000		0	0	0		0	0 +2,000
New Bal. 2.	2,000		0	0	0		0	2,000
New Bal. 3.								
New Bal. 4.								
New Bal. 5.								
New Bal. 6.								
New Bal. 7.								
New Bal. 8.								
New Bal.								

Extra form

Trans. No.	Assets			=	Liabilities		+	Owner's Equity
	Cash	+	Supplies +	Prepaid Insurance =		+	+	
Beg. Bal. 1.								
New Bal. 2.								
New Bal. 3.								
New Bal. 4.								
New Bal. 5.								
New Bal. 6.								
New Bal. 7.								
New Bal. 8.								
New Bal.								

Extra form

Trans. No.	Assets			=	Liabilities	+	Owner's Equity
	Cash	+ Supplies	+ Prepaid Insurance	=	+	+	
Beg. Bal. 1.							
New Bal. 2.							
New Bal. 3.							
New Bal. 4.							
New Bal. 5.							
New Bal. 6.							
New Bal. 7.							
New Bal. 8.							
New Bal. 9.							
New Bal. 10.							
New Bal. 11.							
New Bal. 12.							
New Bal. 13.							
New Bal. 14.							
New Bal. 15.							
New Bal. 16.							
New Bal.							

1-3 APPLICATION PROBLEM, p. 18

Determining how transactions change an accounting equation

Trans. No.	Assets			=	Liabilities		+	Owner's Equity
	Cash	+ Supplies	+ Prepaid Insurance	=	Accts. Pay. — Seiler Supply	+ Accts. Pay.— Miles Co.	+	Ellie VonSpreecken, Capital
Beg. Bal. 1.	0 +3,000	0	0		0	0		0 +3,000
New Bal. 2.	3,000	0	0		0	0		3,000
New Bal. 3.								
New Bal. 4.								
New Bal. 5.								
New Bal. 6.								
New Bal.								

Extra form

Trans. No.	Assets			=	Liabilities		+	Owner's Equity
	Cash	+ Supplies	+ Prepaid Insurance	=		+	+	
Beg. Bal. 1.								
New Bal. 2.								
New Bal. 3.								
New Bal. 4.								
New Bal. 5.								
New Bal. 6.								
New Bal.								

Extra form

Trans. No.	Assets			=	Liabilities	+	Owner's Equity
	Cash +	Supplies +	Prepaid Insurance =		+	+	
Beg. Bal. 1.							
New Bal. 2.							
New Bal. 3.							
New Bal. 4.							
New Bal. 5.							
New Bal. 6.							
New Bal. 7.							
New Bal. 8.							
New Bal. 9.							
New Bal. 10.							
New Bal. 11.							
New Bal. 12.							
New Bal. 13.							
New Bal. 14.							
New Bal. 15.							
New Bal. 16.							
New Bal.							

1-4 APPLICATION PROBLEM, p. 19

Determining where items are listed on a balance sheet

1	2	3
	Balance Sheet	
Items	Left Side	Right Side
1. Cash	Asset	
2. Michelle Sullivan, Capital		
3. Supplies		
4. Prepaid Insurance		
5. Accounts Payable—Action Laundry		
6. Anything owned		
7. Any amount owed		
8. Owner's capital account		

Extra form

1	2	3
	Balance Sheet	
Items	Left Side	Right Side
1.		
2.		
3.		
4.		
5.		
6.		
7.		
8.		

Extra form

	1	2	3
	Items	**Balance Sheet**	
		Left Side	**Right Side**
1.			
2.			
3.			
4.			
5.			
6.			
7.			
8.			
9.			
10.			
11.			
12.			
13.			
14.			
15.			
16.			
17.			
18.			
19.			
20.			
21.			
22.			
23.			
24.			
25.			
26.			
27.			
28.			
29.			
30.			

1-5 APPLICATION PROBLEM, p. 19

Preparing a balance sheet from information in an accounting equation

1-6 MASTERY PROBLEM, p. 19

Determining how transactions change an accounting equation and preparing a balance sheet

1.

Trans. No.	Assets			=	Liabilities	+	Owner's Equity
	Cash	+ Supplies	+ Prepaid Insurance	=	Accts. Pay.— Helfrey Co.	+	Nancy Dirks, Capital
Beg. Bal. 1.	0 +350	0	0		0		0 +350
New Bal. 2.	350	0	0		0		350
New Bal. 3.							
New Bal. 4.							
New Bal. 5.							
New Bal. 6.							
New Bal.							

2.

Extra forms

Trans. No.	Assets				=	Liabilities	+	Owner's Equity
	Cash	+	Supplies	+	Prepaid Insurance	=		+
Beg. Bal. 1.								
New Bal. 2.								
New Bal. 3.								
New Bal. 4.								
New Bal. 5.								
New Bal. 6.								
New Bal.								

1-7 CHALLENGE PROBLEM, p. 20

Applying accounting concepts to determine how transactions change the accounting equation

Trans. No.	Assets			=	Liabilities		+	Owner's Equity
	Cash	+ Supplies	+ Prepaid Insurance	=	Accts. Pay.— Mutual Sav. Bank	+ Accts. Pay.— Nelson Supply Company	+	Gregory Morgan, Capital
Beg. Bal. 1.	0 +1,500	0	0		0	0		0 +1,500
New Bal. 2.	1,500	0	0		0	0		1,500
New Bal. 3.								
New Bal. 4.								
New Bal. 5.								
New Bal. 6.								
New Bal. 7.								
New Bal.								

Extra form

Trans. No.	Assets			=	Liabilities		+	Owner's Equity
	Cash	+ Supplies	+ Prepaid Insurance	=		+	+	
Beg. Bal. 1.								
New Bal. 2.								
New Bal. 3.								
New Bal. 4.								
New Bal. 5.								
New Bal. 6.								
New Bal. 7.								
New Bal.								

Extra form

Trans. No.	Assets			=	Liabilities	+	Owner's Equity
	Cash	+ Supplies	+ Prepaid Insurance	=	+	+	
Beg. Bal. 1.							
New Bal. 2.							
New Bal. 3.							
New Bal. 4.							
New Bal. 5.							
New Bal. 6.							
New Bal. 7.							
New Bal. 8.							
New Bal. 9.							
New Bal. 10.							
New Bal. 11.							
New Bal. 12.							
New Bal. 13.							
New Bal. 14.							
New Bal. 15.							
New Bal.							

2-1 WORK TOGETHER, p. 29

Determining how transactions change an accounting equation

Trans. No.	Assets				=	Liabilities	+	Owner's Equity
	Cash	+ Accts. Rec.—Bowman Co.	+ Supplies	+ Prepaid Insurance	=	Accts. Pay.—Maxwell Co.	+	Susan Sanders, Capital
1.								
2.								
3.								
4.								

Extra form

Trans. No.	Assets				=	Liabilities	+	Owner's Equity
	Cash	+	+ Supplies	+ Prepaid Insurance	=		+	
1.								
2.								
3.								
4.								
5.								
6.								
7.								
8.								

Determining how transactions change an accounting equation

Trans. No.	Assets				= Liabilities +	Owner's Equity
	Cash	Accts. Rec.— + O'Leary Co. +	Supplies +	Prepaid Insurance =	Accts. Pay.— Barrett Co. +	Sue Marist, Capital
1.						
2.						
3.						
4.						

Extra form

Trans. No.	Assets				= Liabilities +	Owner's Equity
	Cash +	+	Supplies +	Prepaid Insurance =	+	
1.						
2.						
3.						
4.						
5.						
6.						
7.						
8.						

2-2 WORK TOGETHER, p. 31

Preparing a balance sheet

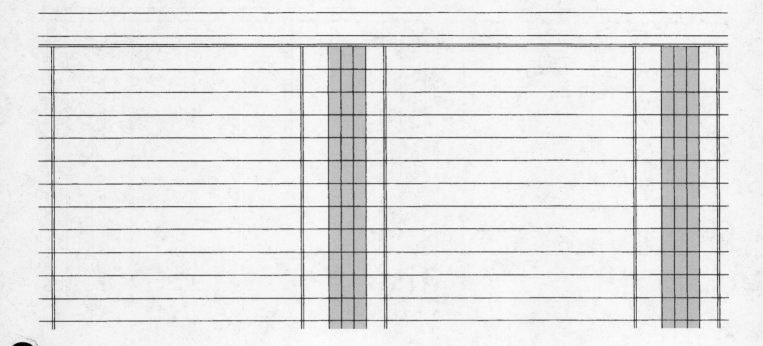

Extra form

Preparing a balance sheet

Extra form

2-1 APPLICATION PROBLEM, p. 33

Determining how revenue, expense, and withdrawal transactions change an accounting equation

Trans. No.	Assets				= Liabilities	+	Owner's Equity
	Cash	+	Accts. Rec.— Lisa Lee	+ Supplies +	Prepaid Insurance =	Accts. Pay.— Kline Co.	+	Peter Smith, Capital
Beg. Bal. 1.	625 −300		−0−	375	300	200		1,100 −300 (expense)
New Bal. 2.	325		−0−	375	300	200		800
New Bal. 3.								
New Bal. 4.								
New Bal. 5.								
New Bal. 6.								
New Bal. 7.								
New Bal. 8.								
New Bal.								

Extra form

Trans. No.	Assets				= Liabilities	+	Owner's Equity
	Cash	+		+ Supplies	+ Prepaid Insurance =		+	
Beg. Bal. 1.								
New Bal. 2.								
New Bal. 3.								
New Bal. 4.								
New Bal. 5.								
New Bal. 6.								
New Bal.								

Extra form

Trans. No.	Assets				=	Liabilities +	Owner's Equity
	Cash +	+	Supplies +	Prepaid Insurance =		+	
Beg. Bal. 1.							
New Bal. 2.							
New Bal. 3.							
New Bal. 4.							
New Bal. 5.							
New Bal. 6.							
New Bal. 7.							
New Bal. 8.							
New Bal. 9.							
New Bal. 10.							
New Bal. 11.							
New Bal. 12.							
New Bal. 13.							
New Bal. 14.							
New Bal. 15.							
New Bal.							

2-2 APPLICATION PROBLEM, p. 34

Determining how transactions change an accounting equation

Trans. No.	Assets							= Liabilities	+	Owner's Equity
	Cash	+	Accts. Rec.—Suburban Rental	+	Supplies	+	Prepaid Insurance	= Accts. Pay.—Teale Co.	+	Doris Becker, Capital
Beg. Bal. 1.	500 −50		−0−		260		300	100		960 −50 (expense)
New Bal. 2.	450		−0−		260		300	100		910
New Bal. 3.										
New Bal. 4.										
New Bal. 5.										
New Bal. 6.										
New Bal. 7.										
New Bal. 8.										
New Bal. 9.										
New Bal. 10.										
New Bal. 11.										
New Bal. 12.										
New Bal.										

Extra form

Trans. No.	Assets				= Liabilities +	Owner's Equity
	Cash +	+	Supplies +	Prepaid Insurance =	+	
Beg. Bal. 1.						
New Bal. 2.						
New Bal. 3.						
New Bal. 4.						
New Bal. 5.						
New Bal. 6.						
New Bal. 7.						
New Bal. 8.						
New Bal. 9.						
New Bal. 10.						
New Bal. 11.						
New Bal. 12.						
New Bal. 13.						
New Bal. 14.						
New Bal. 15.						
New Bal.						

2-3 **APPLICATION PROBLEM, p. 35**

Preparing a balance sheet

Extra form

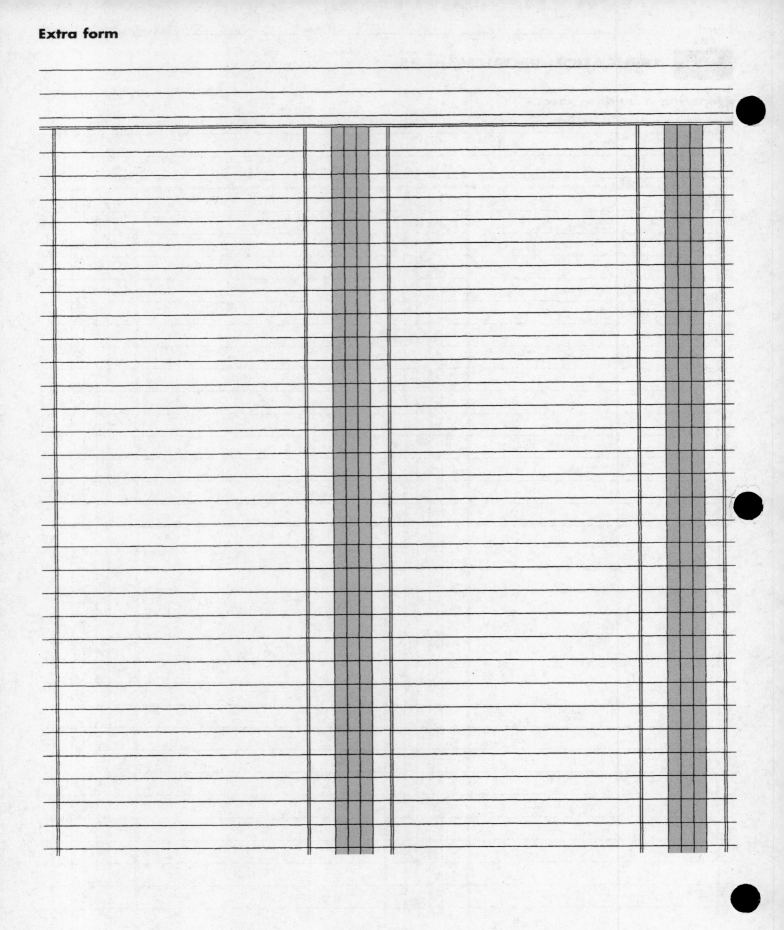

2-4 MASTERY PROBLEM, p. 35

Determining how transactions change an accounting equation and preparing a balance sheet

1.

Trans. No.	Assets				= Liabilities +	Owner's Equity
	Cash	+ Accts. Rec.— + Dorothy Romano	Supplies +	Prepaid Insurance =	Accts. Pay.— Sickle Co. +	Mikaela Mundt, Capital
Beg. Bal. 1.	1,400 −100	–0–	300	400	1,500	600 −100 (expense)
New Bal. 2.	1,300	–0–	300	400	1,500	500
New Bal. 3.						
New Bal. 4.						
New Bal. 5.						
New Bal. 6.						
New Bal. 7.						
New Bal. 8.						
New Bal. 9.						
New Bal. 10.						
New Bal. 11.						
New Bal. 12.						
New Bal. 13.						
New Bal.						

2. _____

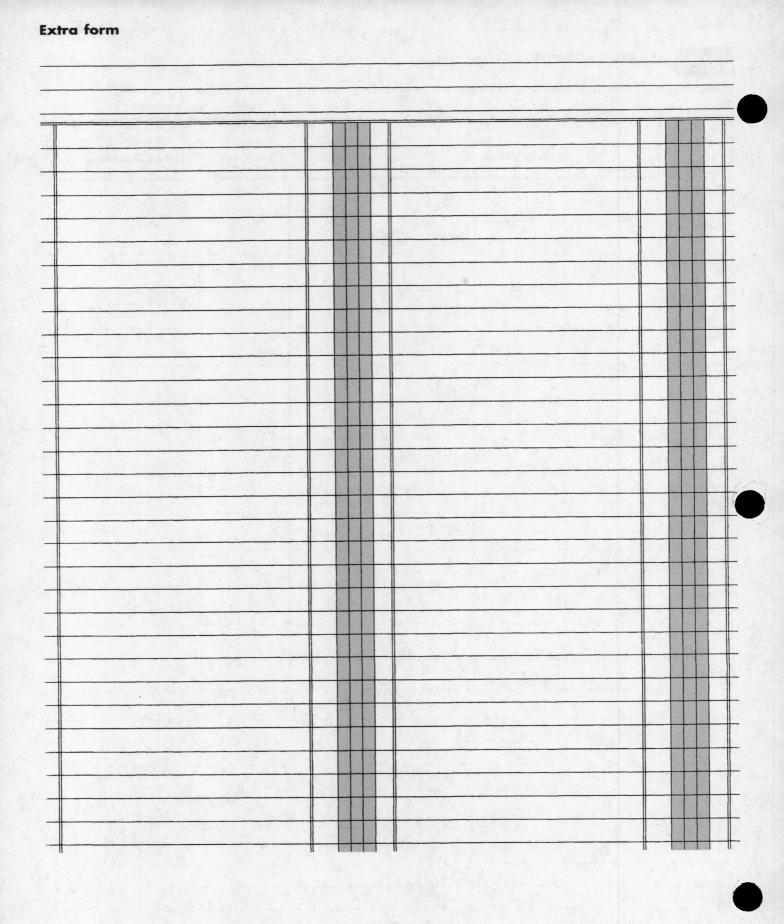

2-5 CHALLENGE PROBLEM, p. 36

Determining how transactions change an accounting equation

1.

Trans. No.	Assets				= Liabilities +	Owner's Equity
	Cash	Accts. Rec.— + Mary Lou Pier +	Supplies +	Prepaid Insurance =	Accts. Pay.— Kollasch Co. +	Zachary Martin, Capital
Beg. Bal. 1.	8,552	1,748	1,485	615	3,145	9,255
New Bal. 2.						
New Bal. 3.						
New Bal. 4.						
New Bal.						

2.

_____

_____

_____

_____

_____

_____

_____

_____

_____

_____

_____

_____

Extra form

Trans. No.	Assets				= Liabilities +	Owner's Equity
	Cash +	+	Supplies +	Prepaid Insurance =	+	
Beg. Bal. 1.						
New Bal. 2.						
New Bal. 3.						
New Bal. 4.						
New Bal. 5.						
New Bal. 6.						
New Bal. 7.						
New Bal. 8.						
New Bal. 9.						
New Bal. 10.						
New Bal. 11.						
New Bal. 12.						
New Bal. 13.						
New Bal. 14.						
New Bal. 15.						
New Bal.						

3-1 WORK TOGETHER, p. 44

Determining the normal balance, increase, and decrease sides for accounts

Extra forms

Determining the normal balance, increase, and decrease sides for accounts

Extra forms

3-2 WORK TOGETHER, p. 50

Analyzing a transaction into its debit and credit parts

April

1. _____|_____   1. _____|_____

2. _____|_____   2. _____|_____

5. _____|_____   5. _____|_____

6. _____|_____   6. _____|_____

9. _____|_____   9. _____|_____

Extra forms

_____|_____   _____|_____

_____|_____   _____|_____

Analyzing a transaction into its debit and credit parts

Sept.

1.
_____|_____

1.
_____|_____

4.
_____|_____

4.
_____|_____

5.
_____|_____

5.
_____|_____

6.
_____|_____

6.
_____|_____

11.
_____|_____

11.
_____|_____

Extra forms

_____|_____

_____|_____

_____|_____

_____|_____

3-3 WORK TOGETHER, p. 56

Analyzing revenue, expense, and withdrawal transactions into debit and credit parts

April

10.

10.

11.

11.

14.

14.

18.

18.

20.

20.

Extra forms

Analyzing revenue, expense, and withdrawal transactions into debit and credit parts

Sept.

13. _____ | _____   13. _____ | _____

15. _____ | _____   15. _____ | _____

16. _____ | _____   16. _____ | _____

18. _____ | _____   18. _____ | _____

21. _____ | _____   21. _____ | _____

Extra forms

_____ | _____   _____ | _____

_____ | _____   _____ | _____

3-1 **APPLICATION PROBLEM, p. 58**

Determining the normal balance, increase, and decrease sides for accounts

1	2	3	4	5	6	7	8
Account	Account Classification	Account's Normal Balance		Increase Side		Decrease Side	
		Debit	Credit	Debit	Credit	Debit	Credit
Cash	Asset	✔		✔			✔

Extra form

	1	2	3	4	5	6	7	8
	Account	Account Classification	Account's Normal Balance		Increase Side		Decrease Side	
			Debit	Credit	Debit	Credit	Debit	Credit

3-2 APPLICATION PROBLEM, p. 58

Analyzing transactions into debit and credit parts

March

1.

Cash	
1,500.00	

John Burke, Capital	
	1,500.00

5.

1.

8.

3.

3-3 APPLICATION PROBLEM, p. 59

Analyzing revenue, expense, and withdrawal transactions into debit and credit parts

March

11.

12.

14.

18.

19.

Extra forms

3-4 APPLICATION PROBLEM, p. 59

Analyzing revenue, expense, and withdrawal transactions into debit and credit parts

March

25. _____

_____

26. _____

27. _____

28. _____

29. _____

3-5 MASTERY PROBLEM, p. 60

Analyzing transactions into debit and credit parts

3-6 CHALLENGE PROBLEM, p. 61

Analyzing transactions recorded in T accounts

1	2	3	4	5	6
Trans. No.	Accounts Affected	Account Classification	Entered in Account as a		Description of Transaction
			Debit	Credit	
1.	Cash	Asset	✔		Received cash from owner as an investment
	Carol Burns, Capital	Owner's Equity		✔	
2.					
3.					
4.					
5.					
6.					
7.					
8.					
9.					
10.					
11.					
12.					
13.					

Extra form

1	2	3	4	5	6
Trans. No.	Accounts Affected	Account Classification	Entered in Account as a		Description of Transaction
			Debit	Credit	
1.					
2.					
3.					
4.					
5.					
6.					
7.					
8.					
9.					
10.					
11.					
12.					
13.					

4-1, 4-2, 4-3, and 4-4 **WORK TOGETHER, pp. 71, 75, 81, 87**

4-1 Journalizing entries into a five-column journal
4-2 Journalizing entries into a five-column journal
4-3 Journalizing transactions that affect owner's equity into a five-column journal
4-4 Proving and ruling a journal

JOURNAL

PAGE

DATE	ACCOUNT TITLE	DOC. NO.	POST. REF.	GENERAL DEBIT 1	GENERAL CREDIT 2	SALES CREDIT 3	CASH DEBIT 4	CASH CREDIT 5
1								
2								
3								
4								
5								
6								
7								
8								
9								
10								
11								
12								
13								
14								
15								

Extra form

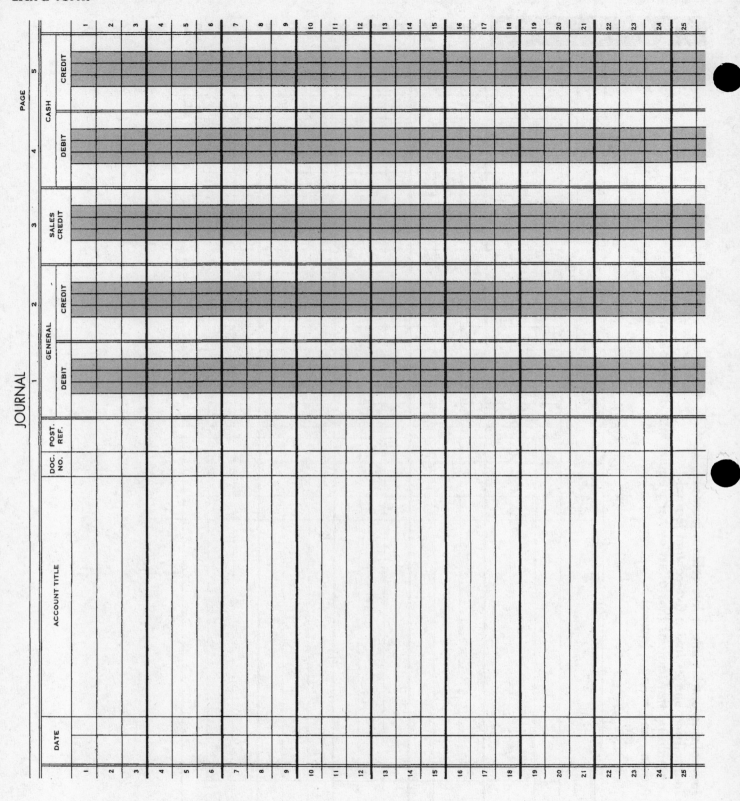

JOURNAL

PAGE

Name _____ Date _____ Class _____

WORK TOGETHER (concluded)

JOURNAL

PAGE _____

	1	2	3	4	5
DATE	ACCOUNT TITLE	DOC. NO.	POST. REF.	GENERAL DEBIT	GENERAL CREDIT

(Column headers: GENERAL — DEBIT (1), CREDIT (2); SALES CREDIT (3); CASH — DEBIT (4), CREDIT (5))

Prove page 1 of the journal:

Column	Debit Column Totals	Credit Column Totals
General	_____	_____
Sales		_____
Cash	_____	_____
Totals	_____	_____

Prove page 2 of the journal:

Column	Debit Column Totals	Credit Column Totals
General	_____	_____
Sales		_____
Cash	_____	_____
Totals	_____	_____

Prove cash:

Cash on hand at the beginning of the month .... _____
Plus total cash received during the month .... _____
Equals Total .... _____
Less total cash paid during the month .... _____
Equals cash balance at the end of the month .... _____
Checkbook balance on the next unused check stub .... _____

Extra form

JOURNAL

PAGE

DATE	ACCOUNT TITLE	DOC. NO.	POST. REF.	GENERAL DEBIT 1	GENERAL CREDIT 2	SALES CREDIT 3	CASH DEBIT 4	CASH CREDIT 5

4-1, 4-2, 4-3, and 4-4 ON YOUR OWN, pp. 71, 75, 81, 87

4-1 Journalizing entries into a five-column journal
4-2 Journalizing entries into a five-column journal
4-3 Journalizing transactions that affect owner's equity into a five-column journal
4-4 Proving and ruling a journal

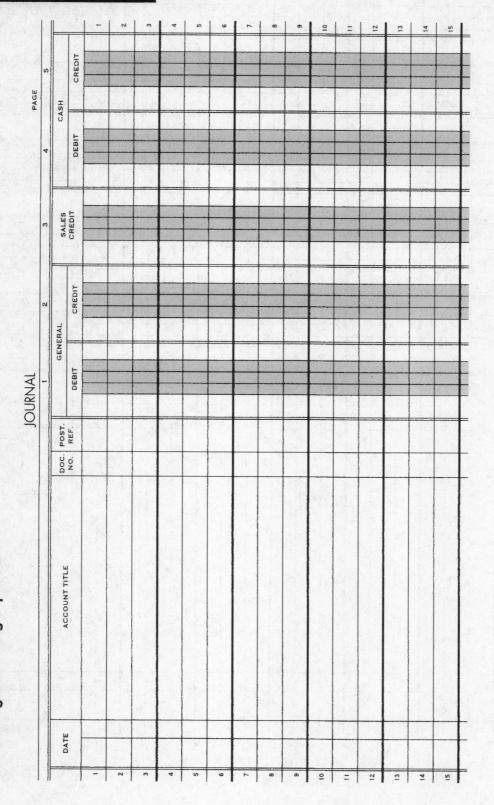

JOURNAL

JOURNAL

PAGE

DATE	ACCOUNT TITLE	DOC. NO.	POST. REF.	GENERAL		SALES CREDIT	CASH	
				DEBIT 1	CREDIT 2	3	DEBIT 4	CREDIT 5
1								
2								
3								
4								
5								
6								
7								
8								
9								
10								
11								
12								
13								
14								
15								
16								
17								
18								
19								
20								
21								
22								
23								
24								
25								

ON YOUR OWN (concluded)

JOURNAL

			GENERAL		SALES		CASH		
	DOC. NO.	POST. REF.	DEBIT 1	CREDIT 2	CREDIT 3		DEBIT 4	CREDIT 5	

PAGE

ACCOUNT TITLE

DATE

Prove page 1 of the journal:

	Debit	Credit
Column	Column Totals	Column Totals
General	_____	_____
Sales	_____	_____
Cash	_____	_____
Totals	_____	_____

Prove page 2 of the journal:

	Debit	Credit
Column	Column Totals	Column Totals
General	_____	_____
Sales	_____	_____
Cash	_____	_____
Totals	_____	_____

Prove cash:

Cash on hand at the beginning of the month .... _____
Plus total cash received during the month .... _____
Equals Total .... _____
Less total cash paid during the month .... _____
Equals cash balance at the end of the month .... _____
Checkbook balance on the next unused check stub ...... _____

Extra form

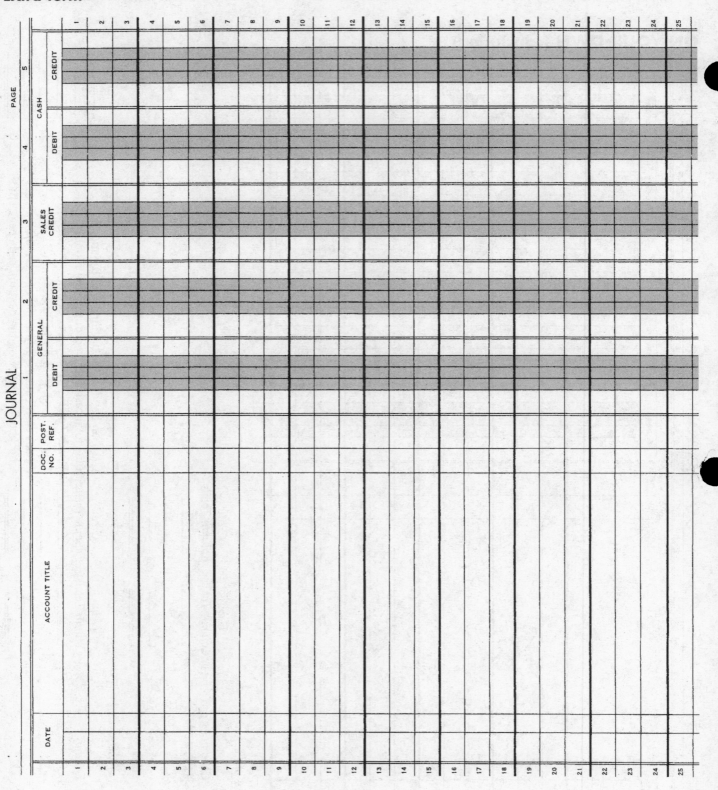

4-1, 4-2, 4-3, and 4-4   APPLICATION PROBLEMS, pp. 89, 90

4-1 Journalizing transactions into a five-column journal
4-2 Journalizing buying insurance, buying on account, and paying on account
4-3 Journalizing transactions that affect owner's equity and receiving cash on account
4-4 Proving and ruling a journal

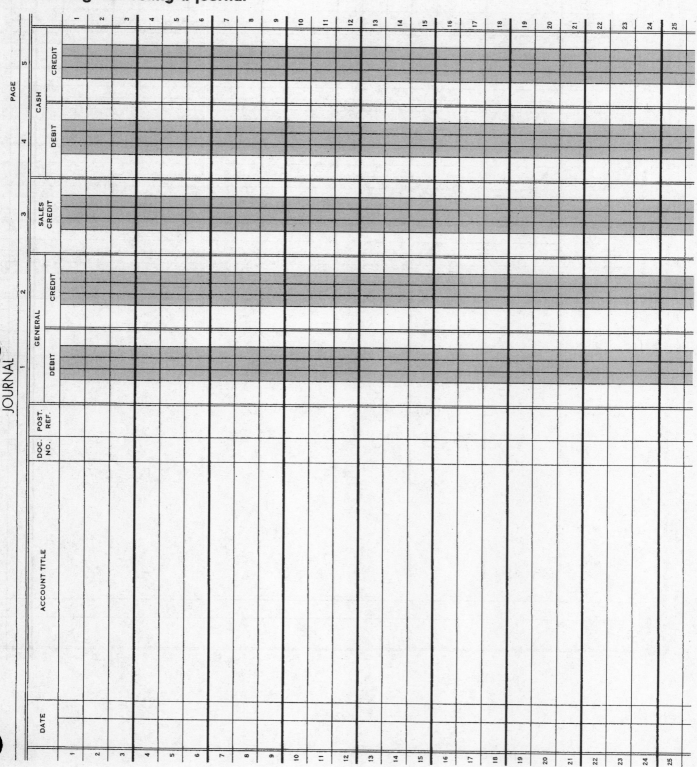

Extra form

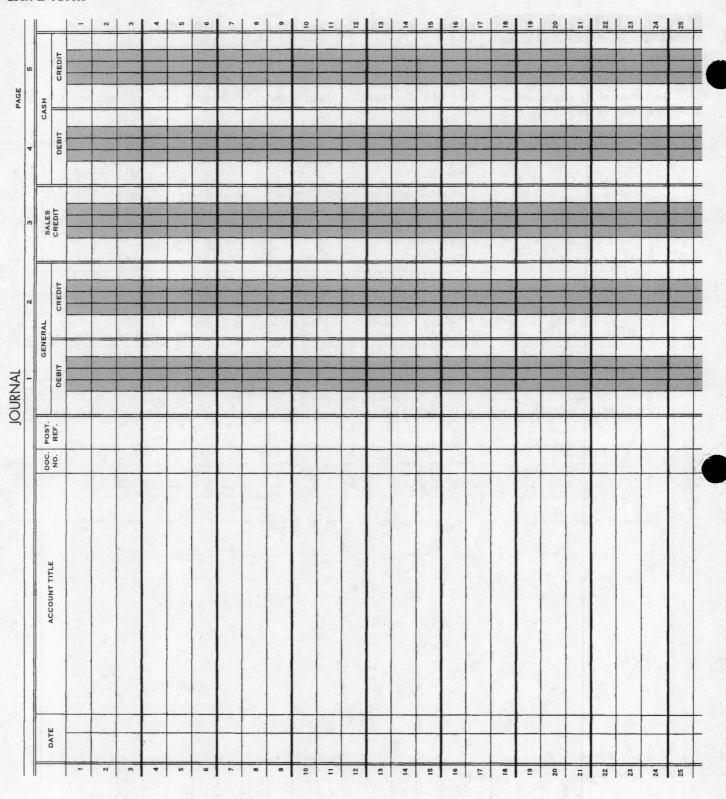

JOURNAL

4-4 APPLICATION PROBLEM (concluded)

JOURNAL

PAGE ___

				GENERAL		SALES CREDIT	CASH	
DATE	ACCOUNT TITLE	DOC. NO.	POST. REF.	DEBIT	CREDIT		DEBIT	CREDIT

Prove page 1 of the journal:

Column	Debit Column Totals	Credit Column Totals
General		
Sales		
Cash		
Totals		

Prove page 2 of the journal:

Column	Debit Column Totals	Credit Column Totals
General		
Sales		
Cash		
Totals		

Prove cash:

Cash on hand at the beginning of the month ....

Plus total cash received during the month ....

Equals Total ....

Less total cash paid during the month ....

Equals cash balance at the end of the month ....

Checkbook balance on the next unused check stub ....

Extra form

JOURNAL

| | | | | | | GENERAL | | SALES CREDIT | CASH | |
| | | | | DEBIT | CREDIT | | DEBIT | CREDIT | | |
DATE	ACCOUNT TITLE	DOC. NO.	POST. REF.	1	2	3	4	5		PAGE
1										1
2										2
3										3
4										4
5										5
6										6
7										7
8										8
9										9
10										10
11										11
12										12
13										13
14										14
15										15
16										16
17										17
18										18
19										19
20										20
21										21
22										22
23										23
24										24
25										25

4-5 APPLICATION PROBLEM, p. 90

Journalizing transactions

JOURNAL

PAGE

			DOC. NO.	POST. REF.	GENERAL		SALES CREDIT	CASH	
DATE	ACCOUNT TITLE				DEBIT 1	CREDIT 2	3	DEBIT 4	CREDIT 5
1									
2									
3									
4									
5									
6									
7									
8									
9									
10									
11									
12									
13									
14									
15									
16									
17									
18									
19									
20									
21									
22									
23									
24									

Extra form

	DATE	ACCOUNT TITLE	DOC. NO.	POST. REF.	GENERAL DEBIT 1	GENERAL CREDIT 2	SALES CREDIT 3	CASH DEBIT 4	CASH CREDIT 5	
1										1
2										2
3										3
4										4
5										5
6										6
7										7
8										8
9										9
10										10
11										11
12										12
13										13
14										14
15										15
16										16
17										17
18										18
19										19
20										20
21										21
22										22
23										23
24										24
25										25

JOURNAL

PAGE

4-6 **MASTERY PROBLEM, p. 91**

Journalizing transactions and proving and ruling a journal

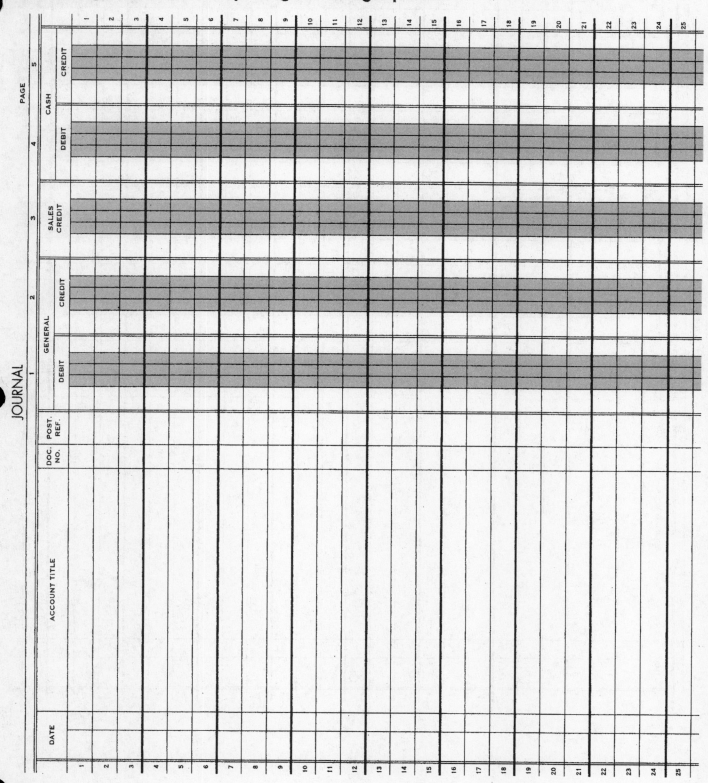

Extra form

JOURNAL

DATE	ACCOUNT TITLE	DOC. NO.	POST. REF.	GENERAL DEBIT 1	GENERAL CREDIT 2	SALES CREDIT 3	CASH DEBIT 4	CASH CREDIT 5
1								
2								
3								
4								
5								
6								
7								
8								
9								
10								
11								
12								
13								
14								
15								
16								
17								
18								
19								
20								
21								
22								
23								
24								
25								

4-6 MASTERY PROBLEM (concluded)

JOURNAL

PAGE 5

			GENERAL		SALES	CASH	
DATE	ACCOUNT TITLE	DOC. NO.	POST. REF.	DEBIT	CREDIT	CREDIT	DEBIT	CREDIT

Prove page 1 of the journal:

	Debit	Credit
Column	Column Totals	Column Totals
General		
Sales		
Cash		
Totals		

Prove page 2 of the journal:

	Debit	Credit
Column	Column Totals	Column Totals
General		
Sales		
Cash		
Totals		

Prove cash:

Cash on hand at the beginning of the month . . . .

Plus total cash received during the month . . . .

Equals Total . . . .

Less total cash paid during the month . . . .

Equals cash balance at the end of the month . . . .

Checkbook balance on the next unused check stub . . . .

Extra form

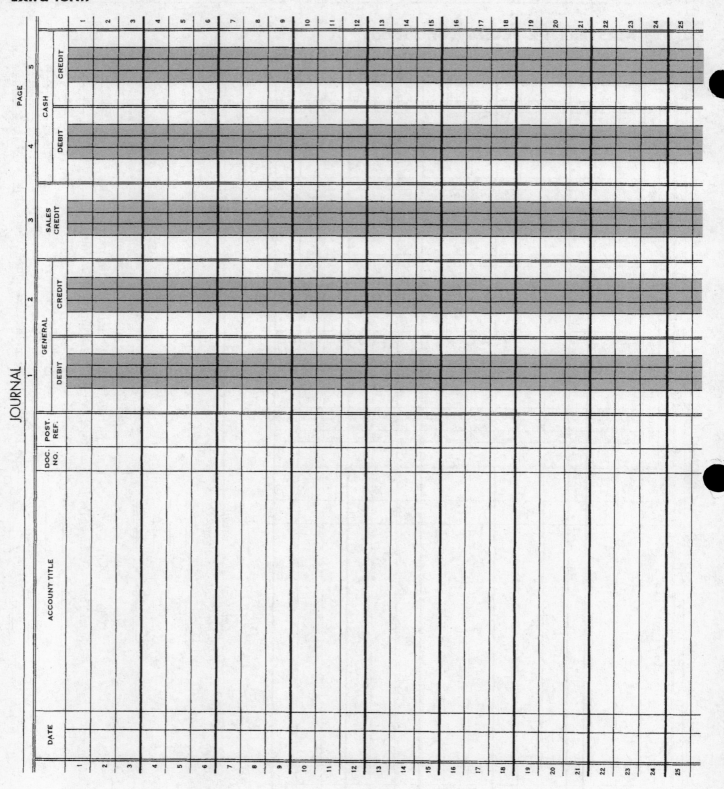

4-7 CHALLENGE PROBLEM, p. 92

Journalizing transactions using a variation of the five-column journal

JOURNAL

		DATE	ACCOUNT TITLE	DOC. NO.	POST. REF.	GENERAL		SALES CREDIT
						DEBIT	CREDIT	

PAGE

CASH — DEBIT (1), CREDIT (2), GENERAL — DEBIT (3), CREDIT (4), SALES CREDIT (5)

Extra form

JOURNAL

PAGE

		DATE	ACCOUNT TITLE	DOC. NO.	POST. REF.	GENERAL		SALES CREDIT	CASH	
						3 DEBIT	4 CREDIT	5	1 DEBIT	2 CREDIT
1										
2										
3										
4										
5										
6										
7										
8										
9										
10										
11										
12										
13										
14										
15										
16										
17										
18										
19										
20										
21										
22										
23										
24										
25										

5-1 WORK TOGETHER, p. 102

Preparing a chart of accounts and opening an account

3.

_____
_____
_____
_____
_____
_____
_____
_____
_____
_____
_____
_____
_____
_____
_____
_____
_____

4.

_____
_____
_____
_____
_____
_____
_____

5.

ACCOUNT _____   ACCOUNT NO. _____

DATE		ITEM	POST. REF.	DEBIT	CREDIT	BALANCE	
						DEBIT	CREDIT

Preparing a chart of accounts and opening an account

6.

_____

7.

_____

8.

ACCOUNT					ACCOUNT NO.	
DATE	ITEM	POST. REF.	DEBIT	CREDIT	BALANCE DEBIT	CREDIT

5-2 Posting separate amounts to a general ledger
5-3 Posting column totals to a general ledger

JOURNAL PAGE 1

DATE		ACCOUNT TITLE	DOC. NO.	POST. REF.	GENERAL DEBIT (1)	GENERAL CREDIT (2)	SALES CREDIT (3)	CASH DEBIT (4)	CASH CREDIT (5)
20-- Mar.	1	Leonard Witkowski, Capital	R1			5000 00		5000 00	
	3	Prepaid Insurance	C1		660 00				660 00
	4	Supplies	M1		78 00				
		Accts. Payable—Joshua's Supplies				78 00			
	8		T8	✔			675 00	675 00	
	9	Accts. Receivable—Danielle Braastad	S1		163 00		163 00		
	12	Rent Expense	C2		375 00				375 00
	15	Accts. Payable—Joshua's Supplies	C3		50 00				50 00
	16	Accts. Receivable—Danielle Braastad	R2			100 00		100 00	
	25	Leonard Witkowski, Drawing	C4		1000 00				1000 00
	31	Totals			2326 00 (✔)	5178 00 (✔)	838 00	5775 00	2085 00

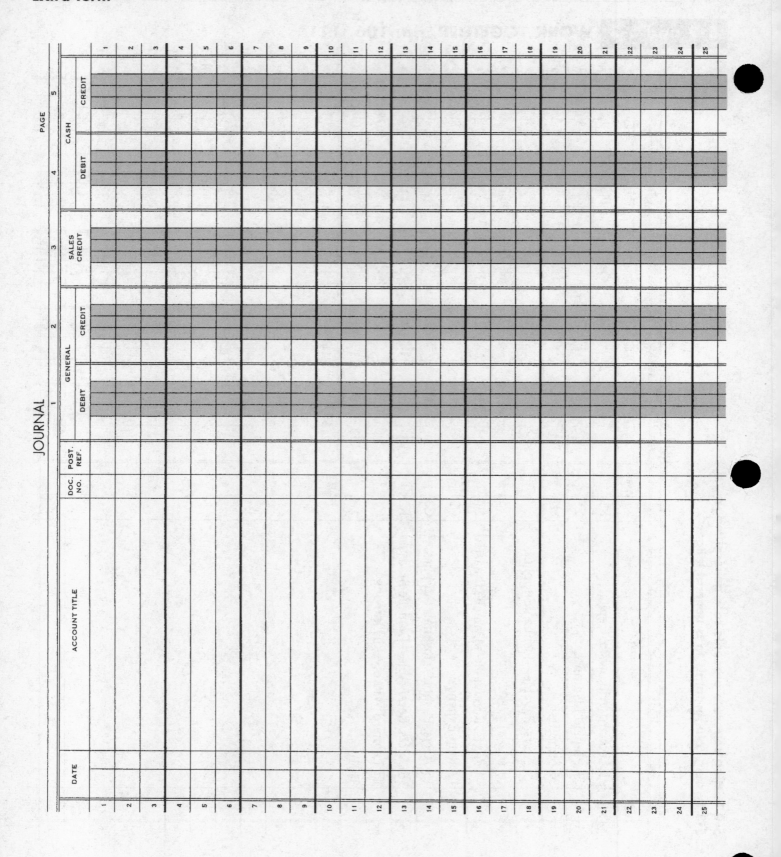

5-2 and 5-3 **WORK TOGETHER (continued)**

GENERAL LEDGER

ACCOUNT Cash   ACCOUNT NO. 110

DATE		ITEM	POST. REF.	DEBIT	CREDIT	BALANCE	
						DEBIT	CREDIT

ACCOUNT Accounts Receivable—Danielle Braastad   ACCOUNT NO. 120

DATE		ITEM	POST. REF.	DEBIT	CREDIT	BALANCE	
						DEBIT	CREDIT

ACCOUNT Supplies   ACCOUNT NO. 130

DATE		ITEM	POST. REF.	DEBIT	CREDIT	BALANCE	
						DEBIT	CREDIT

ACCOUNT Prepaid Insurance   ACCOUNT NO. 140

DATE		ITEM	POST. REF.	DEBIT	CREDIT	BALANCE	
						DEBIT	CREDIT

ACCOUNT Accounts Payable—Joshua's Supplies   ACCOUNT NO. 210

DATE		ITEM	POST. REF.	DEBIT	CREDIT	BALANCE	
						DEBIT	CREDIT

GENERAL LEDGER

ACCOUNT Leonard Witkowski, Capital   ACCOUNT NO. 310

DATE	ITEM	POST. REF.	DEBIT	CREDIT	BALANCE	
					DEBIT	CREDIT

ACCOUNT Leonard Witkowski, Drawing   ACCOUNT NO. 320

DATE	ITEM	POST. REF.	DEBIT	CREDIT	BALANCE	
					DEBIT	CREDIT

ACCOUNT Sales   ACCOUNT NO. 410

DATE	ITEM	POST. REF.	DEBIT	CREDIT	BALANCE	
					DEBIT	CREDIT

ACCOUNT Rent Expense   ACCOUNT NO. 510

DATE	ITEM	POST. REF.	DEBIT	CREDIT	BALANCE	
					DEBIT	CREDIT

ACCOUNT   ACCOUNT NO.

DATE	ITEM	POST. REF.	DEBIT	CREDIT	BALANCE	
					DEBIT	CREDIT

5-2 and 5-3 ON YOUR OWN, pp. 106, 111

5-2 Posting separate amounts to a general ledger
5-3 Posting column totals to a general ledger

JOURNAL PAGE 1

DATE	ACCOUNT TITLE	DOC. NO.	POST. REF.	GENERAL DEBIT	GENERAL CREDIT	SALES CREDIT	CASH DEBIT	CASH CREDIT	
Sept. 1	Melanie Komoko, Capital	R1			2500 00		2500 00		1
4	Supplies	M1		67 00					2
	Accounts Payable—Signs Plus				67 00				3
7	Prepaid Insurance	C1		333 00				333 00	4
10	Accounts Receivable—Brenden Otto	S1		195 00		195 00			5
13		T13	✓			1100 00	1100 00		6
18	Utilities Expense	C2		49 00				49 00	7
21	Accounts Payable—Signs Plus	C3		35 00				35 00	8
27	Accounts Receivable—Brenden Otto	R2			100 00		100 00		9
30	Melanie Komoko, Drawing	C4		300 00				300 00	10
30	Totals			979 00	2667 00	1295 00	3700 00	717 00	11
									12
									13
									14
									15
									16
									17
									18
									19
									20
									21
									22
									23

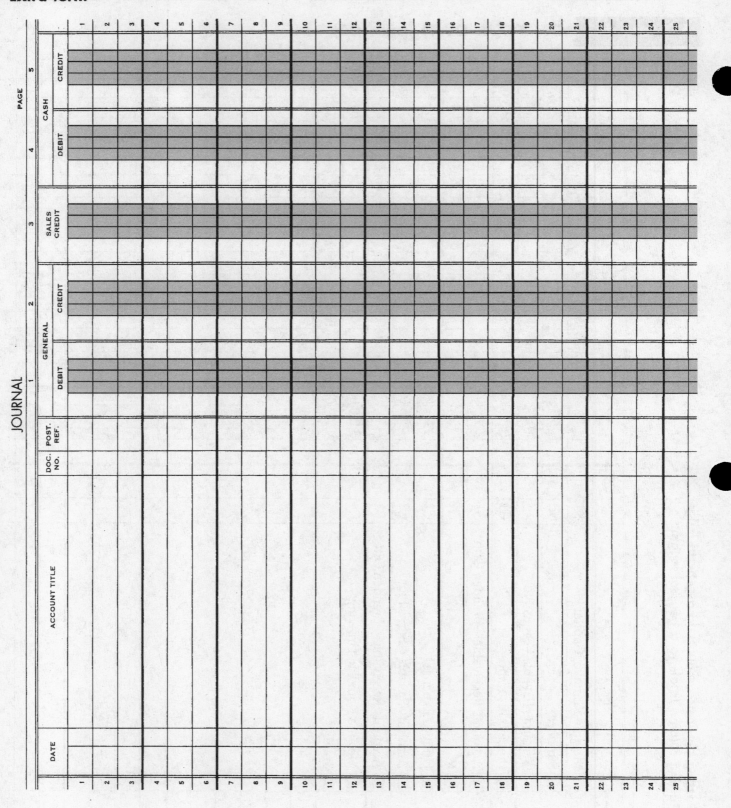

5-2 and 5-3 ON YOUR OWN (continued)

GENERAL LEDGER

ACCOUNT Cash   ACCOUNT NO. 110

DATE	ITEM	POST. REF.	DEBIT	CREDIT	BALANCE DEBIT	BALANCE CREDIT

ACCOUNT Accounts Receivable—Brenden Otto   ACCOUNT NO. 120

DATE	ITEM	POST. REF.	DEBIT	CREDIT	BALANCE DEBIT	BALANCE CREDIT

ACCOUNT Supplies   ACCOUNT NO. 130

DATE	ITEM	POST. REF.	DEBIT	CREDIT	BALANCE DEBIT	BALANCE CREDIT

ACCOUNT Prepaid Insurance   ACCOUNT NO. 140

DATE	ITEM	POST. REF.	DEBIT	CREDIT	BALANCE DEBIT	BALANCE CREDIT

ACCOUNT Accounts Payable—Signs Plus   ACCOUNT NO. 210

DATE	ITEM	POST. REF.	DEBIT	CREDIT	BALANCE DEBIT	BALANCE CREDIT

GENERAL LEDGER

ACCOUNT Melanie Komoko, Capital   ACCOUNT NO. 310

DATE	ITEM	POST. REF.	DEBIT	CREDIT	BALANCE DEBIT	BALANCE CREDIT

ACCOUNT Melanie Komoko, Drawing   ACCOUNT NO. 320

DATE	ITEM	POST. REF.	DEBIT	CREDIT	BALANCE DEBIT	BALANCE CREDIT

ACCOUNT Sales   ACCOUNT NO. 410

DATE	ITEM	POST. REF.	DEBIT	CREDIT	BALANCE DEBIT	BALANCE CREDIT

ACCOUNT Utilities Expense   ACCOUNT NO. 510

DATE	ITEM	POST. REF.	DEBIT	CREDIT	BALANCE DEBIT	BALANCE CREDIT

ACCOUNT   ACCOUNT NO.

DATE	ITEM	POST. REF.	DEBIT	CREDIT	BALANCE DEBIT	BALANCE CREDIT

5-4 **WORK TOGETHER, p. 117**

Journalizing correcting entries

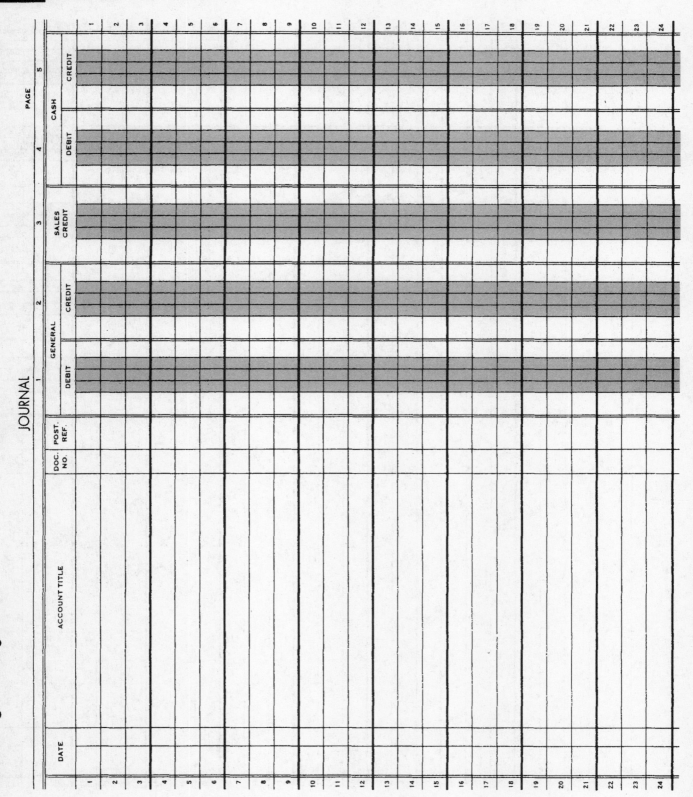

Journalizing correcting entries

JOURNAL

PAGE

DATE	ACCOUNT TITLE	DOC. NO.	POST. REF.	GENERAL DEBIT	GENERAL CREDIT	SALES CREDIT	CASH DEBIT	CASH CREDIT

5-1 APPLICATION PROBLEM, p. 119

Preparing a chart of accounts and opening an account

1. _____

_____
_____
_____
_____
_____
_____
_____
_____
_____
_____
_____
_____
_____
_____
_____
_____

2. _____

_____
_____
_____

3.

ACCOUNT _____   ACCOUNT NO. _____

DATE	ITEM	POST. REF.	DEBIT	CREDIT	BALANCE DEBIT	BALANCE CREDIT

ACCOUNT _____   ACCOUNT NO. _____

DATE	ITEM	POST. REF.	DEBIT	CREDIT	BALANCE DEBIT	BALANCE CREDIT

Extra forms

_____
_____
_____
_____
_____
_____
_____
_____
_____
_____
_____
_____
_____
_____
_____
_____
_____
_____
_____
_____

ACCOUNT   ACCOUNT NO.

DATE	ITEM	POST. REF.	DEBIT	CREDIT	BALANCE	
					DEBIT	CREDIT

ACCOUNT   ACCOUNT NO.

DATE	ITEM	POST. REF.	DEBIT	CREDIT	BALANCE	
					DEBIT	CREDIT

5-2 Posting separate amounts to a general ledger
5-3 Posting column totals to a general ledger

JOURNAL PAGE 1

	DATE	ACCOUNT TITLE	DOC. NO.	POST. REF.	GENERAL DEBIT	GENERAL CREDIT	SALES CREDIT	CASH DEBIT	CASH CREDIT
1	Oct. 1	Michael Byrum, Capital	R1			1500 00		1500 00	
2	4	Prepaid Insurance	C1		60 00				60 00
3	10	Supplies	M1		55 00				
4		Accounts Pay.—Golden Gate Supply				55 00			
5	12		T12	✔			382 00	382 00	
6	15	Accounts Receivable—Cheri Frank	S1		42 00		42 00		
7	19	Advertising Expense	C2		25 00				25 00
8	20	Accounts Pay.—Golden Gate Supply	C3		30 00				30 00
9	27	Accounts Receivable—Cheri Frank	R2			21 00		21 00	
10	31	Michael Byrum, Drawing	C4		150 00				150 00
11	31	Totals			362 00 (✔)	1576 00 (✔)	424 00	1903 00	265 00
12									
13									
14									
15									
16									
17									
18									
19									
20									
21									
22									
23									

Extra form

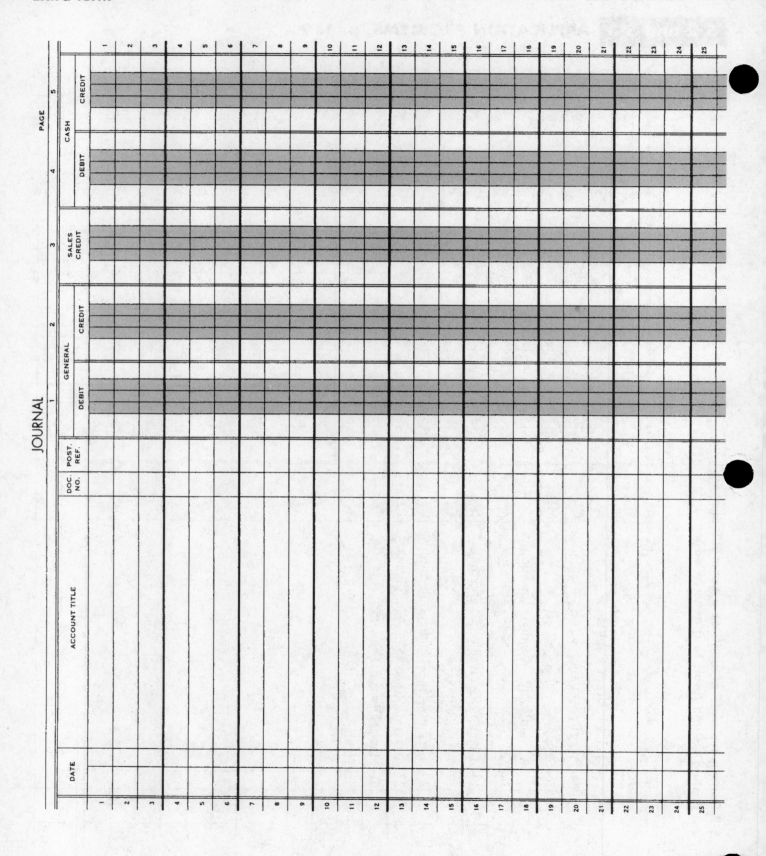

5-2 and 5-3 APPLICATION PROBLEMS (continued)

GENERAL LEDGER

ACCOUNT Cash   ACCOUNT NO. 110

DATE		ITEM	POST. REF.	DEBIT	CREDIT	BALANCE	
						DEBIT	CREDIT

ACCOUNT Accounts Receivable—Cheri Frank   ACCOUNT NO. 120

DATE		ITEM	POST. REF.	DEBIT	CREDIT	BALANCE	
						DEBIT	CREDIT

ACCOUNT Supplies   ACCOUNT NO. 130

DATE		ITEM	POST. REF.	DEBIT	CREDIT	BALANCE	
						DEBIT	CREDIT

ACCOUNT Prepaid Insurance   ACCOUNT NO. 140

DATE		ITEM	POST. REF.	DEBIT	CREDIT	BALANCE	
						DEBIT	CREDIT

ACCOUNT Accounts Payable—Golden Gate Supply   ACCOUNT NO. 210

DATE		ITEM	POST. REF.	DEBIT	CREDIT	BALANCE	
						DEBIT	CREDIT

GENERAL LEDGER

ACCOUNT Michael Byrum, Capital   ACCOUNT NO. 310

DATE	ITEM	POST. REF.	DEBIT	CREDIT	BALANCE DEBIT	BALANCE CREDIT

ACCOUNT Michael Byrum, Drawing   ACCOUNT NO. 320

DATE	ITEM	POST. REF.	DEBIT	CREDIT	BALANCE DEBIT	BALANCE CREDIT

ACCOUNT Sales   ACCOUNT NO. 410

DATE	ITEM	POST. REF.	DEBIT	CREDIT	BALANCE DEBIT	BALANCE CREDIT

ACCOUNT Advertising Expense   ACCOUNT NO. 510

DATE	ITEM	POST. REF.	DEBIT	CREDIT	BALANCE DEBIT	BALANCE CREDIT

ACCOUNT   ACCOUNT NO

DATE	ITEM	POST. REF.	DEBIT	CREDIT	BALANCE DEBIT	BALANCE CREDIT

5-4 APPLICATION PROBLEM, p. 119

Journalizing correcting entries

JOURNAL

					DOC. NO.	POST. REF.	1 GENERAL DEBIT	2 GENERAL CREDIT	3 SALES CREDIT	4 CASH DEBIT	5 CASH CREDIT
DATE	ACCOUNT TITLE										

PAGE

Extra form

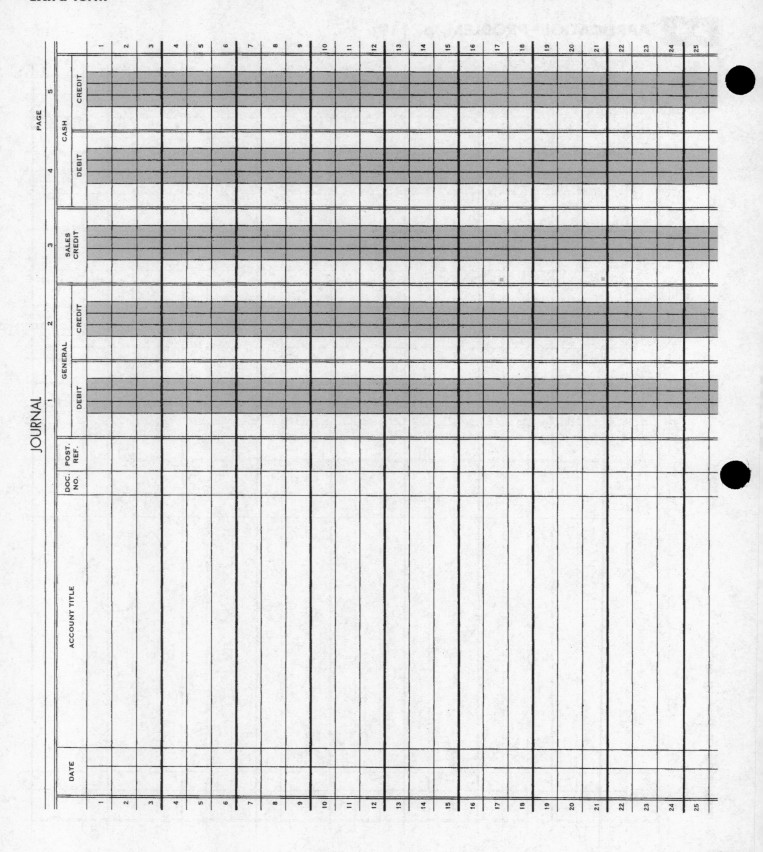

5-5 MASTERY PROBLEM, p. 120

Journalizing transactions and posting to a general ledger

2.–6.

JOURNAL

PAGE 5

DATE	ACCOUNT TITLE	DOC. NO.	POST. REF.	GENERAL DEBIT	GENERAL CREDIT	SALES CREDIT	CASH DEBIT	CASH CREDIT	
									1
									2
									3
									4
									5
									6
									7
									8
									9
									10
									11
									12
									13
									14
									15
									16
									17
									18
									19
									20

3. *Prove the journal:*

Column	Debit Column Totals	Credit Column Totals
General	_____	_____
Sales	_____	_____
Cash	_____	_____
Totals	_____	_____

4. *Prove cash:*

Cash on hand at the beginning of the month ....
Plus total cash received during the month ....
Equals Total ....
Less total cash paid during the month ....
Equals cash balance at the end of the month ....
Checkbook balance on the next unused check stub .....

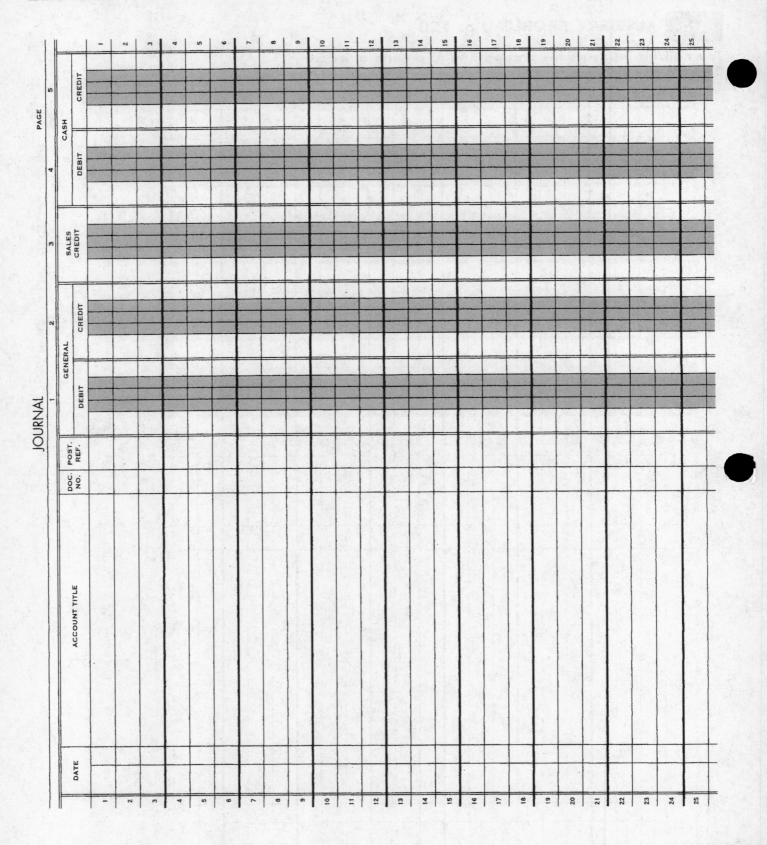

5-5 **MASTERY PROBLEM (continued)**

1., 6.

GENERAL LEDGER

ACCOUNT Cash   ACCOUNT NO. 110

DATE	ITEM	POST. REF.	DEBIT	CREDIT	BALANCE	
					DEBIT	CREDIT

ACCOUNT Accounts Receivable—Alphonse Gutenberg   ACCOUNT NO. 120

DATE	ITEM	POST. REF.	DEBIT	CREDIT	BALANCE	
					DEBIT	CREDIT

ACCOUNT Supplies   ACCOUNT NO. 130

DATE	ITEM	POST. REF.	DEBIT	CREDIT	BALANCE	
					DEBIT	CREDIT

ACCOUNT Accounts Payable—Major Supplies   ACCOUNT NO. 210

DATE	ITEM	POST. REF.	DEBIT	CREDIT	BALANCE	
					DEBIT	CREDIT

ACCOUNT Allan Derner, Capital   ACCOUNT NO. 310

DATE	ITEM	POST. REF.	DEBIT	CREDIT	BALANCE	
					DEBIT	CREDIT

ACCOUNT Allan Derner, Drawing   ACCOUNT NO. 320

DATE	ITEM	POST. REF.	DEBIT	CREDIT	BALANCE	
					DEBIT	CREDIT

1., 6.

GENERAL LEDGER

ACCOUNT Sales   ACCOUNT NO. 410

DATE	ITEM	POST. REF.	DEBIT	CREDIT	BALANCE DEBIT	BALANCE CREDIT

ACCOUNT Advertising Expense   ACCOUNT NO. 510

DATE	ITEM	POST. REF.	DEBIT	CREDIT	BALANCE DEBIT	BALANCE CREDIT

ACCOUNT Miscellaneous Expense   ACCOUNT NO. 520

DATE	ITEM	POST. REF.	DEBIT	CREDIT	BALANCE DEBIT	BALANCE CREDIT

ACCOUNT Rent Expense   ACCOUNT NO. 530

DATE	ITEM	POST. REF.	DEBIT	CREDIT	BALANCE DEBIT	BALANCE CREDIT

ACCOUNT   ACCOUNT NO.

DATE	ITEM	POST. REF.	DEBIT	CREDIT	BALANCE DEBIT	BALANCE CREDIT

5-6   CHALLENGE PROBLEM, p. 120

Posting using a variation of the five-column journal

JOURNAL   PAGE 5

Date	Account Title	Doc. No.	Post. Ref.	Debit General	Debit Cash	Credit General	Credit Sales	Credit Cash
20-- Mar. 1	Nathan Jackson, Capital	R1			8000 00	8000 00		
3	Rent Expense	C1		350 00				350 00
5	Miscellaneous Expense	C2		5 00				5 00
9	Accounts Receivable—Joelle Chu	S1		250 00			250 00	
11	Supplies	C3		400 00				400 00
13	✔	T13	✔		450 00		450 00	
16	Supplies	M1		700 00				
18	Accounts Payable—Hartwood Supplies					700 00		
18	Accounts Payable—Hartwood Supplies	C4		350 00				350 00
19	Utilities Expense	C5		60 00				60 00
20	✔	T20	✔		1100 00		1100 00	
23	Advertising Expense	C6		50 00				50 00
23	Supplies	C7		150 00				150 00
27	Supplies	C8		150 00				150 00
27	✔	T27	✔		1830 00		1830 00	
30	Nathan Jackson, Drawing	C9		400 00				400 00
31	✔	T31	✔		410 00		410 00	
31	Totals			2865 00 (✔)	11790 00	8700 00 (✔)	4040 00	1915 00

Extra form

JOURNAL

5-6 CHALLENGE PROBLEM (continued)

GENERAL LEDGER

ACCOUNT Cash   ACCOUNT NO. 110

DATE	ITEM	POST. REF.	DEBIT	CREDIT	BALANCE	
					DEBIT	CREDIT

ACCOUNT Accounts Receivable—Joelle Chu   ACCOUNT NO. 120

DATE	ITEM	POST. REF.	DEBIT	CREDIT	BALANCE	
					DEBIT	CREDIT

ACCOUNT Supplies   ACCOUNT NO. 130

DATE	ITEM	POST. REF.	DEBIT	CREDIT	BALANCE	
					DEBIT	CREDIT

ACCOUNT Accounts Payable—Hartwood Supplies   ACCOUNT NO. 210

DATE	ITEM	POST. REF.	DEBIT	CREDIT	BALANCE	
					DEBIT	CREDIT

ACCOUNT Nathan Jackson, Capital   ACCOUNT NO. 310

DATE	ITEM	POST. REF.	DEBIT	CREDIT	BALANCE	
					DEBIT	CREDIT

GENERAL LEDGER

ACCOUNT Nathan Jackson, Drawing   ACCOUNT NO. 320

DATE	ITEM	POST. REF.	DEBIT	CREDIT	BALANCE DEBIT	BALANCE CREDIT

ACCOUNT Sales   ACCOUNT NO. 410

DATE	ITEM	POST. REF.	DEBIT	CREDIT	BALANCE DEBIT	BALANCE CREDIT

ACCOUNT Advertising Expense   ACCOUNT NO. 510

DATE	ITEM	POST. REF.	DEBIT	CREDIT	BALANCE DEBIT	BALANCE CREDIT

ACCOUNT Miscellaneous Expense   ACCOUNT NO. 520

DATE	ITEM	POST. REF.	DEBIT	CREDIT	BALANCE DEBIT	BALANCE CREDIT

ACCOUNT Rent Expense   ACCOUNT NO. 530

DATE	ITEM	POST. REF.	DEBIT	CREDIT	BALANCE DEBIT	BALANCE CREDIT

ACCOUNT Utilities Expense   ACCOUNT NO. 540

DATE	ITEM	POST. REF.	DEBIT	CREDIT	BALANCE DEBIT	BALANCE CREDIT

6-1 WORK TOGETHER, p. 130

Endorsing and writing checks

4.

a.

```
ENDORSE HERE

X _____

_____

_____

_____

DO NOT WRITE, STAMP, OR SIGN BELOW THIS LINE
RESERVED FOR FINANCIAL INSTITUTION USE
```

b.

```
ENDORSE HERE

X _____

_____

_____

_____

DO NOT WRITE, STAMP, OR SIGN BELOW THIS LINE
RESERVED FOR FINANCIAL INSTITUTION USE
```

c.

```
ENDORSE HERE

X _____

_____

_____

_____

DO NOT WRITE, STAMP, OR SIGN BELOW THIS LINE
RESERVED FOR FINANCIAL INSTITUTION USE
```

5., 6., 7a.

```
NO. 78          $ _____
Date: _____ 20 __
To: _____
For: _____
     _____

BAL. BRO'T. FOR'D. ...........
AMT. DEPOSITED ....  [    Date    ]
SUBTOTAL ....................
OTHER:
     _____
     _____
SUBTOTAL ....................
AMT. THIS CHECK ............
BAL. CAR'D. FOR'D. ...........
```

```
Balsam Lake Accounting                    NO. 78      93-109
154 Main Street                                       929
Balsam Lake, WI 54810
                                     _____ 20 _____
PAY TO THE
 ORDER OF _____  $ _____

_____ DOLLARS

👥 Peoples national bank        For Classroom Use Only
        Balsam Lake, WI 54810

FOR _____     _____

⑈0929010940⑈  291⑊36118⑊
```

7b.

```
NO. 79          $ _____
Date: _____ 20 __
To: _____
For: _____
     _____

BAL. BRO'T. FOR'D. ...........
AMT. DEPOSITED ....  [    Date    ]
SUBTOTAL ....................
OTHER:
     _____
     _____
SUBTOTAL ....................
AMT. THIS CHECK ............
BAL. CAR'D. FOR'D. ...........
```

```
Balsam Lake Accounting                    NO. 79      93-109
154 Main Street                                       929
Balsam Lake, WI 54810
                                     _____ 20 _____
PAY TO THE
 ORDER OF _____  $ _____

_____ DOLLARS

👥 Peoples national bank        For Classroom Use Only
        Balsam Lake, WI 54810

FOR _____     _____

⑈0929010940⑈  291⑊36118⑊
```

Endorsing and writing checks

8.

a.

```
ENDORSE HERE

X


_____

_____

_____

DO NOT WRITE, STAMP, OR SIGN BELOW THIS LINE
RESERVED FOR FINANCIAL INSTITUTION USE
```

b.

```
ENDORSE HERE

X


_____

_____

_____

DO NOT WRITE, STAMP, OR SIGN BELOW THIS LINE
RESERVED FOR FINANCIAL INSTITUTION USE
```

9., 10., 11a.

```
NO. 345          $ _____
Date: _____ 20 ___
To: _____
For: _____
      _____

BAL. BRO'T. FOR'D. . . . . . . . . .
AMT. DEPOSITED . . . .  [  |  |  ]
                          Date
SUBTOTAL . . . . . . . . . . . . . . . . .
OTHER:
      _____
      _____
SUBTOTAL . . . . . . . . . . . . . . . . .
AMT. THIS CHECK . . . . . . . . . . .
BAL. CAR'D. FOR'D. . . . . . . . . . . .
```

```
DRESSER HAIR CARE                    NO. 345    79-1058
1250 State Street                                 981
Dresser, WI 54009              _____ 20 _____

PAY TO THE
ORDER OF _____ $ _____

_____ DOLLARS

ʍʍʍ County Bank          For Classroom Use Only
       Dresser, WI 54009

FOR _____    _____

⑆098110588⑆  291⑈36118⑈
```

11b.

```
NO. 346          $ _____
Date: _____ 20 ___
To: _____
For: _____
      _____

BAL. BRO'T. FOR'D. . . . . . . . . .
AMT. DEPOSITED . . . .  [  |  |  ]
                          Date
SUBTOTAL . . . . . . . . . . . . . . . . .
OTHER:
      _____
SUBTOTAL . . . . . . . . . . . . . . . . .
AMT. THIS CHECK . . . . . . . . . . .
BAL. CAR'D. FOR'D. . . . . . . . . . . .
```

```
DRESSER HAIR CARE                    NO. 346    79-1058
1250 State Street                                 981
Dresser, WI 54009              _____ 20 _____

PAY TO THE
ORDER OF _____ $ _____

_____ DOLLARS

ʍʍʍ County Bank          For Classroom Use Only
       Dresser, WI 54009

FOR _____    _____

⑆098110588⑆  291⑈36118⑈
```

6-2 WORK TOGETHER, p. 135

Reconciling a bank statement and recording a bank service charge

3.

RECONCILIATION OF BANK STATEMENT

_____ (Date)

Balance On Check Stub No. ____ . . . . $ | |

DEDUCT BANK CHARGES:

Description	Amount	
	$	

Total bank charges ▶

Adjusted Check Stub Balance . . . . $ | |

Balance On Bank Statement . . . . $ | |

ADD OUTSTANDING DEPOSITS:

Date	Amount	
	$	

Total outstanding deposits ▶

SUBTOTAL . . . . $ | |

DEDUCT OUTSTANDING CHECKS:

Ck. No.	Amount	Ck. No.	Amount

Total outstanding checks ▶

Adjusted Bank Balance . . . . $ | |

4.

NO. **106**	$ _____
Date: _____ 20 _ _	
To: _____	
For: _____	
BAL. BRO'T. FOR'D.	1,575	00
AMT. DEPOSITED . . . . [Date]		
SUBTOTAL	1,575	00
OTHER:		
_____		
_____		
SUBTOTAL		
AMT. THIS CHECK		
BAL. CAR'D. FOR'D.		

5.

JOURNAL   PAGE

	DATE	ACCOUNT TITLE	DOC. NO.	POST. REF.	GENERAL DEBIT	GENERAL CREDIT	SALES CREDIT	CASH DEBIT	CASH CREDIT	
14										14
15										15
16										16

Reconciling a bank statement and recording a bank service charge

6.

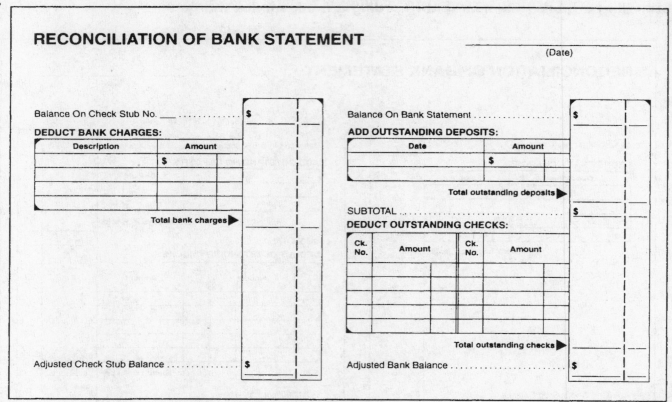

RECONCILIATION OF BANK STATEMENT

_____
(Date)

Balance On Check Stub No. ___ .... $

DEDUCT BANK CHARGES:

Description	Amount
	$

Total bank charges ▶

Balance On Bank Statement .... $

ADD OUTSTANDING DEPOSITS:

Date	Amount
	$

Total outstanding deposits ▶

SUBTOTAL .... $

DEDUCT OUTSTANDING CHECKS:

Ck. No.	Amount	Ck. No.	Amount

Total outstanding checks ▶

Adjusted Check Stub Balance .... $

Adjusted Bank Balance .... $

7.

NO. **218**	$	
Date:		20 - -
To:		
For:		
BAL. BRO'T. FOR'D.	3,578	00
AMT. DEPOSITED		
SUBTOTAL	3,578	00
OTHER:		
SUBTOTAL		
AMT. THIS CHECK		
BAL. CAR'D. FOR'D.		

8.

JOURNAL

PAGE

	DATE	ACCOUNT TITLE	DOC. NO.	POST. REF.	GENERAL DEBIT	GENERAL CREDIT	SALES CREDIT	CASH DEBIT	CASH CREDIT	
17										17
18										18
19										19

Name _____ Date _____ Class _____

6-3 **WORK TOGETHER, p. 140**

Recording dishonored checks, electronic funds transfers, and debit card purchases

JOURNAL   PAGE

	DATE	ACCOUNT TITLE	DOC. NO.	POST. REF.	GENERAL DEBIT	GENERAL CREDIT	SALES CREDIT	CASH DEBIT	CASH CREDIT	
3										3
4										4
5										5
6										6
7										7
8										8
9										9
10										10
11										11
12										12
13										13
14										14
15										15
16										16
17										17
18										18

Extra form

JOURNAL   PAGE

	DATE	ACCOUNT TITLE	DOC. NO.	POST. REF.	GENERAL DEBIT	GENERAL CREDIT	SALES CREDIT	CASH DEBIT	CASH CREDIT	
1										1
2										2
3										3
4										4
5										5
6										6
7										7
8										8
9										9
10										10
11										11
12										12
13										13
14										14
15										15
16										16
17										17
18										18

Recording dishonored checks, electronic funds transfers, and debit card purchases

JOURNAL   PAGE

	DATE	ACCOUNT TITLE	DOC. NO.	POST. REF.	GENERAL DEBIT	GENERAL CREDIT	SALES CREDIT	CASH DEBIT	CASH CREDIT	
15										15
16										16
17										17
18										18
19										19
20										20
21										21
22										22
23										23
24										24
25										25
26										26
27										27
28										28
29										29
30										30

Extra form

JOURNAL   PAGE

	DATE	ACCOUNT TITLE	DOC. NO.	POST. REF.	GENERAL DEBIT	GENERAL CREDIT	SALES CREDIT	CASH DEBIT	CASH CREDIT	
1										1
2										2
3										3
4										4
5										5
6										6
7										7
8										8
9										9
10										10
11										11
12										12
13										13
14										14
15										15
16										16
17										17
18										18

6-4   WORK TOGETHER, p. 144

Establishing and replenishing a petty cash fund

JOURNAL   PAGE

	DATE	ACCOUNT TITLE	DOC. NO.	POST. REF.	GENERAL DEBIT	GENERAL CREDIT	SALES CREDIT	CASH DEBIT	CASH CREDIT	
1										1
2										2
3										3
4										4
5										5
6										6
7										7
8										8
9										9
10										10
11										11
12										12
13										13
14										14
15										15
16										16
17										17

Extra form

JOURNAL   PAGE

	DATE	ACCOUNT TITLE	DOC. NO.	POST. REF.	GENERAL DEBIT	GENERAL CREDIT	SALES CREDIT	CASH DEBIT	CASH CREDIT	
1										1
2										2
3										3
4										4
5										5
6										6
7										7
8										8
9										9
10										10
11										11
12										12
13										13
14										14
15										15
16										16
17										17

Establishing and replenishing a petty cash fund

JOURNAL   PAGE

	DATE		ACCOUNT TITLE	DOC. NO.	POST. REF.	GENERAL DEBIT	GENERAL CREDIT	SALES CREDIT	CASH DEBIT	CASH CREDIT	
1											1
2											2
3											3
4											4
5											5
6											6
7											7
8											8
9											9
10											10
11											11
12											12
13											13
14											14
15											15
16											16
17											17

Extra form

JOURNAL   PAGE

	DATE		ACCOUNT TITLE	DOC. NO.	POST. REF.	GENERAL DEBIT	GENERAL CREDIT	SALES CREDIT	CASH DEBIT	CASH CREDIT	
1											1
2											2
3											3
4											4
5											5
6											6
7											7
8											8
9											9
10											10
11											11
12											12
13											13
14											14
15											15
16											16
17											17

6-1 APPLICATION PROBLEM, p. 146

Endorsing and writing checks

1. **a.**

```
┌─────────────────────────────────┐
│ ENDORSE HERE                    │
│ X                               │
│                                 │
│                                 │
│                                 │
│                                 │
│ DO NOT WRITE, STAMP, OR SIGN BELOW THIS LINE │
│   RESERVED FOR FINANCIAL INSTITUTION USE     │
└─────────────────────────────────┘
```

b.

```
┌─────────────────────────────────┐
│ ENDORSE HERE                    │
│ X                               │
│                                 │
│                                 │
│                                 │
│                                 │
│ DO NOT WRITE, STAMP, OR SIGN BELOW THIS LINE │
│   RESERVED FOR FINANCIAL INSTITUTION USE     │
└─────────────────────────────────┘
```

c.

```
┌─────────────────────────────────┐
│ ENDORSE HERE                    │
│ X                               │
│                                 │
│                                 │
│                                 │
│ DO NOT WRITE, STAMP, OR SIGN BELOW THIS LINE │
│   RESERVED FOR FINANCIAL INSTITUTION USE     │
└─────────────────────────────────┘
```

Extra forms

```
┌─────────────────────────────────┐
│ ENDORSE HERE                    │
│ X                               │
│                                 │
│                                 │
│                                 │
│ DO NOT WRITE, STAMP, OR SIGN BELOW THIS LINE │
│   RESERVED FOR FINANCIAL INSTITUTION USE     │
└─────────────────────────────────┘
```

```
┌─────────────────────────────────┐
│ ENDORSE HERE                    │
│ X                               │
│                                 │
│                                 │
│                                 │
│ DO NOT WRITE, STAMP, OR SIGN BELOW THIS LINE │
│   RESERVED FOR FINANCIAL INSTITUTION USE     │
└─────────────────────────────────┘
```

2., 3., 4a.

NO. **608**	$ _____
Date: _____ 20___	
To: _____	
For: _____	

BAL. BRO'T. FOR'D.		
AMT. DEPOSITED .... [Date]		
SUBTOTAL		
OTHER:		
_____		
_____		
SUBTOTAL		
AMT. THIS CHECK		
BAL. CAR'D. FOR'D.		

Accounting Tutors
707 Oak Street
Minneapolis, MN 55447

NO. **608**   17-432/910

_____ 20 _____

PAY TO THE
ORDER OF _____ $ _____

_____ DOLLARS

First National Bank
Minneapolis, MN 55447

For Classroom Use Only

FOR _____   _____

⑆091004329⑆ 291⑈36118⑈

4b.

NO. **609**	$ _____
Date: _____ 20___	
To: _____	
For: _____	

BAL. BRO'T. FOR'D.		
AMT. DEPOSITED .... [Date]		
SUBTOTAL		
OTHER:		
_____		
_____		
SUBTOTAL		
AMT. THIS CHECK		
BAL. CAR'D. FOR'D.		

Accounting Tutors
707 Oak Street
Minneapolis, MN 55447

NO. **609**   17-432/910

_____ 20 _____

PAY TO THE
ORDER OF _____ $ _____

_____ DOLLARS

First National Bank
Minneapolis, MN 55447

For Classroom Use Only

FOR _____   _____

⑆091004329⑆ 291⑈36118⑈

4c.

NO. **610**	$ _____
Date: _____ 20___	
To: _____	
For: _____	

BAL. BRO'T. FOR'D.		
AMT. DEPOSITED .... [Date]		
SUBTOTAL		
OTHER:		
_____		
_____		
SUBTOTAL		
AMT. THIS CHECK		
BAL. CAR'D. FOR'D.		

Accounting Tutors
707 Oak Street
Minneapolis, MN 55447

NO. **610**   17-432/910

_____ 20 _____

PAY TO THE
ORDER OF _____ $ _____

_____ DOLLARS

First National Bank
Minneapolis, MN 55447

For Classroom Use Only

FOR _____   _____

⑆091004329⑆ 291⑈36118⑈

6-2 APPLICATION PROBLEM, p. 146

Reconciling a bank statement and recording a bank service charge

1.

RECONCILIATION OF BANK STATEMENT

_____
(Date)

Balance On Check Stub No. ____ . . . . $

DEDUCT BANK CHARGES:

Description	Amount	
	$	

Total bank charges ▶

Adjusted Check Stub Balance . . . . $

Balance On Bank Statement . . . . $

ADD OUTSTANDING DEPOSITS:

Date	Amount	
	$	

Total outstanding deposits ▶

SUBTOTAL . . . . $

DEDUCT OUTSTANDING CHECKS:

Ck. No.	Amount	Ck. No.	Amount

Total outstanding checks ▶

Adjusted Bank Balance . . . . $

2.

NO. **312**	$ _____

Date: _____ 20 _ _

To: _____

For: _____

BAL. BRO'T. FOR'D.	2,675	99
AMT. DEPOSITED . . . . Date		
SUBTOTAL	2,675	99
OTHER:		
_____		
_____		
SUBTOTAL		
AMT. THIS CHECK		
BAL. CAR'D. FOR'D.		

3.

JOURNAL   PAGE

	DATE	ACCOUNT TITLE	DOC. NO.	POST. REF.	GENERAL DEBIT	GENERAL CREDIT	SALES CREDIT	CASH DEBIT	CASH CREDIT	
1										1
2										2
3										3
4										4

RECONCILIATION OF BANK STATEMENT

_____
(Date)

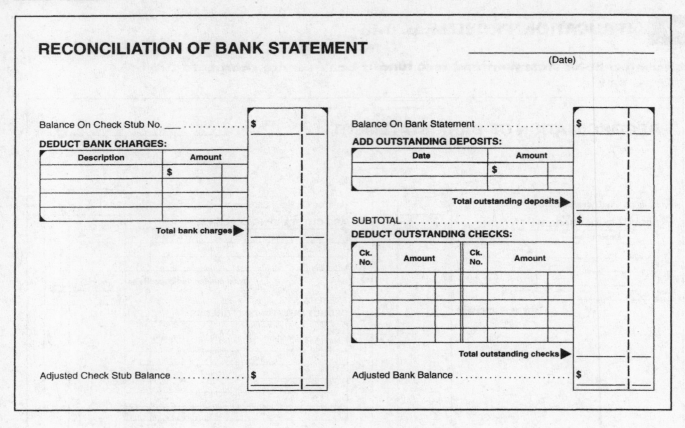

Balance On Check Stub No. ____ .... $

DEDUCT BANK CHARGES:

Description	Amount	
	$	

Total bank charges ▶

Adjusted Check Stub Balance .... $

Balance On Bank Statement .... $

ADD OUTSTANDING DEPOSITS:

Date	Amount	
	$	

Total outstanding deposits ▶

SUBTOTAL . . . . $

DEDUCT OUTSTANDING CHECKS:

Ck. No.	Amount	Ck. No.	Amount	

Total outstanding checks ▶

Adjusted Bank Balance .... $

JOURNAL

PAGE _____

	DATE	ACCOUNT TITLE	DOC. NO.	POST. REF.	GENERAL DEBIT	GENERAL CREDIT	SALES CREDIT	CASH DEBIT	CASH CREDIT	
1										1
2										2
3										3
4										4
5										5
6										6
7										7
8										8
9										9
10										10
11										11
12										12
13										13
14										14
15										15
16										16
17										17
18										18

6-3 APPLICATION PROBLEM, p. 146

Recording dishonored checks, electronic funds transfers, and debit card purchases

JOURNAL   PAGE

	DATE	ACCOUNT TITLE	DOC. NO.	POST. REF.	GENERAL DEBIT	GENERAL CREDIT	SALES CREDIT	CASH DEBIT	CASH CREDIT	
12										12
13										13
14										14
15										15
16										16
17										17
18										18
19										19
20										20
21										21
22										22
23										23
24										24
25										25
26										26
27										27

Extra form

JOURNAL   PAGE

	DATE	ACCOUNT TITLE	DOC. NO.	POST. REF.	GENERAL DEBIT	GENERAL CREDIT	SALES CREDIT	CASH DEBIT	CASH CREDIT	
1										1
2										2
3										3
4										4
5										5
6										6
7										7
8										8
9										9
10										10
11										11
12										12
13										13
14										14
15										15
16										16
17										17

Extra forms

JOURNAL

JOURNAL

	DATE	ACCOUNT TITLE	DOC. NO.	POST. REF.	GENERAL DEBIT (1)	GENERAL CREDIT (2)	SALES CREDIT (3)	CASH DEBIT (4)	CASH CREDIT (5)	
1										1
2										2
3										3
4										4
5										5
6										6
7										7
8										8
9										9
10										10
11										11
12										12
13										13
14										14
15										15
16										16
17										17
18										18

JOURNAL

	DATE	ACCOUNT TITLE	DOC. NO.	POST. REF.	GENERAL DEBIT (1)	GENERAL CREDIT (2)	SALES CREDIT (3)	CASH DEBIT (4)	CASH CREDIT (5)	
1										1
2										2
3										3
4										4
5										5
6										6
7										7
8										8
9										9
10										10
11										11
12										12
13										13
14										14
15										15
16										16
17										17
18										18

6-4 APPLICATION PROBLEM, p. 147

Establishing and replenishing a petty cash fund

JOURNAL

PAGE

	DATE	ACCOUNT TITLE	DOC. NO.	POST. REF.	GENERAL DEBIT	GENERAL CREDIT	SALES CREDIT	CASH DEBIT	CASH CREDIT	
4										4
5										5
6										6
7										7
8										8
9										9
10										10
11										11
12										12
13										13
14										14
15										15
16										16
17										17
18										18
19										19
20										20

Extra form

JOURNAL

PAGE

	DATE	ACCOUNT TITLE	DOC. NO.	POST. REF.	GENERAL DEBIT	GENERAL CREDIT	SALES CREDIT	CASH DEBIT	CASH CREDIT	
1										1
2										2
3										3
4										4
5										5
6										6
7										7
8										8
9										9
10										10
11										11
12										12
13										13
14										14
15										15
16										16
17										17
18										18

Extra forms

JOURNAL

	DATE	ACCOUNT TITLE	DOC. NO.	POST. REF.	GENERAL DEBIT (1)	GENERAL CREDIT (2)	SALES CREDIT (3)	CASH DEBIT (4)	CASH CREDIT (5)	
1										1
2										2
3										3
4										4
5										5
6										6
7										7
8										8
9										9
10										10
11										11
12										12
13										13
14										14
15										15
16										16
17										17
18										18

JOURNAL

	DATE	ACCOUNT TITLE	DOC. NO.	POST. REF.	GENERAL DEBIT (1)	GENERAL CREDIT (2)	SALES CREDIT (3)	CASH DEBIT (4)	CASH CREDIT (5)	
1										1
2										2
3										3
4										4
5										5
6										6
7										7
8										8
9										9
10										10
11										11
12										12
13										13
14										14
15										15
16										16
17										17
18										18

6-5 MASTERY PROBLEM, p. 147

Reconciling a bank statement; journalizing a bank service charge, a dishonored check, and petty cash transactions

1., 3.

JOURNAL   PAGE

	DATE	ACCOUNT TITLE	DOC. NO.	POST. REF.	GENERAL DEBIT	GENERAL CREDIT	SALES CREDIT	CASH DEBIT	CASH CREDIT	
1										1
2										2
3										3
4										4
5										5
6										6
7										7
8										8
9										9
10										10
11										11
12										12
13										13
14										14
15										15

2.

RECONCILIATION OF BANK STATEMENT

_____ (Date)

Balance On Check Stub No. ____ .... $ |

DEDUCT BANK CHARGES:

Description	Amount
	$

Total bank charges ▶

Adjusted Check Stub Balance .... $ |

Balance On Bank Statement .... $ |

ADD OUTSTANDING DEPOSITS:

Date	Amount
	$

Total outstanding deposits ▶

SUBTOTAL .... $ |

DEDUCT OUTSTANDING CHECKS:

Ck. No.	Amount	Ck. No.	Amount

Total outstanding checks ▶

Adjusted Bank Balance .... $ |

Extra forms

JOURNAL   PAGE

DATE	ACCOUNT TITLE	DOC. NO.	POST. REF.	GENERAL		SALES CREDIT	CASH	
				DEBIT	CREDIT		DEBIT	CREDIT
1									1
2									2
3									3
4									4
5									5
6									6
7									7
8									8
9									9
10									10
11									11
12									12
13									13
14									14
15									15
16									16
17									17
18									18

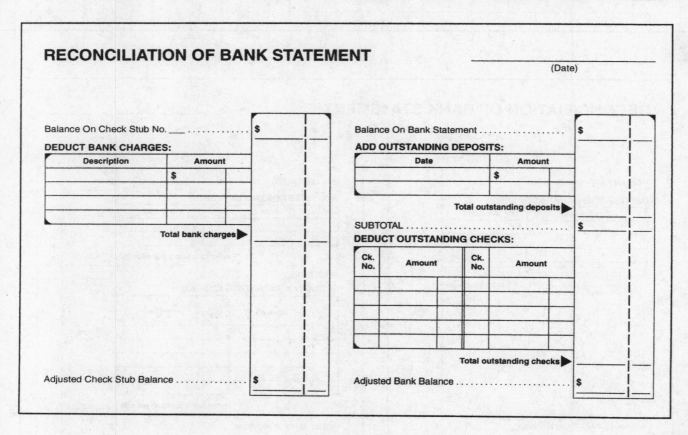

RECONCILIATION OF BANK STATEMENT

_____
(Date)

Balance On Check Stub No. ____ . . . . $ |

DEDUCT BANK CHARGES:

Description	Amount	
	$	

Total bank charges ▶

Adjusted Check Stub Balance . . . . $ |

Balance On Bank Statement . . . . $ |

ADD OUTSTANDING DEPOSITS:

Date	Amount	
	$	

Total outstanding deposits ▶

SUBTOTAL . . . . $ |

DEDUCT OUTSTANDING CHECKS:

Ck. No.	Amount	Ck. No.	Amount

Total outstanding checks ▶

Adjusted Bank Balance . . . . $ |

6-6   CHALLENGE PROBLEM, p. 148

Reconciling a bank statement and recording a bank service charge

1., 2.

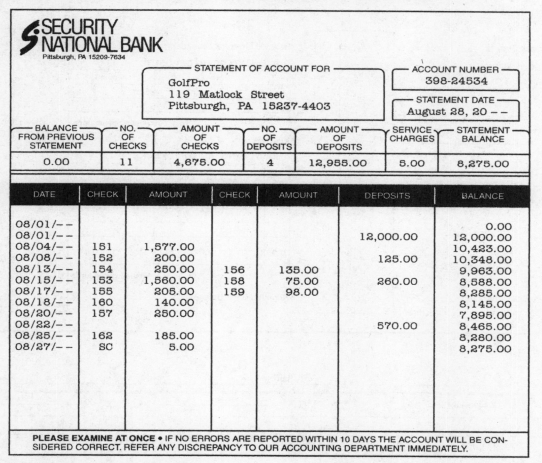

RECONCILIATION OF BANK STATEMENT

_____
(Date)

Balance On Check Stub No. ____ .... $

DEDUCT BANK CHARGES:

Description	Amount	
	$	

Total bank charges ▶

Adjusted Check Stub Balance .... $

Balance On Bank Statement .... $

ADD OUTSTANDING DEPOSITS:

Date	Amount	
	$	

Total outstanding deposits ▶

SUBTOTAL .... $

DEDUCT OUTSTANDING CHECKS:

Ck. No.	Amount	Ck. No.	Amount

Total outstanding checks ▶

Adjusted Bank Balance .... $

JOURNAL

PAGE ____

DATE	ACCOUNT TITLE	DOC. NO.	POST. REF.	GENERAL DEBIT	GENERAL CREDIT	SALES CREDIT	CASH DEBIT	CASH CREDIT	
									1
									2
									3
									4
									5
									6
									7
									8
									9
									10
									11
									12
									13
									14
									15
									16
									17
									18

6-6 CHALLENGE PROBLEM (continued)

1., 2., 4.

NO. 151	$ 1,577.00
Date: August 1,	20--
To: Montag Company	
For: Supplies	

BAL. BRO'T. FOR'D.	0	00
AMT. DEPOSITED ... 8 1 -- Date	12,000	00
SUBTOTAL	12,000	00
OTHER:		
SUBTOTAL	12,000	00
AMT. THIS CHECK	1,577	00
BAL. CAR'D. FOR'D.	10,423	00

NO. 152	$ 200.00
Date: August 5,	20--
To: Plain Company	
For: Rent	

BAL. BRO'T. FOR'D.	10,423	00
AMT. DEPOSITED .... Date		
SUBTOTAL	10,423	00
OTHER:		
SUBTOTAL	10,423	00
AMT. THIS CHECK	200	00
BAL. CAR'D. FOR'D.	10,223	00

NO. 153	$ 1,560.00
Date: August 8,	20--
To: Thomson Company	
For: Supplies	

BAL. BRO'T. FOR'D.	10,223	00
AMT. DEPOSITED .... 8 8 -- Date	125	00
SUBTOTAL	10,348	00
OTHER:		
SUBTOTAL	10,348	00
AMT. THIS CHECK	1,560	00
BAL. CAR'D. FOR'D.	8,788	00

NO. 154	$ 250.00
Date: August 8,	20--
To: Metro Insurance Company	
For: Insurance	

BAL. BRO'T. FOR'D.	8,788	00
AMT. DEPOSITED .... Date		
SUBTOTAL	8,788	00
OTHER:		
SUBTOTAL	8,788	00
AMT. THIS CHECK	250	00
BAL. CAR'D. FOR'D.	8,538	00

NO. 155	$ 205.00
Date: August 10,	20--
To: City Electric Company	
For: Utilities	

BAL. BRO'T. FOR'D.	8,538	00
AMT. DEPOSITED .... Date		
SUBTOTAL	8,538	00
OTHER:		
SUBTOTAL	8,538	00
AMT. THIS CHECK	205	00
BAL. CAR'D. FOR'D.	8,333	00

NO. 156	$ 135.00
Date: August 10,	20--
To: Patterson Supplies	
For: Payment on account	

BAL. BRO'T. FOR'D.	8,333	00
AMT. DEPOSITED .... Date		
SUBTOTAL	8,333	00
OTHER:		
SUBTOTAL	8,333	00
AMT. THIS CHECK	135	00
BAL. CAR'D. FOR'D.	8,198	00

NO. 157	$ 250.00
Date: August 13,	20--
To: John Walker	
For: Owner's withdrawal	

BAL. BRO'T. FOR'D.	8,198	00
AMT. DEPOSITED .... Date		
SUBTOTAL	8,198	00
OTHER:		
SUBTOTAL	8,198	00
AMT. THIS CHECK	250	00
BAL. CAR'D. FOR'D.	7,948	00

NO. 158	$ 75.00
Date: August 14,	20--
To: Pennsylvania Telephone Company	
For: Utilities	

BAL. BRO'T. FOR'D.	7,948	00
AMT. DEPOSITED .... Date		
SUBTOTAL	7,948	00
OTHER:		
SUBTOTAL	7,948	00
AMT. THIS CHECK	75	00
BAL. CAR'D. FOR'D.	7,873	00

NO. 159	$ 98.00
Date: August 15,	20--
To: Ace Cleaning Company	
For: Cleaning	

BAL. BRO'T. FOR'D.	7,873	00
AMT. DEPOSITED .... Date		
SUBTOTAL	7,873	00
OTHER:		
SUBTOTAL	7,873	00
AMT. THIS CHECK	98	00
BAL. CAR'D. FOR'D.	7,775	00

1., 2., 4.

NO. 160	$ 140.00	
Date: August 15,		20--
To: Tri-State Agency		
For: Miscellaneous		
BAL. BRO'T. FOR'D.	7,775	00
AMT. DEPOSITED 8/15--	260	00
SUBTOTAL	8,035	00
OTHER:		
SUBTOTAL	8,035	00
AMT. THIS CHECK	140	00
BAL. CAR'D. FOR'D.	7,895	00

NO. 161	$ 375.00	
Date: August 19,		20--
To: Pittsburgh Enquirer		
For: Advertising		
BAL. BRO'T. FOR'D.	7,895	00
AMT. DEPOSITED		
SUBTOTAL	7,895	00
OTHER:		
SUBTOTAL	7,895	00
AMT. THIS CHECK	375	00
BAL. CAR'D. FOR'D.	7,520	00

NO. 162	$ 185.00	
Date: August 22,		20--
To: Dowd Company		
For: Payment on account		
BAL. BRO'T. FOR'D.	7,520	00
AMT. DEPOSITED 8/22--	570	00
SUBTOTAL	8,090	00
OTHER:		
SUBTOTAL	8,090	00
AMT. THIS CHECK	185	00
BAL. CAR'D. FOR'D.	7,905	00

NO. 163	$ 17.00	
Date: August 23,		20--
To: Jason North		
For: Miscellaneous		
BAL. BRO'T. FOR'D.	7,905	00
AMT. DEPOSITED		
SUBTOTAL	7,905	00
OTHER:		
SUBTOTAL	7,905	00
AMT. THIS CHECK	17	00
BAL. CAR'D. FOR'D.	7,888	00

NO. 164	$ 250.00	
Date: August 28,		20--
To: John Walker		
For: Owner's withdrawal		
BAL. BRO'T. FOR'D.	7,888	00
AMT. DEPOSITED 8/28--	430	00
SUBTOTAL	8,318	00
OTHER:		
SUBTOTAL	8,318	00
AMT. THIS CHECK	250	00
BAL. CAR'D. FOR'D.	8,068	00

NO. 165	$	
Date:		20--
To:		
For:		
BAL. BRO'T. FOR'D.	8,068	00
AMT. DEPOSITED		
SUBTOTAL	8,068	00
OTHER:		
SUBTOTAL		
AMT. THIS CHECK		
BAL. CAR'D. FOR'D.		

6-6 **CHALLENGE PROBLEM (concluded)**

2.

RECONCILIATION OF BANK STATEMENT

_____
(Date)

Balance On Check Stub No. ____ .... $ | |

DEDUCT BANK CHARGES:

Description	Amount
	$

Total bank charges ▶

Adjusted Check Stub Balance .... $

Balance On Bank Statement .... $ | |

ADD OUTSTANDING DEPOSITS:

Date	Amount
	$

Total outstanding deposits ▶

SUBTOTAL .... $

DEDUCT OUTSTANDING CHECKS:

Ck. No.	Amount	Ck. No.	Amount

Total outstanding checks ▶

Adjusted Bank Balance .... $

3.

JOURNAL   PAGE

	DATE	ACCOUNT TITLE	DOC. NO.	POST. REF.	GENERAL DEBIT	GENERAL CREDIT	SALES CREDIT	CASH DEBIT	CASH CREDIT	
1										1
2										2
3										3
4										4
5										5
6										6
7										7
8										8
9										9
10										10
11										11
12										12
13										13
14										14
15										15
16										16

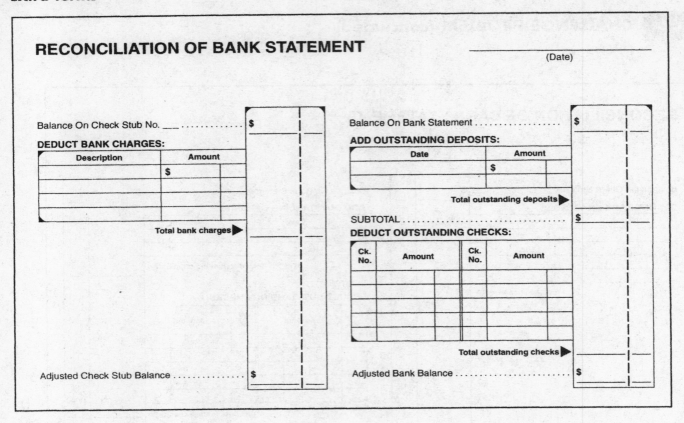

RECONCILIATION OF BANK STATEMENT

_____
(Date)

Balance On Check Stub No. ____ . . . . $ | |

DEDUCT BANK CHARGES:

Description	Amount	
	$	

Total bank charges ▶

Adjusted Check Stub Balance . . . . $ | |

Balance On Bank Statement . . . . $ | |

ADD OUTSTANDING DEPOSITS:

Date	Amount	
	$	

Total outstanding deposits ▶

SUBTOTAL . . . . $ | |

DEDUCT OUTSTANDING CHECKS:

Ck. No.	Amount	Ck. No.	Amount

Total outstanding checks ▶

Adjusted Bank Balance . . . . $ | |

JOURNAL

PAGE

	DATE	ACCOUNT TITLE	DOC. NO.	POST. REF.	GENERAL DEBIT (1)	GENERAL CREDIT (2)	SALES CREDIT (3)	CASH DEBIT (4)	CASH CREDIT (5)	
1										1
2										2
3										3
4										4
5										5
6										6
7										7
8										8
9										9
10										10
11										11
12										12
13										13
14										14
15										15
16										16
17										17
18										18

REINFORCEMENT ACTIVITY 1
PART A, p. 151

An Accounting Cycle for a Proprietorship: Journalizing and Posting Transactions
1., 2., 3.

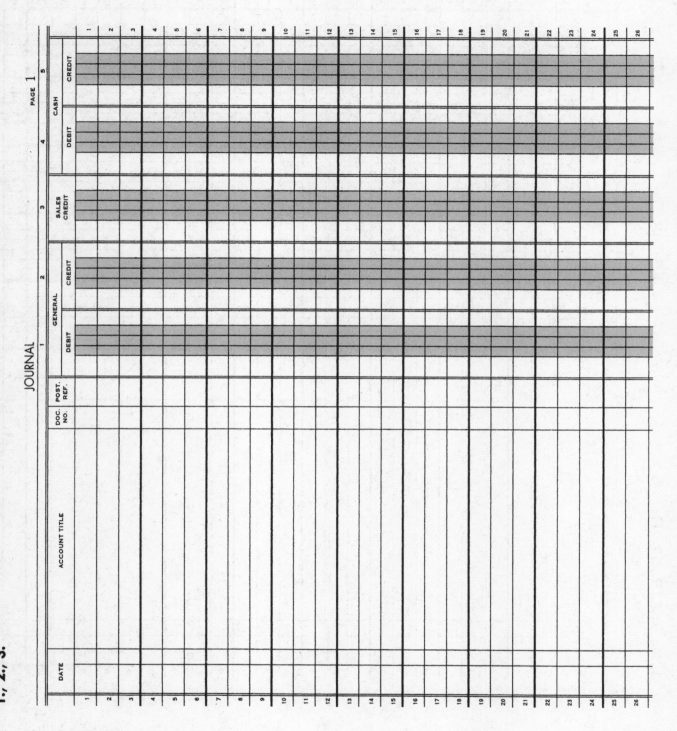

JOURNAL

PAGE 1

2., 4., 6., 7., 9., 10., 11.

JOURNAL

PAGE 2

DATE	ACCOUNT TITLE	DOC. NO.	POST. REF.	GENERAL DEBIT 1	GENERAL CREDIT 2	SALES CREDIT 3	CASH DEBIT 4	CASH CREDIT 5
									1
									2
									3
									4
									5
									6
									7
									8
									9
									10
									11
									12
									13
									14
									15
									16
									17
									18
									19
									20
									21
									22
									23
									24
									25
									26

REINFORCEMENT ACTIVITY 1

PART A (continued)

5.

RECONCILIATION OF BANK STATEMENT

_____
(Date)

Balance On Check Stub No. _____ . . . . $

DEDUCT BANK CHARGES:

Description	Amount	
	$	

Total bank charges ▶

Adjusted Check Stub Balance . . . . $

Balance On Bank Statement . . . . $

ADD OUTSTANDING DEPOSITS:

Date	Amount	
	$	

Total outstanding deposits ▶

SUBTOTAL . . . . $

DEDUCT OUTSTANDING CHECKS:

Ck. No.	Amount	Ck. No.	Amount	

Total outstanding checks ▶

Adjusted Bank Balance . . . . $

2. *Prove page 1 of the journal:*

Column	Debit Column Totals	Credit Column Totals
General		
Sales	_____	_____
Cash	_____	_____
Totals	_____	_____

7. *Prove page 2 of the journal:*

Column	Debit Column Totals	Credit Column Totals
General		
Sales	_____	_____
Cash	_____	_____
Totals	_____	_____

8. *Prove cash:*

Cash on hand at the beginning of the month . . . .
Plus total cash received during the month . . . . _____
Equals Total . . . . _____
Less total cash paid during the month . . . . _____
Equals cash balance at the end of the month . . . . _____
Checkbook balance on the next unused check stub . . . . _____

REINFORCEMENT ACTIVITY 1

PART A (continued)

The general ledger prepared in Reinforcement Activity 1, Part A, is needed to complete Reinforcement Activity 1, Part B.

3., 10., 11., 19., 20.   **GENERAL LEDGER**

ACCOUNT Cash   ACCOUNT NO. 110

DATE	ITEM	POST. REF.	DEBIT	CREDIT	BALANCE DEBIT	BALANCE CREDIT

ACCOUNT Petty Cash   ACCOUNT NO. 120

DATE	ITEM	POST. REF.	DEBIT	CREDIT	BALANCE DEBIT	BALANCE CREDIT

ACCOUNT Accounts Receivable—Breck School   ACCOUNT NO. 130

DATE	ITEM	POST. REF.	DEBIT	CREDIT	BALANCE DEBIT	BALANCE CREDIT

ACCOUNT Accounts Receivable—Lincoln School   ACCOUNT NO. 140

DATE	ITEM	POST. REF.	DEBIT	CREDIT	BALANCE DEBIT	BALANCE CREDIT

ACCOUNT Supplies   ACCOUNT NO. 150

DATE	ITEM	POST. REF.	DEBIT	CREDIT	BALANCE DEBIT	BALANCE CREDIT

ACCOUNT Prepaid Insurance   ACCOUNT NO. 160

DATE	ITEM	POST. REF.	DEBIT	CREDIT	BALANCE DEBIT	BALANCE CREDIT

REINFORCEMENT ACTIVITY 1
PART A (continued)
3., 10., 11., 19., 20.

GENERAL LEDGER

ACCOUNT Accounts Payable—Dunnel Supplies   ACCOUNT NO. 210

DATE	ITEM	POST. REF.	DEBIT	CREDIT	BALANCE DEBIT	BALANCE CREDIT

ACCOUNT Accounts Payable—Voiles Office Supplies   ACCOUNT NO. 220

DATE	ITEM	POST. REF.	DEBIT	CREDIT	BALANCE DEBIT	BALANCE CREDIT

ACCOUNT Caleb Christianson, Capital   ACCOUNT NO. 310

DATE	ITEM	POST. REF.	DEBIT	CREDIT	BALANCE DEBIT	BALANCE CREDIT

ACCOUNT Caleb Christianson, Drawing   ACCOUNT NO. 320

DATE	ITEM	POST. REF.	DEBIT	CREDIT	BALANCE DEBIT	BALANCE CREDIT

ACCOUNT Income Summary   ACCOUNT NO. 330

DATE	ITEM	POST. REF.	DEBIT	CREDIT	BALANCE DEBIT	BALANCE CREDIT

ACCOUNT Sales   ACCOUNT NO. 410

DATE	ITEM	POST. REF.	DEBIT	CREDIT	BALANCE DEBIT	BALANCE CREDIT

ACCOUNT Advertising Expense   ACCOUNT NO. 510

DATE	ITEM	POST. REF.	DEBIT	CREDIT	BALANCE DEBIT	BALANCE CREDIT

REINFORCEMENT ACTIVITY 1

PART A (continued)

The general ledger prepared in Reinforcement Activity 1, Part A, is needed to complete Reinforcement Activity 1, Part B.

3., 10., 11., 19., 20.   GENERAL LEDGER

ACCOUNT Insurance Expense   ACCOUNT NO. 520

DATE	ITEM	POST. REF.	DEBIT	CREDIT	BALANCE DEBIT	BALANCE CREDIT

ACCOUNT Miscellaneous Expense   ACCOUNT NO. 530

DATE	ITEM	POST. REF.	DEBIT	CREDIT	BALANCE DEBIT	BALANCE CREDIT

ACCOUNT Rent Expense   ACCOUNT NO. 540

DATE	ITEM	POST. REF.	DEBIT	CREDIT	BALANCE DEBIT	BALANCE CREDIT

ACCOUNT Repair Expense   ACCOUNT NO. 550

DATE	ITEM	POST. REF.	DEBIT	CREDIT	BALANCE DEBIT	BALANCE CREDIT

ACCOUNT Supplies Expense   ACCOUNT NO. 560

DATE	ITEM	POST. REF.	DEBIT	CREDIT	BALANCE DEBIT	BALANCE CREDIT

ACCOUNT Utilities Expense   ACCOUNT NO. 570

DATE	ITEM	POST. REF.	DEBIT	CREDIT	BALANCE DEBIT	BALANCE CREDIT

7-1, 7-2, and 7-3 WORK TOGETHER, pp. 158, 164, 169

7-1 Recording the trial balance on a work sheet
7-2 Planning adjustments on a work sheet
7-3 Completing a work sheet

ACCOUNT TITLE	TRIAL BALANCE		ADJUSTMENTS		INCOME STATEMENT		BALANCE SHEET	
	DEBIT	CREDIT	DEBIT	CREDIT	DEBIT	CREDIT	DEBIT	CREDIT
	1	2	3	4	5	6	7	8

7-1 Recording the trial balance on a work sheet
7-2 Planning adjustments on a work sheet
7-3 Completing a work sheet

ACCOUNT TITLE	TRIAL BALANCE		ADJUSTMENTS		INCOME STATEMENT		BALANCE SHEET	
	DEBIT	CREDIT	DEBIT	CREDIT	DEBIT	CREDIT	DEBIT	CREDIT
	1	2	3	4	5	6	7	8

COPYRIGHT © SOUTH-WESTERN CENGAGE LEARNING

7-4   WORK TOGETHER, p. 173

Finding and correcting errors in accounting records

4., 5.   **GENERAL LEDGER**

ACCOUNT Cash   ACCOUNT NO. 110

DATE		ITEM	POST. REF.	DEBIT	CREDIT	BALANCE DEBIT	BALANCE CREDIT
Sept.	1		1	4 0 0 0 00		4 0 0 0 00	
	30		2	7 0 0 0 00		15 0 0 0 00	
	30		2		6 7 5 0 00	8 0 0 0 00	

ACCOUNT Accounts Receivable—Sharon Mann   ACCOUNT NO. 120

DATE		ITEM	POST. REF.	DEBIT	CREDIT	BALANCE DEBIT	BALANCE CREDIT
Sept.	12		1	1 0 0 0 00		1 0 0 0 00	

ACCOUNT Supplies   ACCOUNT NO. 130

DATE		ITEM	POST. REF.	DEBIT	CREDIT	BALANCE DEBIT	BALANCE CREDIT
Sept.	2		1	6 0 0 00		6 0 0 00	
	25		2	4 2 5 00		7 2 5 00	

ACCOUNT Prepaid Insurance   ACCOUNT NO. 140

DATE		ITEM	POST. REF.	DEBIT	CREDIT	BALANCE DEBIT	BALANCE CREDIT
Sept.	3		1	1 5 0 00		1 5 0 00	
	20		2	1 5 0 00		4 0 0 00	

ACCOUNT Accounts Payable—Powers Supply   ACCOUNT NO. 210

DATE		ITEM	POST. REF.	DEBIT	CREDIT	BALANCE DEBIT	BALANCE CREDIT
Sept.	4		1		3 0 0 00		3 0 0 00
	15		2	1 5 0 00			1 5 0 00

ACCOUNT Paul Coty, Capital   ACCOUNT NO. 310

DATE		ITEM	POST. REF.	DEBIT	CREDIT	BALANCE DEBIT	BALANCE CREDIT
Sept.	1		1		5 0 0 0 00		5 0 0 0 00

4., 5.   **GENERAL LEDGER**

ACCOUNT Paul Coty, Drawing   ACCOUNT NO. 320

DATE		ITEM	POST. REF.	DEBIT	CREDIT	BALANCE	
						DEBIT	CREDIT
Sept.	30		2	3 0 0 00		3 0 0 00	

ACCOUNT Income Summary   ACCOUNT NO. 330

DATE		ITEM	POST. REF.	DEBIT	CREDIT	BALANCE	
						DEBIT	CREDIT

ACCOUNT Sales   ACCOUNT NO. 410

DATE		ITEM	POST. REF.	DEBIT	CREDIT	BALANCE	
						DEBIT	CREDIT
Sept.	30		2		1 9 0 0 00		1 8 7 5 00

ACCOUNT Insurance Expense   ACCOUNT NO. 510

DATE		ITEM	POST. REF.	DEBIT	CREDIT	BALANCE	
						DEBIT	CREDIT

ACCOUNT Miscellaneous Expense   ACCOUNT NO. 520

DATE		ITEM	POST. REF.	DEBIT	CREDIT	BALANCE	
						DEBIT	CREDIT
Sept.	9		1	1 5 0 00		1 5 0 00	
	27		2	2 5 00		1 2 5 00	

ACCOUNT Supplies Expense   ACCOUNT NO. 530

DATE		ITEM	POST. REF.	DEBIT	CREDIT	BALANCE	
						DEBIT	CREDIT

7-4 **WORK TOGETHER (continued)**

4. **ERRORS**

_____
_____
_____
_____
_____
_____
_____
_____
_____
_____
_____
_____
_____
_____
_____
_____
_____
_____
_____
_____
_____
_____
_____
_____
_____
_____
_____
_____
_____
_____
_____
_____

4. **ERRORS**

_____

_____

_____

_____

_____

_____

_____

_____

_____

_____

_____

_____

_____

_____

_____

_____

_____

_____

_____

_____

_____

_____

_____

_____

_____

_____

_____

_____

_____

7-4 WORK TOGETHER (continued)

4.

#	Account Title	Trial Balance Debit	Trial Balance Credit	Adjustments Debit	Adjustments Credit	Income Statement Debit	Income Statement Credit	Balance Sheet Debit	Balance Sheet Credit
1	Cash	8000 00						8000 00	
2	Accts. Rec.—Sharon Mann	1000 00						1000 00	
3	Supplies	725 00		(a) 390 00				1115 00	
4	Prepaid Insurance	400 00		(b) 95 00				495 00	
5	Accts. Pay.—Powers Supply		150 00						150 00
6	Paul Coty, Capital		5000 00						5000 00
7	Paul Coty, Drawing	300 00							300 00
8	Income Summary								
9	Sales		1875 00				1875 00		
10	Insurance Expense				(b) 95 00		95 00		
11	Miscellaneous Expense	125 00				152 00			
12	Supplies Expense				(a) 390 00		390 00		
13		10550 00	7025 00	485 00	485 00	152 00	2360 00	10610 00	5450 00
14	Net Income					2208 00			5160 00
15						2360 00	2360 00	10610 00	10610 00
16									
17									
18									
19									
20									
21									

ACCOUNT TITLE	TRIAL BALANCE		ADJUSTMENTS		INCOME STATEMENT		BALANCE SHEET	
	DEBIT	CREDIT	DEBIT	CREDIT	DEBIT	CREDIT	DEBIT	CREDIT
	1	2	3	4	5	6	7	8

7-4 WORK TOGETHER (concluded)

6.

ACCOUNT TITLE	TRIAL BALANCE		ADJUSTMENTS		INCOME STATEMENT		BALANCE SHEET	
	DEBIT	CREDIT	DEBIT	CREDIT	DEBIT	CREDIT	DEBIT	CREDIT
1								
2								
3								
4								
5								
6								
7								
8								
9								
10								
11								
12								
13								
14								
15								
16								
17								
18								
19								
20								
21								

ACCOUNT TITLE		TRIAL BALANCE		ADJUSTMENTS		INCOME STATEMENT		BALANCE SHEET	
		DEBIT	CREDIT	DEBIT	CREDIT	DEBIT	CREDIT	DEBIT	CREDIT
		1	2	3	4	5	6	7	8

7-4 ON YOUR OWN, p. 173

Finding and correcting errors in accounting records

7., 8. GENERAL LEDGER

ACCOUNT Cash ACCOUNT NO. 110

DATE	ITEM	POST. REF.	DEBIT	CREDIT	BALANCE DEBIT	BALANCE CREDIT
20-- Nov. 1		1	11 000 00		11 000 00	
30		2	6 495 00		17 945 00	
30		2		5 550 00	12 395 00	

ACCOUNT Supplies ACCOUNT NO. 120

DATE	ITEM	POST. REF.	DEBIT	CREDIT	BALANCE DEBIT	BALANCE CREDIT
20-- Nov. 2		1	400 00		40 00	
25		2	100 00		140 00	

ACCOUNT Prepaid Insurance ACCOUNT NO. 130

DATE	ITEM	POST. REF.	DEBIT	CREDIT	BALANCE DEBIT	BALANCE CREDIT
20-- Nov. 3		1	250 00		520 00	

ACCOUNT Accounts Payable—NW Electric ACCOUNT NO. 210

DATE	ITEM	POST. REF.	DEBIT	CREDIT	BALANCE DEBIT	BALANCE CREDIT
20-- Nov. 4		1		500 00		500 00
15		2	150 00			650 00

ACCOUNT Marlene Lewis, Capital ACCOUNT NO. 310

DATE	ITEM	POST. REF.	DEBIT	CREDIT	BALANCE DEBIT	BALANCE CREDIT
20-- Nov. 1		1		11 000 00		11 000 00

7., 8.   **GENERAL LEDGER**

ACCOUNT Marlene Lewis, Drawing   ACCOUNT NO. 320

DATE	ITEM	POST. REF.	DEBIT	CREDIT	BALANCE DEBIT	BALANCE CREDIT
Nov. 30		2	400 00		400 00	

ACCOUNT Income Summary   ACCOUNT NO. 330

DATE	ITEM	POST. REF.	DEBIT	CREDIT	BALANCE DEBIT	BALANCE CREDIT

ACCOUNT Sales   ACCOUNT NO. 410

DATE	ITEM	POST. REF.	DEBIT	CREDIT	BALANCE DEBIT	BALANCE CREDIT
Nov. 30		2		1900 00		1900 00

ACCOUNT Insurance Expense   ACCOUNT NO. 510

DATE	ITEM	POST. REF.	DEBIT	CREDIT	BALANCE DEBIT	BALANCE CREDIT

ACCOUNT Miscellaneous Expense   ACCOUNT NO. 520

DATE	ITEM	POST. REF.	DEBIT	CREDIT	BALANCE DEBIT	BALANCE CREDIT
Nov. 9		1	100 00		100 00	
27		2	55 00		45 00	

ACCOUNT Supplies Expense   ACCOUNT NO. 530

DATE	ITEM	POST. REF.	DEBIT	CREDIT	BALANCE DEBIT	BALANCE CREDIT

7-4 **ON YOUR OWN** (continued)

7. **ERRORS**

7. **ERRORS**

7-4 ON YOUR OWN (continued)

Internet Access

Work Sheet

For Month Ended November 30, 20 --

ACCOUNT TITLE	TRIAL BALANCE DEBIT	TRIAL BALANCE CREDIT	ADJUSTMENTS DEBIT	ADJUSTMENTS CREDIT	INCOME STATEMENT DEBIT	INCOME STATEMENT CREDIT	BALANCE SHEET DEBIT	BALANCE SHEET CREDIT	
1 Cash	12395 00						12395 00		1
2 Supplies	140 00		(a) 90 00				230 00		2
3 Prepaid Insurance	520 00		(b) 104 00				642 00		3
4 Accts. Pay.—NW Electric		650 00						650 00	4
5 Marlene Lewis, Capital		11000 00						11000 00	5
6 Marlene Lewis, Drawing	400 00							400 00	6
7 Income Summary									7
8 Sales		1900 00				1900 00			8
9 Insurance Expense				(b) 104 00		104 00			9
10 Miscellaneous Expense	45 00				54 00				10
11 Supplies Expense				(a) 90 00	54 00	90 00			11
12	13500 00	13550 00	194 00	194 00	54 00	2094 00	13267 00	1205 00	12
13 Net Income					2040 00			1217 00	13
14					2094 00	2094 00	13267 00	13267 00	14
15									15
16									16
17									17
18									18
19									19
20									20
21									21

Extra form

ACCOUNT TITLE		TRIAL BALANCE		ADJUSTMENTS		INCOME STATEMENT		BALANCE SHEET	
		1 DEBIT	2 CREDIT	3 DEBIT	4 CREDIT	5 DEBIT	6 CREDIT	7 DEBIT	8 CREDIT

7-4 **ON YOUR OWN (concluded)**

9.

ACCOUNT TITLE		TRIAL BALANCE		ADJUSTMENTS		INCOME STATEMENT		BALANCE SHEET	
		1 DEBIT	2 CREDIT	3 DEBIT	4 CREDIT	5 DEBIT	6 CREDIT	7 DEBIT	8 CREDIT
1									
2									
3									
4									
5									
6									
7									
8									
9									
10									
11									
12									
13									
14									
15									
16									
17									
18									
19									
20									
21									

Extra form

ACCOUNT TITLE	TRIAL BALANCE		ADJUSTMENTS		INCOME STATEMENT		BALANCE SHEET	
	DEBIT 1	CREDIT 2	DEBIT 3	CREDIT 4	DEBIT 5	CREDIT 6	DEBIT 7	CREDIT 8
1								
2								
3								
4								
5								
6								
7								
8								
9								
10								
11								
12								
13								
14								
15								
16								
17								
18								
19								
20								
21								
22								
23								

7-1, 7-2, and 7-3 APPLICATION PROBLEMS, p. 175

7-1 Recording the trial balance on a work sheet
7-2 Planning adjustments on a work sheet
7-3 Completing a work sheet

ACCOUNT TITLE	TRIAL BALANCE		ADJUSTMENTS		INCOME STATEMENT		BALANCE SHEET	
	DEBIT	CREDIT	DEBIT	CREDIT	DEBIT	CREDIT	DEBIT	CREDIT
	1	2	3	4	5	6	7	8

ACCOUNT TITLE	TRIAL BALANCE		ADJUSTMENTS		INCOME STATEMENT		BALANCE SHEET	
	1 DEBIT	2 CREDIT	3 DEBIT	4 CREDIT	5 DEBIT	6 CREDIT	7 DEBIT	8 CREDIT

7-4 APPLICATION PROBLEM, p. 176

Finding and correcting errors in accounting records

1., 2.   **GENERAL LEDGER**

ACCOUNT **Cash**   ACCOUNT NO. 110

DATE		ITEM	POST. REF.	DEBIT	CREDIT	BALANCE DEBIT	BALANCE CREDIT
20-- Apr.	1		1	8 5 0 0 00		8 5 0 0 00	
	30		2	1 5 3 5 00		10 3 0 5 00	
	30		2		2 3 4 0 00	7 9 6 5 00	

ACCOUNT **Supplies**   ACCOUNT NO. 120

DATE		ITEM	POST. REF.	DEBIT	CREDIT	BALANCE DEBIT	BALANCE CREDIT
20-- Apr.	2		1	5 0 0 00		5 0 00	

ACCOUNT **Prepaid Insurance**   ACCOUNT NO. 130

DATE		ITEM	POST. REF.	DEBIT	CREDIT	BALANCE DEBIT	BALANCE CREDIT
20-- Apr.	3		1	6 3 0 00		6 3 0 00	

ACCOUNT **Accounts Payable—Archer Supplies**   ACCOUNT NO. 210

DATE		ITEM	POST. REF.	DEBIT	CREDIT	BALANCE DEBIT	BALANCE CREDIT
20-- Apr.	4		1		7 0 0 00		7 0 0 00
	15		2	2 0 0 00			5 0 0 00

ACCOUNT **Ervin Watkins, Capital**   ACCOUNT NO. 310

DATE		ITEM	POST. REF.	DEBIT	CREDIT	BALANCE DEBIT	BALANCE CREDIT
20-- Apr.	1		1		8 5 0 0 00		5 8 0 0 00

1., 2.   **GENERAL LEDGER**

ACCOUNT Ervin Watkins, Drawing   ACCOUNT NO. 320

DATE	ITEM	POST. REF.	DEBIT	CREDIT	BALANCE DEBIT	BALANCE CREDIT
20-- Apr. 30		2	6 0 0 00		6 0 0 00	

ACCOUNT Income Summary   ACCOUNT NO. 330

DATE	ITEM	POST. REF.	DEBIT	CREDIT	BALANCE DEBIT	BALANCE CREDIT

ACCOUNT Sales   ACCOUNT NO. 410

DATE	ITEM	POST. REF.	DEBIT	CREDIT	BALANCE DEBIT	BALANCE CREDIT
20-- Apr. 30		2		9 0 0 00		9 9 0 00

ACCOUNT Insurance Expense   ACCOUNT NO. 510

DATE	ITEM	POST. REF.	DEBIT	CREDIT	BALANCE DEBIT	BALANCE CREDIT

ACCOUNT Miscellaneous Expense   ACCOUNT NO. 520

DATE	ITEM	POST. REF.	DEBIT	CREDIT	BALANCE DEBIT	BALANCE CREDIT
20-- Apr. 9		1	3 5 0 00			3 5 0 00
27		2	1 2 5 00			2 2 5 00

ACCOUNT Supplies Expense   ACCOUNT NO. 530

DATE	ITEM	POST. REF.	DEBIT	CREDIT	BALANCE DEBIT	BALANCE CREDIT

7-4 **APPLICATION PROBLEM** (continued)

1. ERRORS

1.   ERRORS

7-4 APPLICATION PROBLEM (continued)

Ever Clean

Work Sheet

For Month Ended April 30, 20 – –

	ACCOUNT TITLE	TRIAL BALANCE DEBIT	TRIAL BALANCE CREDIT	ADJUSTMENTS DEBIT	ADJUSTMENTS CREDIT	INCOME STATEMENT DEBIT	INCOME STATEMENT CREDIT	BALANCE SHEET DEBIT	BALANCE SHEET CREDIT
1	Cash	7 9 6 5 00						7 9 5 6 00	
2	Supplies	5 0 00			(a) 2 1 0 00				2 5 0 00
3	Prepaid Insurance	6 3 0 00			(b) 3 0 0 00			2 4 0 00	
4	Accts. Pay.—Archer Supplies		5 0 0 00						5 0 0 00
5	Ervin Watkins, Capital		5 8 0 0 00						5 8 0 00
6	Ervin Watkins, Drawing	6 0 0 00						6 0 0 00	
7	Income Summary								
8	Sales		9 9 0 00				9 9 0 00		
9	Insurance Expense			(b) 3 0 0 00	(b) 2 1 0 00		2 1 0 00		
10	Miscellaneous Expense	2 2 5 00				2 2 5 00			
11	Supplies Expense			5 1 0 00		3 0 0 00			
12		9 4 7 0 00	7 2 9 0 00	5 1 0 00	5 1 0 00	5 2 5 00	1 2 0 0 00	8 7 9 6 00	6 5 5 00
13	Net Income					6 7 5 00			2 2 4 6 00
14						1 2 0 0 00	1 2 0 0 00	8 7 9 6 00	8 7 9 6 00
15									
16									
17									
18									
19									
20									
21									

ACCOUNT TITLE	TRIAL BALANCE		ADJUSTMENTS		INCOME STATEMENT		BALANCE SHEET	
	DEBIT 1	CREDIT 2	DEBIT 3	CREDIT 4	DEBIT 5	CREDIT 6	DEBIT 7	CREDIT 8

7-4 APPLICATION PROBLEM (concluded)

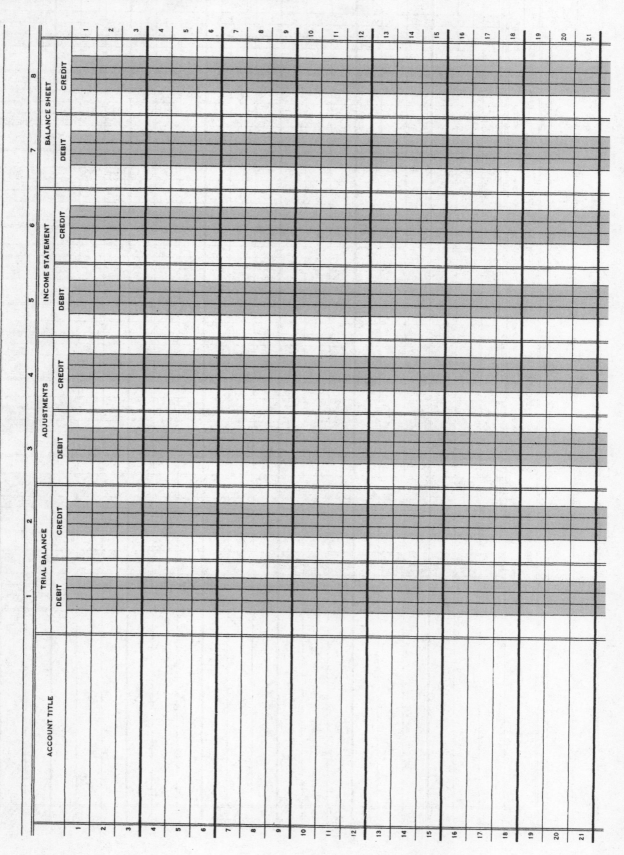

			ACCOUNT TITLE	1	2	3	4	5	6	7	8	9	10	11	12	13	14	15	16	17	18	19	20	21	22	23
TRIAL BALANCE	1	DEBIT																								
	2	CREDIT																								
ADJUSTMENTS	3	DEBIT																								
	4	CREDIT																								
INCOME STATEMENT	5	DEBIT																								
	6	CREDIT																								
BALANCE SHEET	7	DEBIT																								
	8	CREDIT																								

7-5 **MASTERY PROBLEM, p. 176**

Completing a work sheet

ACCOUNT TITLE	TRIAL BALANCE		ADJUSTMENTS		INCOME STATEMENT		BALANCE SHEET	
	DEBIT	CREDIT	DEBIT	CREDIT	DEBIT	CREDIT	DEBIT	CREDIT
	1	2	3	4	5	6	7	8
1								
2								
3								
4								
5								
6								
7								
8								
9								
10								
11								
12								
13								
14								
15								
16								
17								
18								
19								
20								
21								

Extra form

ACCOUNT TITLE	TRIAL BALANCE		ADJUSTMENTS		INCOME STATEMENT		BALANCE SHEET	
	DEBIT	CREDIT	DEBIT	CREDIT	DEBIT	CREDIT	DEBIT	CREDIT
1								
2								
3								
4								
5								
6								
7								
8								
9								
10								
11								
12								
13								
14								
15								
16								
17								
18								
19								
20								
21								
22								
23								

7-6 CHALLENGE PROBLEM, p. 177

Completing a work sheet

ACCOUNT TITLE	TRIAL BALANCE		ADJUSTMENTS		INCOME STATEMENT		BALANCE SHEET	
	DEBIT	CREDIT	DEBIT	CREDIT	DEBIT	CREDIT	DEBIT	CREDIT
1								
2								
3								
4								
5								
6								
7								
8								
9								
10								
11								
12								
13								
14								
15								
16								
17								
18								
19								
20								
21								

ACCOUNT TITLE	TRIAL BALANCE		ADJUSTMENTS		INCOME STATEMENT		BALANCE SHEET	
	DEBIT 1	CREDIT 2	DEBIT 3	CREDIT 4	DEBIT 5	CREDIT 6	DEBIT 7	CREDIT 8
1								
2								
3								
4								
5								
6								
7								
8								
9								
10								
11								
12								
13								
14								
15								
16								
17								
18								
19								
20								
21								
22								
23								

8-1 WORK TOGETHER, p. 186

Preparing an income statement

ACCOUNT TITLE	INCOME STATEMENT DEBIT	INCOME STATEMENT CREDIT	BALANCE SHEET DEBIT	BALANCE SHEET CREDIT	
11 Sales		5 5 1 1 00			11
12 Advertising Expense	8 2 1 00				12
13 Insurance Expense	3 0 0 00				13
14 Miscellaneous Expense	3 4 7 00				14
15 Supplies Expense	7 1 3 00				15
16	2 1 8 1 00	5 5 1 1 00	11 0 6 0 00	7 7 3 0 00	16
17 Net Income	3 3 3 0 00			3 3 3 0 00	17
18	5 5 1 1 00	5 5 1 1 00	11 0 6 0 00	11 0 6 0 00	18
19					19
20					20
21					21
22					22

Preparing an income statement

	ACCOUNT TITLE	INCOME STATEMENT		BALANCE SHEET		
		DEBIT (5)	CREDIT (6)	DEBIT (7)	CREDIT (8)	
12	Sales		6 3 4 7 00			12
13	Insurance Expense	3 0 0 00				13
14	Miscellaneous Expense	9 6 2 00				14
15	Supplies Expense	5 2 0 00				15
16	Utilities Expense	1 4 1 4 00				16
17		3 1 9 6 00	6 3 4 7 00	9 1 9 8 00	6 0 4 7 00	17
18	Net Income	3 1 5 1 00			3 1 5 1 00	18
19		6 3 4 7 00	6 3 4 7 00	9 1 9 8 00	9 1 9 8 00	19
20						20
21						21
22						22
23						23

					% OF SALES

8-2 WORK TOGETHER, p. 191

Preparing a balance sheet

	ACCOUNT TITLE	BALANCE SHEET	
		DEBIT	CREDIT
1	Cash	9 5 0 0 00	
2	Petty Cash	1 0 0 00	
3	Accts. Rec.—Betsy Russell	1 6 5 0 00	
4	Accts. Rec.—Charles Healy	1 4 0 3 00	
5	Supplies	2 2 0 00	
6	Prepaid Insurance	6 4 0 00	
7	Accts. Pay.—Lindgren Supply		5 4 8 00
8	Accts. Pay.—Taxes By Thomas		1 1 1 00
9	Ken Cherniak, Capital		11 8 1 0 00
10	Ken Cherniak, Drawing	8 5 5 00	
11	Income Summary		
18		14 3 6 8 00	12 4 6 9 00
19	Net Income		1 8 9 9 00
20		14 3 6 8 00	14 3 6 8 00
21			
22			

Preparing a balance sheet

	ACCOUNT TITLE			BALANCE SHEET		
				DEBIT	CREDIT	
1	Cash			6 4 0 0 00		1
2	Petty Cash			1 0 0 00		2
3	Accts. Rec.—Debbie McDonald			6 5 7 00		3
4	Accts. Rec.—Howard Kiklas			5 9 9 00		4
5	Supplies			1 5 5 00		5
6	Prepaid Insurance			3 0 0 00		6
7	Accts. Pay.—Bailey's Supply				1 8 7 00	7
8	Accts. Pay.—Freida's on Fulton				1 2 6 00	8
9	Jane Wisen, Capital				6 4 3 0 00	9
10	Jane Wisen, Drawing			1 5 0 0 00		10
16				9 7 1 1 00	6 7 4 3 00	16
17	Net Income				2 9 6 8 00	17
18				9 7 1 1 00	9 7 1 1 00	18
19						19
20						20
21						21

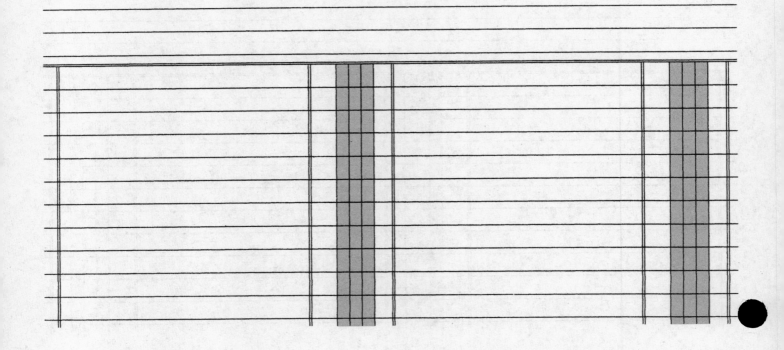

8-1   APPLICATION PROBLEM, p. 193

Preparing an income statement

							% OF SALES

Extra form

							% OF SALES

8-2 APPLICATION PROBLEM, p. 193

Preparing a balance sheet

8-3 MASTERY PROBLEM, p. 194

Preparing financial statements with a net loss

1., 2.

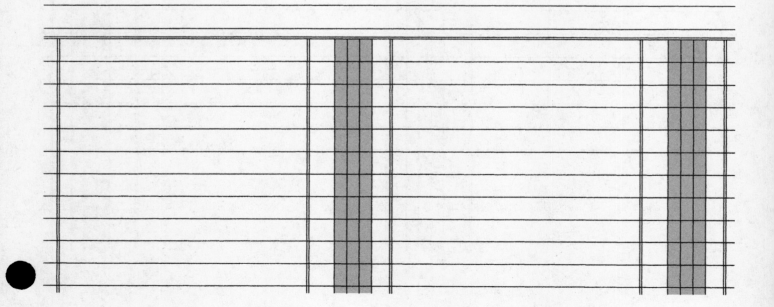

3.

Extra forms

8-4 **CHALLENGE PROBLEM, p. 194**

Preparing financial statements with two sources of revenue and a net loss

1., 2.

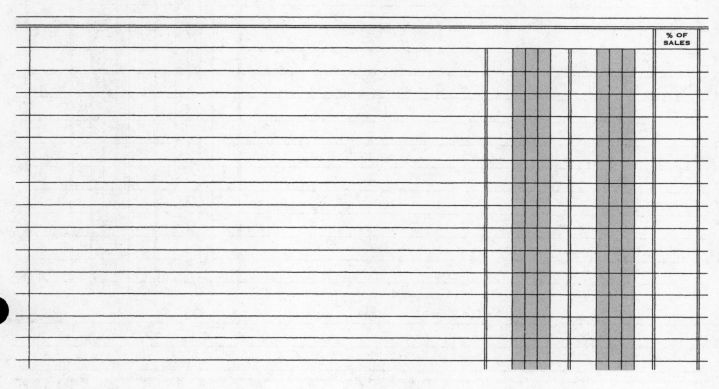

3.

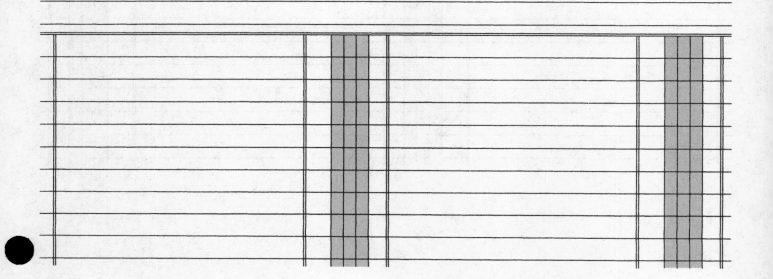

			% OF SALES

9-1 and 9-2 WORK TOGETHER, pp. 202, 209

9-1 Journalizing and posting adjusting entries
9-2 Journalizing and posting closing entries

#	ACCOUNT TITLE	ADJUSTMENTS DEBIT	ADJUSTMENTS CREDIT	INCOME STATEMENT DEBIT	INCOME STATEMENT CREDIT	BALANCE SHEET DEBIT	BALANCE SHEET CREDIT
1	Cash					735000	
2	Accts. Rec.—Romelle Woods					37200	
3	Accts. Rec.—Wyatt Ames					8800	
4	Supplies		(a) 713000			25000	
5	Prepaid Insurance		(b) 30000			90000	
6	Accts. Pay.—Colin Gas						97500
7	Accts. Pay.—Grand Uniforms						21200
8	Darlene Wong, Capital						654300
9	Darlene Wong, Drawing					210000	
10	Income Summary						
11	Sales				551100		
12	Advertising Expense			82100			
13	Insurance Expense	(b) 30000		30000			
14	Miscellaneous Expense			34700			
15	Supplies Expense	(a) 713000		71300			
16		1013000	1013000	218100	551100	1106000	773000
17	Net Income			333000			333000
18				551100	551100	1106000	1106000

9-1 Journalizing and posting adjusting entries
9-2 Journalizing and posting closing entries

	ACCOUNT TITLE	ADJUSTMENTS DEBIT	ADJUSTMENTS CREDIT	INCOME STATEMENT DEBIT	INCOME STATEMENT CREDIT	BALANCE SHEET DEBIT	BALANCE SHEET CREDIT
1	Cash					6072.00	
2	Petty Cash					175.00	
3	Accts. Rec.—Terry Jo Hugo					356.00	
4	Accts. Rec.—Jean Asmus					128.00	
5	Supplies		(a) 5200.00			117.00	
6	Prepaid Insurance		(b) 3000.00			600.00	
7	Accts. Pay.—Jaeger Repair						758.00
8	Accts. Pay.—Dakota Supply						129.00
9	Keith Altobelli, Capital						5160.00
10	Keith Altobelli, Drawing					175.00	
11	Income Summary						
12	Sales				6347.00		
13	Insurance Expense	(b) 3000.00		300.00			
14	Miscellaneous Expense			962.00			
15	Supplies Expense	(a) 5200.00		520.00			
16	Utilities Expense			1414.00			
17		820.00	820.00	3196.00	6347.00	9198.00	6047.00
18	Net Income			3151.00			3151.00
19				6347.00	6347.00	9198.00	9198.00
20							
21							
22							

9-1 and 9-2   WORK TOGETHER (continued)

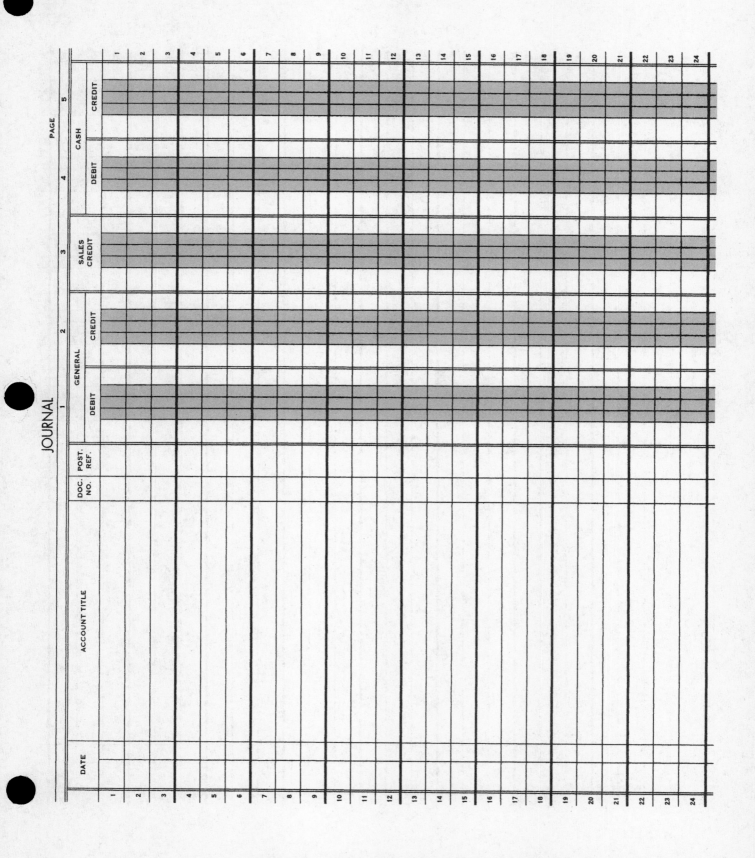

(On Your Own is continued on pages 182–184.)

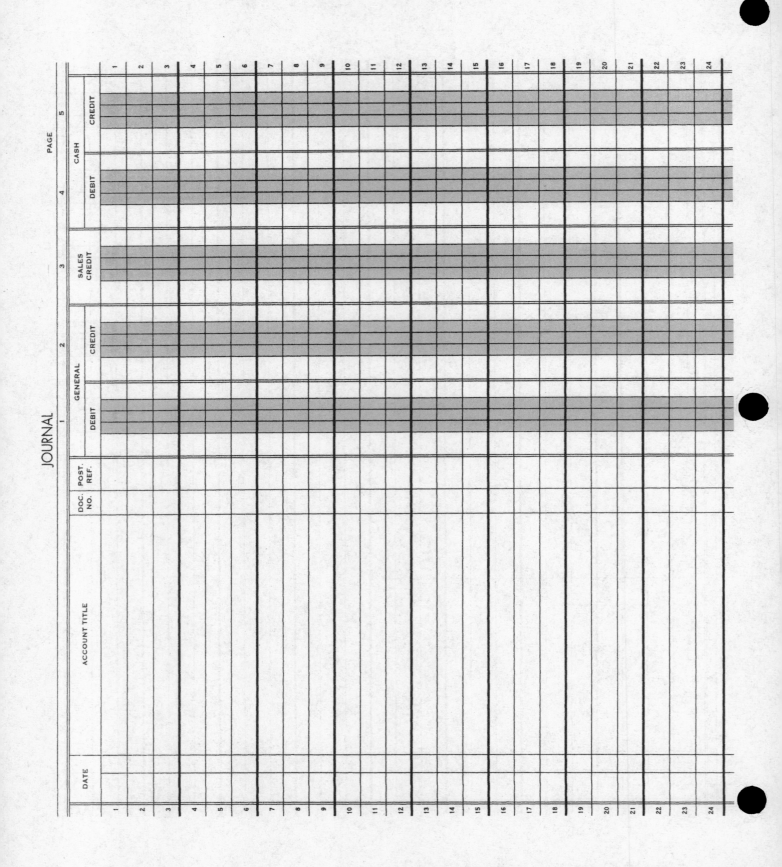

GENERAL LEDGER

ACCOUNT Cash   **ACCOUNT NO.** 110

DATE		ITEM	POST. REF.	DEBIT	CREDIT	BALANCE	
						DEBIT	CREDIT
July 31	20--	Balance	✔			7 3 5 0 00	

ACCOUNT Accounts Receivable—Romelle Woods   **ACCOUNT NO.** 120

DATE		ITEM	POST. REF.	DEBIT	CREDIT	BALANCE	
						DEBIT	CREDIT
July 31	20--	Balance	✔			3 7 2 00	

ACCOUNT Accounts Receivable—Wyatt Ames   **ACCOUNT NO.** 130

DATE		ITEM	POST. REF.	DEBIT	CREDIT	BALANCE	
						DEBIT	CREDIT
July 31	20--	Balance	✔			8 8 00	

ACCOUNT Supplies   **ACCOUNT NO.** 140

DATE		ITEM	POST. REF.	DEBIT	CREDIT	BALANCE	
						DEBIT	CREDIT
July 31	20--	Balance	✔			9 6 3 00	

ACCOUNT Prepaid Insurance   **ACCOUNT NO.** 150

DATE		ITEM	POST. REF.	DEBIT	CREDIT	BALANCE	
						DEBIT	CREDIT
July 31	20--	Balance	✔			1 2 0 0 00	

ACCOUNT Accounts Payable—Colin Gas   **ACCOUNT NO.** 210

DATE		ITEM	POST. REF.	DEBIT	CREDIT	BALANCE	
						DEBIT	CREDIT
July 31	20--	Balance	✔				9 7 5 00

GENERAL LEDGER

ACCOUNT Accounts Payable—Grand Uniforms   ACCOUNT NO. 220

DATE	ITEM	POST. REF.	DEBIT	CREDIT	BALANCE DEBIT	BALANCE CREDIT
July 31 (20--)	Balance	✔				2 1 2 00

ACCOUNT Darlene Wong, Capital   ACCOUNT NO. 310

DATE	ITEM	POST. REF.	DEBIT	CREDIT	BALANCE DEBIT	BALANCE CREDIT
July 31 (20--)	Balance	✔				6 5 4 3 00

ACCOUNT Darlene Wong, Drawing   ACCOUNT NO. 320

DATE	ITEM	POST. REF.	DEBIT	CREDIT	BALANCE DEBIT	BALANCE CREDIT
July 31 (20--)	Balance	✔			2 1 0 0 00	

ACCOUNT Income Summary   ACCOUNT NO. 330

DATE	ITEM	POST. REF.	DEBIT	CREDIT	BALANCE DEBIT	BALANCE CREDIT

ACCOUNT Sales   ACCOUNT NO. 410

DATE	ITEM	POST. REF.	DEBIT	CREDIT	BALANCE DEBIT	BALANCE CREDIT
July 31 (20--)	Balance	✔				5 5 1 1 00

ACCOUNT Advertising Expense   ACCOUNT NO. 510

DATE	ITEM	POST. REF.	DEBIT	CREDIT	BALANCE DEBIT	BALANCE CREDIT
July 31 (20--)	Balance	✔			8 2 1 00	

9-1 and 9-2   WORK TOGETHER (concluded)

GENERAL LEDGER

ACCOUNT **Insurance Expense**   ACCOUNT NO. 520

DATE	ITEM	POST. REF.	DEBIT	CREDIT	BALANCE DEBIT	BALANCE CREDIT

ACCOUNT **Miscellaneous Expense**   ACCOUNT NO. 530

DATE	ITEM	POST. REF.	DEBIT	CREDIT	BALANCE DEBIT	BALANCE CREDIT
July 20-- 31	Balance	✔			3 4 7 00	

ACCOUNT **Supplies Expense**   ACCOUNT NO. 540

DATE	ITEM	POST. REF.	DEBIT	CREDIT	BALANCE DEBIT	BALANCE CREDIT

ACCOUNT   ACCOUNT NO.

DATE	ITEM	POST. REF.	DEBIT	CREDIT	BALANCE DEBIT	BALANCE CREDIT

ACCOUNT   ACCOUNT NO.

DATE	ITEM	POST. REF.	DEBIT	CREDIT	BALANCE DEBIT	BALANCE CREDIT

ACCOUNT   ACCOUNT NO.

DATE	ITEM	POST. REF.	DEBIT	CREDIT	BALANCE DEBIT	BALANCE CREDIT

GENERAL LEDGER

ACCOUNT Cash   ACCOUNT NO. 110

DATE		ITEM	POST. REF.	DEBIT	CREDIT	BALANCE	
						DEBIT	CREDIT
Feb.	28	Balance	✔			6 0 7 2 00	

ACCOUNT Petty Cash   ACCOUNT NO. 120

DATE		ITEM	POST. REF.	DEBIT	CREDIT	BALANCE	
						DEBIT	CREDIT
Feb.	28	Balance	✔			1 7 5 00	

ACCOUNT Accounts Receivable—Terry Jo Hugo   ACCOUNT NO. 130

DATE		ITEM	POST. REF.	DEBIT	CREDIT	BALANCE	
						DEBIT	CREDIT
Feb.	28	Balance	✔			3 5 6 00	

ACCOUNT Accounts Receivable—Jean Asmus   ACCOUNT NO. 140

DATE		ITEM	POST. REF.	DEBIT	CREDIT	BALANCE	
						DEBIT	CREDIT
Feb.	28	Balance	✔			1 2 8 00	

ACCOUNT Supplies   ACCOUNT NO. 150

DATE		ITEM	POST. REF.	DEBIT	CREDIT	BALANCE	
						DEBIT	CREDIT
Feb.	28	Balance	✔			6 3 7 00	

ACCOUNT Prepaid Insurance   ACCOUNT NO. 160

DATE		ITEM	POST. REF.	DEBIT	CREDIT	BALANCE	
						DEBIT	CREDIT
Feb.	28	Balance	✔			9 0 0 00	

GENERAL LEDGER

ACCOUNT **Accounts Payable—Jaeger Repair**   ACCOUNT NO. 210

DATE	ITEM	POST. REF.	DEBIT	CREDIT	BALANCE DEBIT	BALANCE CREDIT
Feb. 28	Balance	✔				7 5 8 00

ACCOUNT **Accounts Payable—Dakota Supply**   ACCOUNT NO. 220

DATE	ITEM	POST. REF.	DEBIT	CREDIT	BALANCE DEBIT	BALANCE CREDIT
Feb. 28	Balance	✔				1 2 9 00

ACCOUNT **Keith Altobelli, Capital**   ACCOUNT NO. 310

DATE	ITEM	POST. REF.	DEBIT	CREDIT	BALANCE DEBIT	BALANCE CREDIT
Feb. 28	Balance	✔				5 1 6 0 00

ACCOUNT **Keith Altobelli, Drawing**   ACCOUNT NO. 320

DATE	ITEM	POST. REF.	DEBIT	CREDIT	BALANCE DEBIT	BALANCE CREDIT
Feb. 28	Balance	✔			1 7 5 0 00	

ACCOUNT **Income Summary**   ACCOUNT NO. 330

DATE	ITEM	POST. REF.	DEBIT	CREDIT	BALANCE DEBIT	BALANCE CREDIT

ACCOUNT **Sales**   ACCOUNT NO. 410

DATE	ITEM	POST. REF.	DEBIT	CREDIT	BALANCE DEBIT	BALANCE CREDIT
Feb. 28	Balance	✔				6 3 4 7 00

GENERAL LEDGER

ACCOUNT Insurance Expense   ACCOUNT NO. 510

DATE	ITEM	POST. REF.	DEBIT	CREDIT	BALANCE DEBIT	BALANCE CREDIT

ACCOUNT Miscellaneous Expense   ACCOUNT NO. 520

DATE	ITEM	POST. REF.	DEBIT	CREDIT	BALANCE DEBIT	BALANCE CREDIT
Feb. 20-- 28	Balance	✔			9 6 2 00	

ACCOUNT Supplies Expense   ACCOUNT NO. 530

DATE	ITEM	POST. REF.	DEBIT	CREDIT	BALANCE DEBIT	BALANCE CREDIT

ACCOUNT Utilities Expense   ACCOUNT NO. 540

DATE	ITEM	POST. REF.	DEBIT	CREDIT	BALANCE DEBIT	BALANCE CREDIT
Feb. 20-- 28	Balance	✔			1 4 1 4 00	

ACCOUNT   ACCOUNT NO.

DATE	ITEM	POST. REF.	DEBIT	CREDIT	BALANCE DEBIT	BALANCE CREDIT

ACCOUNT   ACCOUNT NO.

DATE	ITEM	POST. REF.	DEBIT	CREDIT	BALANCE DEBIT	BALANCE CREDIT

9-3 WORK TOGETHER, p. 215

Preparing a post-closing trial balance

ACCOUNT TITLE	DEBIT	CREDIT

Preparing a post-closing trial balance

ACCOUNT TITLE	DEBIT	CREDIT

9-1 and 9-2   APPLICATION PROBLEMS, p. 217

9-1 Journalizing and posting adjusting entries
9-2 Journalizing and posting closing entries

JOURNAL

					PAGE
					5

DATE	ACCOUNT TITLE	DOC. NO.	POST. REF.	GENERAL DEBIT	GENERAL CREDIT	SALES CREDIT	CASH DEBIT	CASH CREDIT
				1	2	3	4	5

GENERAL LEDGER

ACCOUNT Cash   ACCOUNT NO. 110

DATE		ITEM	POST. REF.	DEBIT	CREDIT	BALANCE DEBIT	BALANCE CREDIT
20-- Apr.	30	Balance	✔			9 5 0 0 00	

ACCOUNT Petty Cash   ACCOUNT NO. 120

DATE		ITEM	POST. REF.	DEBIT	CREDIT	BALANCE DEBIT	BALANCE CREDIT
20-- Apr.	30	Balance	✔			1 0 0 00	

ACCOUNT Accounts Receivable—Betsy Russell   ACCOUNT NO. 130

DATE		ITEM	POST. REF.	DEBIT	CREDIT	BALANCE DEBIT	BALANCE CREDIT
20-- Apr.	30	Balance	✔			1 6 5 0 00	

ACCOUNT Accounts Receivable—Charles Healy   ACCOUNT NO. 140

DATE		ITEM	POST. REF.	DEBIT	CREDIT	BALANCE DEBIT	BALANCE CREDIT
20-- Apr.	30	Balance	✔			1 4 0 3 00	

ACCOUNT Supplies   ACCOUNT NO. 150

DATE		ITEM	POST. REF.	DEBIT	CREDIT	BALANCE DEBIT	BALANCE CREDIT
20-- Apr.	30	Balance	✔			4 0 0 00	

ACCOUNT Prepaid Insurance   ACCOUNT NO. 160

DATE		ITEM	POST. REF.	DEBIT	CREDIT	BALANCE DEBIT	BALANCE CREDIT
20-- Apr.	30	Balance	✔			8 0 0 00	

9-1 and 9-2   **APPLICATION PROBLEMS (continued)**

GENERAL LEDGER

ACCOUNT Accounts Payable—Lindgren Supply ACCOUNT NO. 210

DATE	ITEM	POST. REF.	DEBIT	CREDIT	BALANCE DEBIT	BALANCE CREDIT
20-- Apr. 30	Balance	✔				5 4 8 00

ACCOUNT Accounts Payable—Taxes By Thomas ACCOUNT NO. 220

DATE	ITEM	POST. REF.	DEBIT	CREDIT	BALANCE DEBIT	BALANCE CREDIT
20-- Apr. 30	Balance	✔				1 1 1 00

ACCOUNT Ken Cherniak, Capital ACCOUNT NO. 310

DATE	ITEM	POST. REF.	DEBIT	CREDIT	BALANCE DEBIT	BALANCE CREDIT
20-- Apr. 30	Balance	✔				11 8 1 0 00

ACCOUNT Ken Cherniak, Drawing ACCOUNT NO. 320

DATE	ITEM	POST. REF.	DEBIT	CREDIT	BALANCE DEBIT	BALANCE CREDIT
20-- Apr. 30	Balance	✔			8 5 5 00	

ACCOUNT Income Summary ACCOUNT NO. 330

DATE	ITEM	POST. REF.	DEBIT	CREDIT	BALANCE DEBIT	BALANCE CREDIT

ACCOUNT Sales ACCOUNT NO. 410

DATE	ITEM	POST. REF.	DEBIT	CREDIT	BALANCE DEBIT	BALANCE CREDIT
20-- Apr. 30	Balance	✔				4 4 0 0 00

GENERAL LEDGER

ACCOUNT Advertising Expense   ACCOUNT NO. 510

DATE		ITEM	POST. REF.	DEBIT	CREDIT	BALANCE DEBIT	BALANCE CREDIT
20-- Apr.	30	Balance	✔			8 0 0 00	

ACCOUNT Insurance Expense   ACCOUNT NO. 520

DATE		ITEM	POST. REF.	DEBIT	CREDIT	BALANCE DEBIT	BALANCE CREDIT

ACCOUNT Miscellaneous Expense   ACCOUNT NO. 530

DATE		ITEM	POST. REF.	DEBIT	CREDIT	BALANCE DEBIT	BALANCE CREDIT
20-- Apr.	30	Balance	✔			3 5 1 00	

ACCOUNT Supplies Expense   ACCOUNT NO. 540

DATE		ITEM	POST. REF.	DEBIT	CREDIT	BALANCE DEBIT	BALANCE CREDIT

ACCOUNT Utilities Expense   ACCOUNT NO. 550

DATE		ITEM	POST. REF.	DEBIT	CREDIT	BALANCE DEBIT	BALANCE CREDIT
20-- Apr.	30	Balance	✔			1 0 1 0 00	

ACCOUNT   ACCOUNT NO.

DATE		ITEM	POST. REF.	DEBIT	CREDIT	BALANCE DEBIT	BALANCE CREDIT

9-3 APPLICATION PROBLEM, p. 218

Preparing a post-closing trial balance

ACCOUNT TITLE	DEBIT	CREDIT

ACCOUNT TITLE	DEBIT	CREDIT

9-4 MASTERY PROBLEM, p. 218

Journalizing and posting adjusting and closing entries; preparing a post-closing trial balance

1., 2.

JOURNAL

DATE	ACCOUNT TITLE	DOC. NO.	POST. REF.	GENERAL DEBIT	GENERAL CREDIT	SALES CREDIT	CASH DEBIT	CASH CREDIT
1								
2								
3								
4								
5								
6								
7								
8								
9								
10								
11								
12								
13								
14								
15								
16								
17								
18								
19								
20								
21								
22								

PAGE 5

1., 2.   **GENERAL LEDGER**

ACCOUNT Cash   ACCOUNT NO. 110

DATE		ITEM	POST. REF.	DEBIT	CREDIT	BALANCE	
						DEBIT	CREDIT
Oct.	31	Balance	✔			6 4 0 0 00	

ACCOUNT Petty Cash   ACCOUNT NO. 120

DATE		ITEM	POST. REF.	DEBIT	CREDIT	BALANCE	
						DEBIT	CREDIT
Oct.	31	Balance	✔			1 0 0 00	

ACCOUNT Accounts Receivable—Debbie McDonald   ACCOUNT NO. 130

DATE		ITEM	POST. REF.	DEBIT	CREDIT	BALANCE	
						DEBIT	CREDIT
Oct.	31	Balance	✔			6 5 7 00	

ACCOUNT Accounts Receivable—Howard Kikles   ACCOUNT NO. 140

DATE		ITEM	POST. REF.	DEBIT	CREDIT	BALANCE	
						DEBIT	CREDIT
Oct.	31	Balance	✔			5 9 9 00	

ACCOUNT Supplies   ACCOUNT NO. 150

DATE		ITEM	POST. REF.	DEBIT	CREDIT	BALANCE	
						DEBIT	CREDIT
Oct.	31	Balance	✔			2 7 5 00	

ACCOUNT Prepaid Insurance   ACCOUNT NO. 160

DATE		ITEM	POST. REF.	DEBIT	CREDIT	BALANCE	
						DEBIT	CREDIT
Oct.	31	Balance	✔			4 5 0 00	

9-4 MASTERY PROBLEM (continued)

1., 2.
GENERAL LEDGER

ACCOUNT Accounts Payable—Bailey's Supply   ACCOUNT NO. 210

DATE		ITEM	POST. REF.	DEBIT	CREDIT	BALANCE DEBIT	BALANCE CREDIT
Oct.	31	Balance	✔				1 8 7 00

ACCOUNT Accounts Payable—Freida's on Fulton   ACCOUNT NO. 220

DATE		ITEM	POST. REF.	DEBIT	CREDIT	BALANCE DEBIT	BALANCE CREDIT
Oct.	31	Balance	✔				1 2 6 00

ACCOUNT Jane Wisen, Capital   ACCOUNT NO. 310

DATE		ITEM	POST. REF.	DEBIT	CREDIT	BALANCE DEBIT	BALANCE CREDIT
Oct.	31	Balance	✔				6 4 3 0 00

ACCOUNT Jane Wisen, Drawing   ACCOUNT NO. 320

DATE		ITEM	POST. REF.	DEBIT	CREDIT	BALANCE DEBIT	BALANCE CREDIT
Oct.	31	Balance	✔			1 5 0 0 00	

ACCOUNT Income Summary   ACCOUNT NO. 330

DATE		ITEM	POST. REF.	DEBIT	CREDIT	BALANCE DEBIT	BALANCE CREDIT

ACCOUNT Sales   ACCOUNT NO. 410

DATE		ITEM	POST. REF.	DEBIT	CREDIT	BALANCE DEBIT	BALANCE CREDIT
Oct.	31	Balance	✔				4 2 3 8 00

1., 2. GENERAL LEDGER

ACCOUNT Advertising Expense · ACCOUNT NO. 510

DATE	ITEM	POST. REF.	DEBIT	CREDIT	BALANCE DEBIT	BALANCE CREDIT
Oct. 31	Balance	✔			3 8 2 00	

ACCOUNT Insurance Expense · ACCOUNT NO. 520

DATE	ITEM	POST. REF.	DEBIT	CREDIT	BALANCE DEBIT	BALANCE CREDIT

ACCOUNT Supplies Expense · ACCOUNT NO. 530

DATE	ITEM	POST. REF.	DEBIT	CREDIT	BALANCE DEBIT	BALANCE CREDIT

ACCOUNT Utilities Expense · ACCOUNT NO. 540

DATE	ITEM	POST. REF.	DEBIT	CREDIT	BALANCE DEBIT	BALANCE CREDIT
Oct. 31	Balance	✔			6 1 8 00	

ACCOUNT · ACCOUNT NO.

DATE	ITEM	POST. REF.	DEBIT	CREDIT	BALANCE DEBIT	BALANCE CREDIT

ACCOUNT · ACCOUNT NO.

DATE	ITEM	POST. REF.	DEBIT	CREDIT	BALANCE DEBIT	BALANCE CREDIT

9-4 **MASTERY PROBLEM (concluded)**

3.

ACCOUNT TITLE	DEBIT	CREDIT

Extra form

ACCOUNT TITLE	DEBIT	CREDIT

9-5 **CHALLENGE PROBLEM, p. 219**

Journalizing and posting adjusting and closing entries with a net loss; preparing a post-closing trial balance

1., 2.

JOURNAL

PAGE ___

DATE	ACCOUNT TITLE	DOC. NO.	POST. REF.	GENERAL DEBIT	GENERAL CREDIT	SALES CREDIT	CASH DEBIT	CASH CREDIT	
									1
									2
									3
									4
									5
									6
									7
									8
									9
									10
									11
									12
									13
									14
									15
									16
									17
									18
									19
									20
									21
									22
									23

1., 2.

GENERAL LEDGER

ACCOUNT Cash   ACCOUNT NO. 110

DATE	ITEM	POST. REF.	DEBIT	CREDIT	BALANCE DEBIT	BALANCE CREDIT
Sept. 30	Balance	✔			7 6 7 8 00	

ACCOUNT Petty Cash   ACCOUNT NO. 120

DATE	ITEM	POST. REF.	DEBIT	CREDIT	BALANCE DEBIT	BALANCE CREDIT
Sept. 30	Balance	✔			1 0 0 00	

ACCOUNT Accounts Receivable—Jennifer Balsa   ACCOUNT NO. 130

DATE	ITEM	POST. REF.	DEBIT	CREDIT	BALANCE DEBIT	BALANCE CREDIT
Sept. 30	Balance	✔			1 6 4 00	

ACCOUNT Supplies   ACCOUNT NO. 140

DATE	ITEM	POST. REF.	DEBIT	CREDIT	BALANCE DEBIT	BALANCE CREDIT
Sept. 30	Balance	✔			2 1 9 0 00	

ACCOUNT Prepaid Insurance   ACCOUNT NO. 150

DATE	ITEM	POST. REF.	DEBIT	CREDIT	BALANCE DEBIT	BALANCE CREDIT
Sept. 30	Balance	✔			8 7 5 00	

ACCOUNT Accounts Payable—Alto Supplies   ACCOUNT NO. 210

DATE	ITEM	POST. REF.	DEBIT	CREDIT	BALANCE DEBIT	BALANCE CREDIT
Sept. 30	Balance	✔				7 3 3 00

9-5   **CHALLENGE PROBLEM (continued)**

1., 2.   **GENERAL LEDGER**

ACCOUNT Jon Mancini, Capital   ACCOUNT NO. 310

DATE	ITEM	POST. REF.	DEBIT	CREDIT	BALANCE DEBIT	BALANCE CREDIT
Sept. 30	Balance	✔				9 50 0 00

ACCOUNT Jon Mancini, Drawing   ACCOUNT NO. 320

DATE	ITEM	POST. REF.	DEBIT	CREDIT	BALANCE DEBIT	BALANCE CREDIT
Sept. 30	Balance	✔			5 0 0 00	

ACCOUNT Income Summary   ACCOUNT NO. 330

DATE	ITEM	POST. REF.	DEBIT	CREDIT	BALANCE DEBIT	BALANCE CREDIT

ACCOUNT Sales   ACCOUNT NO. 410

DATE	ITEM	POST. REF.	DEBIT	CREDIT	BALANCE DEBIT	BALANCE CREDIT
Sept. 30	Balance	✔				4 59 6 00

ACCOUNT Advertising Expense   ACCOUNT NO. 510

DATE	ITEM	POST. REF.	DEBIT	CREDIT	BALANCE DEBIT	BALANCE CREDIT
Sept. 30	Balance	✔			5 5 0 00	

ACCOUNT Insurance Expense   ACCOUNT NO. 520

DATE	ITEM	POST. REF.	DEBIT	CREDIT	BALANCE DEBIT	BALANCE CREDIT

1., 2.

GENERAL LEDGER

ACCOUNT Miscellaneous Expense   ACCOUNT NO. 530

DATE		ITEM	POST. REF.	DEBIT	CREDIT	BALANCE	
						DEBIT	CREDIT
Sept.	30	Balance	✔			5 8 00	

ACCOUNT Supplies Expense   ACCOUNT NO. 540

DATE		ITEM	POST. REF.	DEBIT	CREDIT	BALANCE	
						DEBIT	CREDIT

ACCOUNT Utilities Expense   ACCOUNT NO. 550

DATE		ITEM	POST. REF.	DEBIT	CREDIT	BALANCE	
						DEBIT	CREDIT
Sept.	30	Balance	✔			2 7 1 4 00	

ACCOUNT   ACCOUNT NO.

DATE		ITEM	POST. REF.	DEBIT	CREDIT	BALANCE	
						DEBIT	CREDIT

ACCOUNT   ACCOUNT NO.

DATE		ITEM	POST. REF.	DEBIT	CREDIT	BALANCE	
						DEBIT	CREDIT

ACCOUNT   ACCOUNT NO.

DATE		ITEM	POST. REF.	DEBIT	CREDIT	BALANCE	
						DEBIT	CREDIT

9-5 **CHALLENGE PROBLEM (continued)**

3.

ACCOUNT TITLE	DEBIT	CREDIT

4.

REINFORCEMENT ACTIVITY 1

PART B, p. 222

An Accounting Cycle for a Proprietorship: End-of-Fiscal-Period Work

The general ledger prepared in Reinforcement Activity 1, Part A, is needed to complete Reinforcement Activity 1, Part B.

12., 13., 14., 15., 16.

ACCOUNT TITLE	TRIAL BALANCE		ADJUSTMENTS		INCOME STATEMENT		BALANCE SHEET	
	DEBIT	CREDIT	DEBIT	CREDIT	DEBIT	CREDIT	DEBIT	CREDIT
1								
2								
3								
4								
5								
6								
7								
8								
9								
10								
11								
12								
13								
14								
15								
16								
17								
18								
19								
20								
21								
22								
23								

REINFORCEMENT ACTIVITY 1

PART B (continued)

21. Post-Closing Trial Balance

ACCOUNT TITLE	DEBIT	CREDIT

REINFORCEMENT ACTIVITY 1

PART B (continued)

17. Income Statement

					% OF SALES

18. Balance Sheet

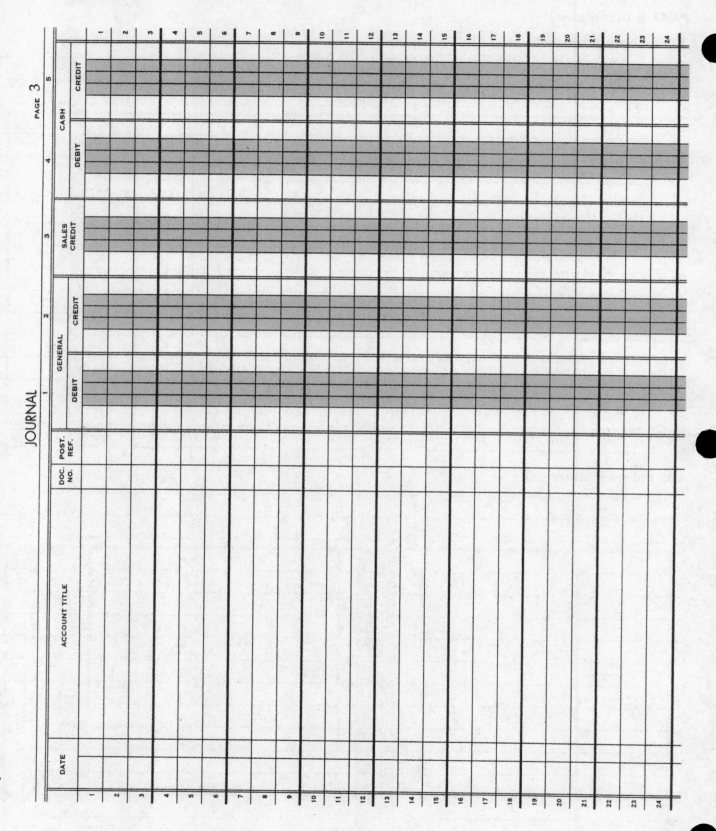

JOURNAL

19., 20.

	SALES CREDIT	SALES TAX PAYABLE CREDIT	ACCOUNTS PAYABLE		PURCHASES DEBIT	CASH		
	5	6	DEBIT 7	CREDIT 8	9	DEBIT 10	CREDIT 11	

PAGE

10-1, 10-2, and 10-3 WORK TOGETHER and ON YOUR OWN, pp. 232, 237, 243

10-1 Journalizing purchases of merchandise for cash
10-2 Journalizing purchases of merchandise on account and buying supplies
10-3 Journalizing cash payments and other transactions

PAGE 10 JOURNAL

	DATE	ACCOUNT TITLE	DOC. NO.	POST. REF.	GENERAL DEBIT	GENERAL CREDIT	ACCOUNTS RECEIVABLE DEBIT	ACCOUNTS RECEIVABLE CREDIT	
1									1
2									2
3									3
4									4
5									5
6									6
7									7
8									8
9									9
10									10
11									11
12									12
13									13
14									14
15									15
16									16
17									17
18									18
19									19
20									20
21									21
22									22
23									23
24									24
25									25
26									26
27									27
28									28
29									29
30									30
31									31
32									32
33									33
34									34
35									35
36									36

10-1, 10-2, and 10-3 WORK TOGETHER and ON YOUR OWN (concluded)

PAGE 10

	5		6		7		8		9		10		11	
	SALES CREDIT		SALES TAX PAYABLE CREDIT		ACCOUNTS PAYABLE DEBIT		ACCOUNTS PAYABLE CREDIT		PURCHASES DEBIT		CASH DEBIT		CASH CREDIT	
1														1
2														2
3														3
4														4
5														5
6														6
7														7
8														8
9														9
10														10
11														11
12														12
13														13
14														14
15														15
16														16
17														17
18														18
19														19
20														20
21														21
22														22
23														23
24														24
25														25
26														26
27														27
28														28
29														29
30														30
31														31
32														32
33														33
34														34
35														35
36														36

JOURNAL

	DATE	ACCOUNT TITLE	DOC. NO.	POST. REF.	GENERAL		ACCOUNTS RECEIVABLE		
					DEBIT	CREDIT	DEBIT	CREDIT	
1									1
2									2
3									3
4									4
5									5
6									6
7									7
8									8
9									9
10									10
11									11
12									12
13									13
14									14
15									15
16									16
17									17
18									18
19									19
20									20
21									21
22									22
23									23
24									24
25									25
26									26
27									27
28									28
29									29
30									30
31									31
32									32

10-1 APPLICATION PROBLEM, p. 245

Journalizing purchases of merchandise for cash

PAGE 17

JOURNAL

PAGE 17

DATE	ACCOUNT TITLE	DOC. NO.	POST. REF.	GENERAL DEBIT	GENERAL CREDIT	ACCOUNTS PAYABLE DEBIT	ACCOUNTS PAYABLE CREDIT	PURCHASES DEBIT	CASH DEBIT	CASH CREDIT

JOURNAL

PAGE

	DATE	ACCOUNT TITLE	DOC. NO.	POST. REF.	1 GENERAL DEBIT	2 GENERAL CREDIT	7 ACCOUNTS PAYABLE DEBIT	8 ACCOUNTS PAYABLE CREDIT	9 PURCHASES DEBIT	10 CASH DEBIT	11 CASH CREDIT	
1												1
2												2
3												3
4												4
5												5
6												6
7												7
8												8
9												9
10												10
11												11
12												12
13												13
14												14
15												15
16												16
17												17
18												18
19												19
20												20
21												21
22												22
23												23
24												24
25												25

PAGE

10-2 APPLICATION PROBLEM, p. 245

Journalizing purchases of merchandise on account and buying supplies

JOURNAL

PAGE 17

	DATE	ACCOUNT TITLE	DOC. NO.	POST. REF.	GENERAL DEBIT 1	GENERAL CREDIT 2
1						
2						
3						
4						
5						
6						
7						
8						
9						
10						
11						
12						
13						
14						
15						
16						
17						
18						
19						
20						
21						
22						
23						

PAGE 17

ACCOUNTS PAYABLE DEBIT 7	ACCOUNTS PAYABLE CREDIT 8	PURCHASES DEBIT 9	CASH DEBIT 10	CASH CREDIT 11

Extra form

JOURNAL

DATE	ACCOUNT TITLE	DOC. NO.	POST. REF.	GENERAL DEBIT	GENERAL CREDIT	ACCOUNTS PAYABLE DEBIT	ACCOUNTS PAYABLE CREDIT	PURCHASES DEBIT	CASH DEBIT	CASH CREDIT

10-3 APPLICATION PROBLEM, p. 245

Journalizing cash payments and other transactions

JOURNAL

PAGE 19

DATE	ACCOUNT TITLE	DOC. NO.	POST. REF.	GENERAL DEBIT 1	GENERAL CREDIT 2

PAGE 19

ACCOUNTS PAYABLE DEBIT 7	ACCOUNTS PAYABLE CREDIT 8	PURCHASES DEBIT 9	CASH DEBIT 10	CASH CREDIT 11

Extra form

JOURNAL

					GENERAL		ACCOUNTS PAYABLE		PURCHASES	CASH	
					DEBIT	CREDIT	DEBIT	CREDIT	DEBIT	DEBIT	CREDIT
DATE	ACCOUNT TITLE	DOC. NO.	POST. REF.		1	2	7	8	9	10	11

10-4 APPLICATION PROBLEM, p. 246

Journalizing purchases, cash payments, and other transactions

JOURNAL

PAGE 22

				GENERAL		ACCOUNTS PAYABLE		PURCHASES DEBIT	CASH	
DATE	ACCOUNT TITLE	DOC. NO.	POST. REF.	DEBIT	CREDIT	DEBIT	CREDIT		DEBIT	CREDIT

Extra form

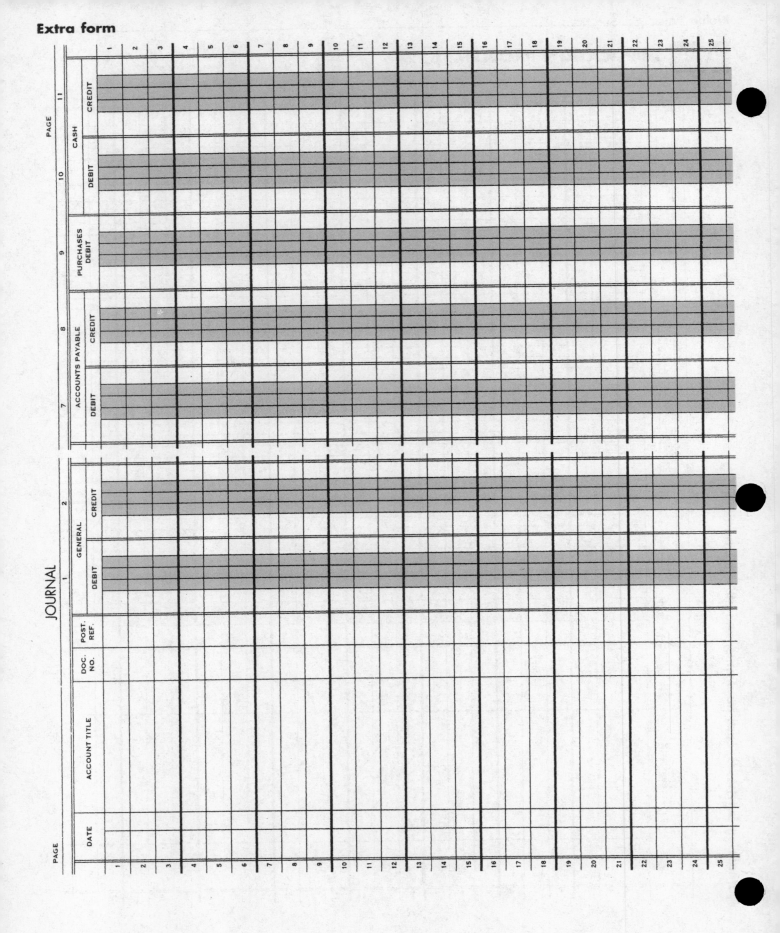

Extra form

	5	6	7	8	9	10	11	
	SALES CREDIT	SALES TAX PAYABLE CREDIT	ACCOUNTS PAYABLE		PURCHASES DEBIT	CASH		
			DEBIT	CREDIT		DEBIT	CREDIT	
1								1
2								2
3								3
4								4
5								5
6								6
7								7
8								8
9								9
10								10
11								11
12								12
13								13
14								14
15								15
16								16
17								17
18								18
19								19
20								20
21								21
22								22
23								23
24								24
25								25
26								26
27								27
28								28
29								29
30								30
31								31
32								32
33								33

10-5 MASTERY PROBLEM, p. 246

Journalizing purchases, cash payments, and other transactions

PAGE 19   JOURNAL

	DATE	ACCOUNT TITLE	DOC. NO.	POST. REF.	GENERAL DEBIT	GENERAL CREDIT	ACCOUNTS RECEIVABLE DEBIT	ACCOUNTS RECEIVABLE CREDIT	
1									1
2									2
3									3
4									4
5									5
6									6
7									7
8									8
9									9
10									10
11									11
12									12
13									13
14									14
15									15
16									16
17									17
18									18
19									19
20									20
21									21
22									22
23									23
24									24
25									25
26									26
27									27
28									28
29									29
30									30
31									31
32									32

10-5 MASTERY PROBLEM (concluded)

	5 SALES CREDIT	6 SALES TAX PAYABLE CREDIT	7 ACCOUNTS PAYABLE DEBIT	8 ACCOUNTS PAYABLE CREDIT	9 PURCHASES DEBIT	10 CASH DEBIT	11 CASH CREDIT	
1								1
2								2
3								3
4								4
5								5
6								6
7								7
8								8
9								9
10								10
11								11
12								12
13								13
14								14
15								15
16								16
17								17
18								18
19								19
20								20
21								21
22								22
23								23
24								24
25								25
26								26
27								27
28								28
29								29
30								30
31								31
32								32

Extra form

JOURNAL

	DATE	ACCOUNT TITLE	DOC. NO.	POST. REF.	GENERAL		ACCOUNTS RECEIVABLE		
					1 DEBIT	2 CREDIT	3 DEBIT	4 CREDIT	
1									1
2									2
3									3
4									4
5									5
6									6
7									7
8									8
9									9
10									10
11									11
12									12
13									13
14									14
15									15
16									16
17									17
18									18
19									19
20									20
21									21
22									22
23									23
24									24
25									25
26									26
27									27
28									28
29									29
30									30
31									31
32									32
33									33

10-6 CHALLENGE PROBLEM, p. 247

1.

Journalizing purchases, cash payments, and other transactions

JOURNAL

PAGE 26

DATE	ACCOUNT TITLE	DOC. NO.	POST. REF.	GENERAL DEBIT (1)	GENERAL CREDIT (2)
1					
2					
3					
4					
5					
6					
7					
8					
9					
10					
11					
12					
13					
14					
15					
16					
17					
18					
19					
20					
21					
22					

PAGE 26

ACCOUNTS PAYABLE DEBIT (7)	ACCOUNTS PAYABLE CREDIT (8)	PURCHASES DEBIT (9)	CASH DEBIT (10)	CASH CREDIT (11)

2.

Extra form

	5	6	7	8	9	10	11
	SALES CREDIT	SALES TAX PAYABLE CREDIT	ACCOUNTS PAYABLE DEBIT	ACCOUNTS PAYABLE CREDIT	PURCHASES DEBIT	CASH DEBIT	CASH CREDIT

11-1 WORK TOGETHER and ON YOUR OWN, p. 259

Journalizing sales and cash receipts

PAGE 9

JOURNAL

	DATE	ACCOUNT TITLE	DOC. NO.	POST. REF.	GENERAL DEBIT	GENERAL CREDIT	ACCOUNTS RECEIVABLE DEBIT	ACCOUNTS RECEIVABLE CREDIT	
1									1
2									2
3									3
4									4
5									5
6									6
7									7
8									8
9									9
10									10
11									11
12									12
13									13
14									14
15									15
16									16
17									17
18									18
19									19
20									20
21									21
22									22
23									23
24									24
25									25
26									26
27									27
28									28
29									29
30									30
31									31

11-1 **WORK TOGETHER and ON YOUR OWN (concluded)**

	5	6	7	8	9	10	11	
	SALES CREDIT	SALES TAX PAYABLE CREDIT	ACCOUNTS PAYABLE DEBIT	ACCOUNTS PAYABLE CREDIT	PURCHASES DEBIT	CASH DEBIT	CASH CREDIT	
1								1
2								2
3								3
4								4
5								5
6								6
7								7
8								8
9								9
10								10
11								11
12								12
13								13
14								14
15								15
16								16
17								17
18								18
19								19
20								20
21								21
22								22
23								23
24								24
25								25
26								26
27								27
28								28
29								29
30								30
31								31

JOURNAL

	DATE	ACCOUNT TITLE	DOC. NO.	POST. REF.	GENERAL		ACCOUNTS RECEIVABLE	
					DEBIT 1	CREDIT 2	DEBIT 3	CREDIT 4
1								
2								
3								
4								
5								
6								
7								
8								
9								
10								
11								
12								
13								
14								
15								
16								
17								
18								
19								
20								
21								
22								
23								
24								
25								
26								
27								
28								
29								
30								
31								
32								
33								

Extra forms

Col. No.	Column Title	Debit Totals	Credit Totals
1	General Debit	_____	
2	General Credit		_____
3	Accounts Receivable Debit	_____	
4	Accounts Receivable Credit		_____
5	Sales Credit		_____
6	Sales Tax Payable Credit		_____
7	Accounts Payable Debit	_____	
8	Accounts Payable Credit		_____
9	Purchases Debit	_____	
10	Cash Debit	_____	
11	Cash Credit		_____
	Totals	======	======

CASH PROOF

Cash on hand at the beginning of the month .... _____

Plus total cash received during the month .... _____

Equals total .... _____

Less total cash paid during the month .... _____

Equals cash balance on hand at end of the month .... ======

Checkbook balance on the next unused check stub .... ======

11-2 WORK TOGETHER, p. 266

Proving and ruling an expanded journal

5.

PAGE 15   JOURNAL

		DATE	ACCOUNT TITLE	DOC. NO.	POST. REF.	GENERAL DEBIT	GENERAL CREDIT	ACCOUNTS RECEIVABLE DEBIT	ACCOUNTS RECEIVABLE CREDIT	
32		18	Carried Forward		✔	3 4 3 4 40	2 5 6 00	2 7 1 3 60	3 1 8 0 00	32

6., 9.

PAGE 16   JOURNAL

		DATE	ACCOUNT TITLE	DOC. NO.	POST. REF.	GENERAL DEBIT	GENERAL CREDIT	ACCOUNTS RECEIVABLE DEBIT	ACCOUNTS RECEIVABLE CREDIT	
1										1
30		31	Totals			12 5 4 8 98	1 6 2 3 22	7 3 7 7 60	6 3 6 0 00	30
31										31
32										32

5.

Col. No.	Column Title	Debit Totals	Credit Totals
1	General Debit	_____	
2	General Credit.		
3	Accounts Receivable Debit	_____	
4	Accounts Receivable Credit		
5	Sales Credit		_____
6	Sales Tax Payable Credit		_____
7	Accounts Payable Debit	_____	
8	Accounts Payable Credit		_____
9	Purchases Debit.	_____	
10	Cash Debit.	_____	
11	Cash Credit		_____
	Totals.	_____	_____

6.

Col. No.	Column Title	Debit Totals	Credit Totals
1	General Debit	_____	
2	General Credit.		
3	Accounts Receivable Debit		_____
4	Accounts Receivable Credit		
5	Sales Credit		_____
6	Sales Tax Payable Credit		_____
7	Accounts Payable Debit		
8	Accounts Payable Credit		
9	Purchases Debit.	_____	
10	Cash Debit.	_____	
11	Cash Credit		_____
	Totals.	_____	_____

11-2 WORK TOGETHER (concluded)

5.

PAGE 15

	5 SALES CREDIT	6 SALES TAX PAYABLE CREDIT	7 ACCOUNTS PAYABLE DEBIT	8 ACCOUNTS PAYABLE CREDIT	9 PURCHASES DEBIT	10 CASH DEBIT	11 CASH CREDIT	
32	11 800 00	708 00	4 288 00	9 352 00	9 610 40	12 974 40	7 724 80	32

6., 9.

PAGE 16

	5 SALES CREDIT	6 SALES TAX PAYABLE CREDIT	7 ACCOUNTS PAYABLE DEBIT	8 ACCOUNTS PAYABLE CREDIT	9 PURCHASES DEBIT	10 CASH DEBIT	11 CASH CREDIT	
1								1
30	25 280 00	1 516 80	8 656 00	12 696 00	11 818 40	25 779 20	18 704 16	30
31								31
32								32

7.

Col. No.	Column Title	Debit Totals	Credit Totals
1	General Debit	_____	
2	General Credit.		_____
3	Accounts Receivable Debit	_____	
4	Accounts Receivable Credit		_____
5	Sales Credit		_____
6	Sales Tax Payable Credit		_____
7	Accounts Payable Debit	_____	
8	Accounts Payable Credit		_____
9	Purchases Debit.	_____	
10	Cash Debit.	_____	
11	Cash Credit		_____
	Totals.	_____	_____

8.

CASH PROOF

Cash on hand at the beginning of the month . . . _____

Plus total cash received during the month . . . . . _____

Equals total . . . . _____

Less total cash paid during the month . . . . _____

Equals cash balance on hand at end of the month . . . . _____

Checkbook balance on the next unused check stub . . . . _____

Proving and ruling an expanded journal

10.

PAGE 17   JOURNAL

	DATE	ACCOUNT TITLE	DOC. NO.	POST. REF.	GENERAL DEBIT (1)	GENERAL CREDIT (2)	ACCOUNTS RECEIVABLE DEBIT (3)	ACCOUNTS RECEIVABLE CREDIT (4)	
32	16	Carried Forward		✔	3 8 6 3 70	2 8 8 00	3 0 5 2 80	3 5 7 7 50	32

11., 14.

PAGE 18   JOURNAL

	DATE	ACCOUNT TITLE	DOC. NO.	POST. REF.	GENERAL DEBIT (1)	GENERAL CREDIT (2)	ACCOUNTS RECEIVABLE DEBIT (3)	ACCOUNTS RECEIVABLE CREDIT (4)	
1									1
28	30	Totals			14 1 1 7 60	1 8 2 6 12	8 2 9 9 80	7 1 5 5 00	28
29									29
30									30

10.

Col. No.	Column Title	Debit Totals	Credit Totals
1	General Debit	_____	
2	General Credit		_____
3	Accounts Receivable Debit	_____	
4	Accounts Receivable Credit		_____
5	Sales Credit		_____
6	Sales Tax Payable Credit		_____
7	Accounts Payable Debit	_____	
8	Accounts Payable Credit		_____
9	Purchases Debit	_____	
10	Cash Debit	_____	
11	Cash Credit		_____
	Totals	_____	_____

11.

Col. No.	Column Title	Debit Totals	Credit Totals
1	General Debit	_____	
2	General Credit		_____
3	Accounts Receivable Debit	_____	
4	Accounts Receivable Credit		_____
5	Sales Credit		_____
6	Sales Tax Payable Credit		_____
7	Accounts Payable Debit	_____	
8	Accounts Payable Credit		_____
9	Purchases Debit	_____	
10	Cash Debit	_____	
11	Cash Credit		_____
	Totals	_____	_____

11-2 ON YOUR OWN (concluded)

10.

PAGE 17

	5 SALES CREDIT	6 SALES TAX PAYABLE CREDIT	7 ACCOUNTS PAYABLE DEBIT	8 ACCOUNTS PAYABLE CREDIT	9 PURCHASES DEBIT	10 CASH DEBIT	11 CASH CREDIT	
32	13 275 00	796 50	4 824 00	10 521 00	10 811 70	14 596 20	8 690 40	32

11., 14.

PAGE 18

	5 SALES CREDIT	6 SALES TAX PAYABLE CREDIT	7 ACCOUNTS PAYABLE DEBIT	8 ACCOUNTS PAYABLE CREDIT	9 PURCHASES DEBIT	10 CASH DEBIT	11 CASH CREDIT	
1								1
28	28 440 00	1 706 40	9 738 00	14 283 00	13 295 70	29 001 60	21 042 18	28
29								29
30								30

12.

Col. No.	Column Title	Debit Totals	Credit Totals
1	General Debit	____	
2	General Credit.........		____
3	Accounts Receivable Debit	____	
4	Accounts Receivable Credit		____
5	Sales Credit...........		____
6	Sales Tax Payable Credit		____
7	Accounts Payable Debit	____	
8	Accounts Payable Credit		____
9	Purchases Debit........	____	
10	Cash Debit............	____	
11	Cash Credit...........		____
	Totals...............	____	____

13.

CASH PROOF

Cash on hand at the beginning of the month... ____

Plus total cash received during the month ..... ____

Equals total .... ____

Less total cash paid during the month .... ____

Equals cash balance on hand at end of the month .... ____

Checkbook balance on the next unused check stub .... ____

Col. No.	Column Title	Debit Totals	Credit Totals
1	General Debit	_____	
2	General Credit		_____
3	Accounts Receivable Debit	_____	
4	Accounts Receivable Credit		_____
5	Sales Credit		_____
6	Sales Tax Payable Credit		_____
7	Accounts Payable Debit	_____	
8	Accounts Payable Credit		_____
9	Purchases Debit	_____	
10	Cash Debit	_____	
11	Cash Credit		_____
	Totals	══════	══════

CASH PROOF

Cash on hand at the beginning of the month ....

Plus total cash received during the month ....

Equals total ....

Less total cash paid during the month ....

Equals cash balance on hand at end of the month ....

Checkbook balance on the next unused check stub ....

	5	6	ACCOUNTS PAYABLE 7	8	9	CASH PAGE 10	11
	SALES CREDIT	SALES TAX PAYABLE CREDIT	DEBIT	CREDIT	PURCHASES DEBIT	DEBIT	CREDIT

11-1 APPLICATION PROBLEM, p. 268

Journalizing sales and cash receipts

PAGE 15

JOURNAL

	DATE	ACCOUNT TITLE	DOC. NO.	POST. REF.	GENERAL		ACCOUNTS RECEIVABLE	
					DEBIT 1	CREDIT 2	DEBIT 3	CREDIT 4
1								
2								
3								
4								
5								
6								
7								
8								
9								
10								
11								
12								
13								
14								
15								
16								
17								
18								
19								
20								
21								
22								
23								
24								
25								
26								
27								
28								
29								
30								
31								

11-1 **APPLICATION PROBLEM (concluded)**

	5	6	7	8	9	10	11	
	SALES CREDIT	SALES TAX PAYABLE CREDIT	ACCOUNTS PAYABLE		PURCHASES DEBIT	CASH		
			DEBIT	CREDIT		DEBIT	CREDIT	
1								1
2								2
3								3
4								4
5								5
6								6
7								7
8								8
9								9
10								10
11								11
12								12
13								13
14								14
15								15
16								16
17								17
18								18
19								19
20								20
21								21
22								22
23								23
24								24
25								25
26								26
27								27
28								28
29								29
30								30
31								31

JOURNAL

	DATE		ACCOUNT TITLE	DOC. NO.	POST. REF.	GENERAL		ACCOUNTS RECEIVABLE		
						1 DEBIT	2 CREDIT	3 DEBIT	4 CREDIT	
1										1
2										2
3										3
4										4
5										5
6										6
7										7
8										8
9										9
10										10
11										11
12										12
13										13
14										14
15										15
16										16
17										17
18										18
19										19
20										20
21										21
22										22
23										23
24										24
25										25
26										26
27										27
28										28
29										29
30										30
31										31
32										32
33										33

Extra form

	5	6	7	8	9	10	11	
	SALES CREDIT	SALES TAX PAYABLE CREDIT	ACCOUNTS PAYABLE		PURCHASES DEBIT	CASH		
			DEBIT	CREDIT		DEBIT	CREDIT	
1								1
2								2
3								3
4								4
5								5
6								6
7								7
8								8
9								9
10								10
11								11
12								12
13								13
14								14
15								15
16								16
17								17
18								18
19								19
20								20
21								21
22								22
23								23
24								24
25								25
26								26
27								27
28								28
29								29
30								30
31								31
32								32
33								33

11-2   APPLICATION PROBLEM, p. 268

Journalizing sales and cash receipts

PAGE 16   JOURNAL

| | DATE | | ACCOUNT TITLE | DOC. NO. | POST. REF. | GENERAL | | ACCOUNTS RECEIVABLE | | |
						DEBIT	CREDIT	DEBIT	CREDIT	
1										1
2										2
3										3
4										4
5										5
6										6
7										7
8										8
9										9
10										10
11										11
12										12
13										13
14										14
15										15
16										16
17										17
18										18
19										19
20										20
21										21
22										22
23										23
24										24
25										25
26										26
27										27
28										28
29										29
30										30
31										31
32										32
33										33

11-2 APPLICATION PROBLEM (concluded)

PAGE 16

	5	6	7	8	9	10	11	
	SALES CREDIT	SALES TAX PAYABLE CREDIT	ACCOUNTS PAYABLE DEBIT	CREDIT	PURCHASES DEBIT	CASH DEBIT	CREDIT	
1								1
2								2
3								3
4								4
5								5
6								6
7								7
8								8
9								9
10								10
11								11
12								12
13								13
14								14
15								15
16								16
17								17
18								18
19								19
20								20
21								21
22								22
23								23
24								24
25								25
26								26
27								27
28								28
29								29
30								30
31								31
32								32
33								33

JOURNAL

	DATE	ACCOUNT TITLE	DOC. NO.	POST. REF.	GENERAL		ACCOUNTS RECEIVABLE		
					1 DEBIT	**2** CREDIT	**3** DEBIT	**4** CREDIT	
1									1
2									2
3									3
4									4
5									5
6									6
7									7
8									8
9									9
10									10
11									11
12									12
13									13
14									14
15									15
16									16
17									17
18									18
19									19
20									20
21									21
22									22
23									23
24									24
25									25
26									26
27									27
28									28
29									29
30									30
31									31
32									32
33									33

Extra forms

Col. No.	Column Title	Debit Totals	Credit Totals
1	General Debit	_____	
2	General Credit		_____
3	Accounts Receivable Debit	_____	
4	Accounts Receivable Credit		
5	Sales Credit		_____
6	Sales Tax Payable Credit		_____
7	Accounts Payable Debit	_____	
8	Accounts Payable Credit		
9	Purchases Debit	_____	_____
10	Cash Debit	_____	
11	Cash Credit		
	Totals	======	======

Col. No.	Column Title	Debit Totals	Credit Totals
1	General Debit	_____	
2	General Credit		
3	Accounts Receivable Debit	_____	
4	Accounts Receivable Credit		
5	Sales Credit		_____
6	Sales Tax Payable Credit		_____
7	Accounts Payable Debit	_____	
8	Accounts Payable Credit		
9	Purchases Debit	_____	_____
10	Cash Debit	_____	
11	Cash Credit		_____
	Totals	======	======

11-3 APPLICATION PROBLEM, p. 269

Proving and ruling an expanded journal

1.

PAGE 13   JOURNAL

	DATE	ACCOUNT TITLE	DOC. NO.	POST. REF.	GENERAL DEBIT	GENERAL CREDIT	ACCOUNTS RECEIVABLE DEBIT	ACCOUNTS RECEIVABLE CREDIT	
32	20	Carried Forward		✔	3 6 4 4 80	4 0 8 00	1 2 6 1 82	2 2 1 7 52	32

2.

PAGE 14   JOURNAL

	DATE	ACCOUNT TITLE	DOC. NO.	POST. REF.	GENERAL DEBIT	GENERAL CREDIT	ACCOUNTS RECEIVABLE DEBIT	ACCOUNTS RECEIVABLE CREDIT	
1									1
2									2
3									3

1.

Col. No.	Column Title	Debit Totals	Credit Totals
1	General Debit		
2	General Credit		
3	Accounts Receivable Debit		
4	Accounts Receivable Credit		
5	Sales Credit		
6	Sales Tax Payable Credit		
7	Accounts Payable Debit		
8	Accounts Payable Credit		
9	Purchases Debit		
10	Cash Debit		
11	Cash Credit		
	Totals		

11-3 **APPLICATION PROBLEM (concluded)**

1.

	5	6	7	8	9	10	11	
	SALES CREDIT	SALES TAX PAYABLE CREDIT	ACCOUNTS PAYABLE		PURCHASES DEBIT	CASH		
			DEBIT	CREDIT		DEBIT	CREDIT	
32	9 9 5 8 40	5 9 7 50	2 2 3 4 40	2 6 0 8 00	2 9 1 2 80	1 1 5 1 1 60	5 7 7 6 00	32

2.

	5	6	7	8	9	10	11	
	SALES CREDIT	SALES TAX PAYABLE CREDIT	ACCOUNTS PAYABLE		PURCHASES DEBIT	CASH		
			DEBIT	CREDIT		DEBIT	CREDIT	
1								1
2								2
3								3

2.

Col. No.	Column Title	Debit Totals	Credit Totals
1	General Debit	_____	
2	General Credit		_____
3	Accounts Receivable Debit	_____	
4	Accounts Receivable Credit		_____
5	Sales Credit		_____
6	Sales Tax Payable Credit		_____
7	Accounts Payable Debit	_____	
8	Accounts Payable Credit		_____
9	Purchases Debit	_____	
10	Cash Debit	_____	
11	Cash Credit		_____
	Totals	========	========

Extra forms

Col. No.	Column Title	Debit Totals	Credit Totals
1	General Debit	_____	
2	General Credit		_____
3	Accounts Receivable Debit	_____	
4	Accounts Receivable Credit		
5	Sales Credit		_____
6	Sales Tax Payable Credit		_____
7	Accounts Payable Debit	_____	
8	Accounts Payable Credit		
9	Purchases Debit	_____	
10	Cash Debit	_____	
11	Cash Credit		_____
	Totals	══════	══════

Col. No.	Column Title	Debit Totals	Credit Totals
1	General Debit	_____	
2	General Credit		_____
3	Accounts Receivable Debit	_____	
4	Accounts Receivable Credit		
5	Sales Credit		_____
6	Sales Tax Payable Credit		_____
7	Accounts Payable Debit		_____
8	Accounts Payable Credit	_____	
9	Purchases Debit		
10	Cash Debit	_____	
11	Cash Credit	_____	_____
	Totals	══════	══════

Col. No.	Column Title	Debit Totals	Credit Totals
1	General Debit	_____	
2	General Credit		_____
3	Accounts Receivable Debit	_____	
4	Accounts Receivable Credit		_____
5	Sales Credit		_____
6	Sales Tax Payable Credit		_____
7	Accounts Payable Debit	_____	
8	Accounts Payable Credit		_____
9	Purchases Debit	_____	
10	Cash Debit	_____	
11	Cash Credit		_____
	Totals	========	========

CASH PROOF

Cash on hand at the beginning of the month . . . . _____

Plus total cash received during the month . . . . _____

Equals total . . . . _____

Less total cash paid during the month . . . . _____

Equals cash balance on hand at end of the month . . . . _____

Checkbook balance on the next unused check stub . . . . _____

11-4 APPLICATION PROBLEM, p. 269

Proving and ruling an expanded journal

1., 3.

PAGE 16   JOURNAL

						1		2		3		4		
	DATE	ACCOUNT TITLE	DOC. NO.	POST. REF.		GENERAL				ACCOUNTS RECEIVABLE				
						DEBIT		CREDIT		DEBIT		CREDIT		
22	31	Totals				4 4 4 7 80		4 5 9 00		1 7 7 2 53		4 0 9 4 64		22
23														23
24														24

1.

Col. No.	Column Title	Debit Totals	Credit Totals
1	General Debit	_____	
2	General Credit		_____
3	Accounts Receivable Debit	_____	
4	Accounts Receivable Credit		_____
5	Sales Credit		_____
6	Sales Tax Payable Credit		_____
7	Accounts Payable Debit	_____	
8	Accounts Payable Credit		_____
9	Purchases Debit	_____	
10	Cash Debit	_____	
11	Cash Credit		_____
	Totals	_____	_____

11-4 APPLICATION PROBLEM (concluded)

1., 3.

PAGE 16

	5	6	7	8	9	10	11	
	SALES CREDIT	SALES TAX PAYABLE CREDIT	ACCOUNTS PAYABLE DEBIT	ACCOUNTS PAYABLE CREDIT	PURCHASES DEBIT	CASH DEBIT	CASH CREDIT	
22	14 5 2 4 20	8 7 1 45	2 5 1 3 70	4 0 5 0 00	4 3 9 2 90	17 7 1 7 76	6 8 4 5 40	22
23								23
24								24

2.

CASH PROOF

Cash on hand at the beginning of the month . . . . _____

Plus total cash received during the month . . . . _____

Equals total . . . . _____

Less total cash paid during the month . . . . _____

Equals cash balance on hand at end of the month . . . . _____

Checkbook balance on the next unused check stub . . . . _____

Col. No.	Column Title	Debit Totals	Credit Totals
1	General Debit	_____	
2	General Credit		_____
3	Accounts Receivable Debit	_____	
4	Accounts Receivable Credit		_____
5	Sales Credit		_____
6	Sales Tax Payable Credit		_____
7	Accounts Payable Debit	_____	
8	Accounts Payable Credit		_____
9	Purchases Debit	_____	
10	Cash Debit	_____	
11	Cash Credit		_____
	Totals	_____	_____

CASH PROOF

Cash on hand at the beginning of the month . . . .   _____

Plus total cash received during the month . . . .   _____

Equals total . . . .   _____

Less total cash paid during the month . . . .   _____

Equals cash balance on hand at end of the month . . . .   _____

Checkbook balance on the next unused check stub . . . .   _____

Extra forms

Col. No.	Column Title	Debit Totals	Credit Totals
1	General Debit	_____	
2	General Credit		
3	Accounts Receivable Debit		_____
4	Accounts Receivable Credit	_____	
5	Sales Credit		_____
6	Sales Tax Payable Credit		_____
7	Accounts Payable Debit		_____
8	Accounts Payable Credit		
9	Purchases Debit		_____
10	Cash Debit	_____	
11	Cash Credit	_____	
	Totals		_____
		======	======

Col. No.	Column Title	Debit Totals	Credit Totals
1	General Debit	_____	
2	General Credit		
3	Accounts Receivable Debit		_____
4	Accounts Receivable Credit	_____	
5	Sales Credit		_____
6	Sales Tax Payable Credit		_____
7	Accounts Payable Debit		_____
8	Accounts Payable Credit		
9	Purchases Debit		_____
10	Cash Debit	_____	
11	Cash Credit	_____	
	Totals		_____
		======	======

11-5 MASTERY PROBLEM, p. 269

Journalizing sales and cash receipts transactions; proving and ruling a journal

1.

PAGE 19   JOURNAL

	DATE	ACCOUNT TITLE	DOC. NO.	POST. REF.	GENERAL DEBIT	GENERAL CREDIT	ACCOUNTS RECEIVABLE DEBIT	ACCOUNTS RECEIVABLE CREDIT	
32	24	Carried Forward		✔	—	—	1 2 6 4 12	1 3 8 0 81	32

2., 3., 4., 5.

PAGE 20   JOURNAL

	DATE	ACCOUNT TITLE	DOC. NO.	POST. REF.	GENERAL DEBIT	GENERAL CREDIT	ACCOUNTS RECEIVABLE DEBIT	ACCOUNTS RECEIVABLE CREDIT	
1									1
2									2
3									3
4									4
5									5
6									6
7									7
8									8

1.

Col. No.	Column Title	Debit Totals	Credit Totals
1	General Debit	_____	
2	General Credit.		_____
3	Accounts Receivable Debit	_____	
4	Accounts Receivable Credit		_____
5	Sales Credit		_____
6	Sales Tax Payable Credit		_____
7	Accounts Payable Debit	_____	
8	Accounts Payable Credit		_____
9	Purchases Debit.	_____	
10	Cash Debit.	_____	
11	Cash Credit		_____
	Totals.	_____	_____

2.

Col. No.	Column Title	Debit Totals	Credit Totals
1	General Debit	_____	
2	General Credit.		_____
3	Accounts Receivable Debit	_____	
4	Accounts Receivable Credit		_____
5	Sales Credit		_____
6	Sales Tax Payable Credit		_____
7	Accounts Payable Debit	_____	
8	Accounts Payable Credit		_____
9	Purchases Debit.	_____	
10	Cash Debit.	_____	
11	Cash Credit		_____
	Totals.	_____	_____

11-5 MASTERY PROBLEM (concluded)

1.

PAGE 19

	5	6	7	8	9	10	11
	SALES CREDIT	SALES TAX PAYABLE CREDIT	ACCOUNTS PAYABLE DEBIT	ACCOUNTS PAYABLE CREDIT	PURCHASES DEBIT	CASH DEBIT	CASH CREDIT
32	12 3 9 7 00	4 9 5 88				13 0 0 9 57		32

2., 3., 4., 5.

PAGE 20

	5	6	7	8	9	10	11	
	SALES CREDIT	SALES TAX PAYABLE CREDIT	ACCOUNTS PAYABLE DEBIT	ACCOUNTS PAYABLE CREDIT	PURCHASES DEBIT	CASH DEBIT	CASH CREDIT	
1								1
2								2
3								3
4								4
5								5
6								6
7								7
8								8

4.

Col. No.	Column Title	Debit Totals	Credit Totals
1	General Debit	_____	
2	General Credit.		_____
3	Accounts Receivable Debit	_____	
4	Accounts Receivable Credit		_____
5	Sales Credit		_____
6	Sales Tax Payable Credit		_____
7	Accounts Payable Debit	_____	
8	Accounts Payable Credit		_____
9	Purchases Debit.	_____	
10	Cash Debit	_____	
11	Cash Credit		_____
	Totals	_____	_____

Extra forms

Col. No.	Column Title	Debit Totals	Credit Totals
1	General Debit	_____	
2	General Credit		_____
3	Accounts Receivable Debit	_____	
4	Accounts Receivable Credit		_____
5	Sales Credit		_____
6	Sales Tax Payable Credit		_____
7	Accounts Payable Debit	_____	
8	Accounts Payable Credit		_____
9	Purchases Debit	_____	
10	Cash Debit	_____	
11	Cash Credit		_____
	Totals	========	========

Col. No.	Column Title	Debit Totals	Credit Totals
1	General Debit	_____	
2	General Credit		_____
3	Accounts Receivable Debit	_____	
4	Accounts Receivable Credit		_____
5	Sales Credit		_____
6	Sales Tax Payable Credit		_____
7	Accounts Payable Debit	_____	
8	Accounts Payable Credit		_____
9	Purchases Debit	_____	
10	Cash Debit	_____	
11	Cash Credit		_____
	Totals	========	========

11-6 CHALLENGE PROBLEM, p. 270

Journalizing transactions; proving and ruling a journal

2.

Col. No.	Column Title	Debit Totals	Credit Totals
1	General Debit	_____	
2	General Credit		_____
3	Accounts Receivable Debit	_____	
4	Accounts Receivable Credit		_____
5	Sales Credit		_____
6	Sales Tax Payable Credit		_____
7	Accounts Payable Debit	_____	
8	Accounts Payable Credit		_____
9	Purchases Debit	_____	
10	Cash Debit	_____	
11	Cash Credit		_____
	Totals	_____	_____

3.

Col. No.	Column Title	Debit Totals	Credit Totals
1	General Debit	_____	
2	General Credit		_____
3	Accounts Receivable Debit	_____	
4	Accounts Receivable Credit		_____
5	Sales Credit		_____
6	Sales Tax Payable Credit		_____
7	Accounts Payable Debit	_____	
8	Accounts Payable Credit		_____
9	Purchases Debit	_____	
10	Cash Debit	_____	
11	Cash Credit		_____
	Totals	_____	_____

1., 2.

JOURNAL

	DATE	ACCOUNT TITLE	DOC. NO.	POST. REF.	GENERAL		ACCOUNTS RECEIVABLE		
					DEBIT	CREDIT	DEBIT	CREDIT	
1									1
2									2
3									3
4									4
5									5
6									6
7									7
8									8
9									9
10									10
11									11
12									12
13									13
14									14
15									15
16									16
17									17
18									18
19									19
20									20
21									21
22									22
23									23
24									24
25									25
26									26
27									27
28									28
29									29
30									30
31									31
32									32

11-6 CHALLENGE PROBLEM (continued)

1., 2.

	5 SALES CREDIT	6 SALES TAX PAYABLE CREDIT	7 ACCOUNTS PAYABLE DEBIT	8 ACCOUNTS PAYABLE CREDIT	9 PURCHASES DEBIT	10 CASH DEBIT	11 CASH CREDIT	
1								1
2								2
3								3
4								4
5								5
6								6
7								7
8								8
9								9
10								10
11								11
12								12
13								13
14								14
15								15
16								16
17								17
18								18
19								19
20								20
21								21
22								22
23								23
24								24
25								25
26								26
27								27
28								28
29								29
30								30
31								31
32								32

3., 4., 5., 7

PAGE 20   JOURNAL

	DATE	ACCOUNT TITLE	DOC. NO.	POST. REF.	GENERAL		ACCOUNTS RECEIVABLE		
					DEBIT	CREDIT	DEBIT	CREDIT	
1									1
2									2
3									3
4									4
5									5
6									6
7									7
8									8
9									9
10									10
11									11
12									12
13									13
14									14
15									15

5.

Col. No.	Column Title	Debit Totals	Credit Totals
1	General Debit		
2	General Credit		
3	Accounts Receivable Debit		
4	Accounts Receivable Credit		
5	Sales Credit		
6	Sales Tax Payable Credit		
7	Accounts Payable Debit		
8	Accounts Payable Credit		
9	Purchases Debit		
10	Cash Debit		
11	Cash Credit		
	Totals		

11-6 **CHALLENGE PROBLEM (concluded)**

3., 4., 5., 7.

PAGE 20

	SALES CREDIT 5	SALES TAX PAYABLE CREDIT 6	ACCOUNTS PAYABLE DEBIT 7	ACCOUNTS PAYABLE CREDIT 8	PURCHASES DEBIT 9	CASH DEBIT 10	CASH CREDIT 11	
1								1
2								2
3								3
4								4
5								5
6								6
7								7
8								8
9								9
10								10
11								11
12								12
13								13
14								14
15								15

6.

CASH PROOF

Cash on hand at the beginning of the month . . . . _____

Plus total cash received during the month . . . . _____

Equals total . . . . _____

Less total cash paid during the month . . . . _____

Equals cash balance on hand at end of the month . . . . _____

Checkbook balance on the next unused check stub . . . . _____

Col. No.	Column Title	Debit Totals	Credit Totals
1	General Debit	_____	
2	General Credit		_____
3	Accounts Receivable Debit	_____	
4	Accounts Receivable Credit		_____
5	Sales Credit		_____
6	Sales Tax Payable Credit		_____
7	Accounts Payable Debit	_____	
8	Accounts Payable Credit		_____
9	Purchases Debit	_____	
10	Cash Debit	_____	
11	Cash Credit		_____
	Totals	_____	_____

CASH PROOF

Cash on hand at the beginning of the month . . . . _____

Plus total cash received during the month . . . . _____

Equals total . . . . _____

Less total cash paid during the month . . . . _____

Equals cash balance on hand at end of the month . . . . _____

Checkbook balance on the next unused check stub . . . . _____

Extra form

	5	6	7	8	9	10	11	
	SALES CREDIT	SALES TAX PAYABLE CREDIT	ACCOUNTS PAYABLE		PURCHASES DEBIT	CASH		
			DEBIT	CREDIT		DEBIT	CREDIT	
1								1
2								2
3								3
4								4
5								5
6								6
7								7
8								8
9								9
10								10
11								11
12								12
13								13
14								14
15								15
16								16
17								17
18								18
19								19
20								20
21								21
22								22
23								23
24								24
25								25
26								26
27								27
28								28
29								29
30								30
31								31
32								32
33								33

12-1, 12-2, and 12-3 WORK TOGETHER, pp. 279, 285, 291

12-1 Posting to a general ledger
12-2 Posting to an accounts payable ledger
12-3 Posting to an accounts receivable ledger

PAGE 16   JOURNAL

	DATE	ACCOUNT TITLE	DOC. NO.	POST. REF.	GENERAL DEBIT (1)	GENERAL CREDIT (2)	ACCOUNTS RECEIVABLE DEBIT (3)	ACCOUNTS RECEIVABLE CREDIT (4)	
1	Oct. 18	Brought Forward		✔	3 4 3 4 40	2 5 6 00	2 7 1 3 60	3 1 8 0 00	1
2	19	Supplies—Office	C290		6 9 60				2
3	19	Regal Designs	P89						3
4	20	Electro-Graphic Supply	C291						4
5	20	Maria Farrell	S84				5 7 6 64		5
6	21	Alfredo Lopez	R104					2 5 4 40	6
30	31	Totals			12 5 4 8 98	1 6 2 3 22	7 3 7 7 60	6 3 6 0 00	30
31									31

12-1, 12-2, and 12-3 ON YOUR OWN, pp. 279, 285, 291

12-1 Posting to a general ledger
12-2 Posting to an accounts payable ledger
12-3 Posting to an accounts receivable ledger

PAGE 18   JOURNAL

	DATE	ACCOUNT TITLE	DOC. NO.	POST. REF.	GENERAL DEBIT (1)	GENERAL CREDIT (2)	ACCOUNTS RECEIVABLE DEBIT (3)	ACCOUNTS RECEIVABLE CREDIT (4)	
1	Nov. 16	Brought Forward		✔	3 8 6 3 70	2 8 8 00	3 0 5 2 80	3 5 7 7 50	1
2	16	Supplies—Store	C320		7 8 30				2
3	17	Can Do Graphics	P99						3
4	17	Art and Things	C321						4
5	18	David Bishop	S92				6 4 8 72		5
6	20	Brandee Sparks	R114					2 8 6 20	6
28	30	Totals			14 1 1 7 60	1 8 2 6 12	8 2 9 9 80	7 1 5 5 00	28
29									29
30									30

12-1, 12-2, and 12-3 WORK TOGETHER (continued)

PAGE 16

	5 SALES CREDIT	6 SALES TAX PAYABLE CREDIT	7 ACCOUNTS PAYABLE DEBIT	8 ACCOUNTS PAYABLE CREDIT	9 PURCHASES DEBIT	10 CASH DEBIT	11 CASH CREDIT	
1	11 800 00	708 00	4 288 00	9 352 00	9 610 40	12 974 40	7 724 80	1
2							69 60	2
3				1 403 20	1 403 20			3
4			776 00				776 00	4
5	544 00	32 64						5
6						254 40		6
30	25 280 00	1 516 80	8 656 00	12 696 00	11 818 40	25 779 20	18 704 16	30
31								31

12-1, 12-2, and 12-3 ON YOUR OWN (continued)

PAGE 18

	5 SALES CREDIT	6 SALES TAX PAYABLE CREDIT	7 ACCOUNTS PAYABLE DEBIT	8 ACCOUNTS PAYABLE CREDIT	9 PURCHASES DEBIT	10 CASH DEBIT	11 CASH CREDIT	
1	13 275 00	796 50	4 824 00	10 521 00	10 811 70	14 596 20	8 690 40	1
2							78 30	2
3				1 578 60	1 578 60			3
4			873 00				873 00	4
5	612 00	36 72						5
6						286 20		6
28	28 440 00	1 706 40	9 738 00	14 283 00	13 295 70	29 001 60	21 042 18	28
29						(1110)		29
30								30

JOURNAL

	DATE	ACCOUNT TITLE	DOC. NO.	POST. REF.	GENERAL		ACCOUNTS RECEIVABLE	
					1 DEBIT	**2** CREDIT	**3** DEBIT	**4** CREDIT
1								
2								
3								
4								
5								
6								
7								
8								
9								
10								
11								
12								
13								
14								
15								
16								
17								
18								
19								
20								
21								
22								
23								
24								
25								
26								
27								
28								
29								
30								
31								
32								
33								

12-1 WORK TOGETHER (concluded)

5., 6., 7.

ACCOUNT Cash   ACCOUNT NO. 1110

DATE		ITEM	POST. REF.	DEBIT	CREDIT	BALANCE	
						DEBIT	CREDIT
Oct.	1	Balance	✔			11 7 6 4 96	

ACCOUNT   ACCOUNT NO.

DATE	ITEM	POST. REF.	DEBIT	CREDIT	BALANCE	
					DEBIT	CREDIT

12-2 WORK TOGETHER (concluded)

4., 5., 6.

VENDOR Electro-Graphic Supply   VENDOR NO. 230

DATE		ITEM	POST. REF.	DEBIT	CREDIT	CREDIT BALANCE
Oct.	1	Balance	✔			7 7 6 00
	6		15		2 5 4 4 00	3 3 2 0 00

VENDOR   VENDOR NO.

DATE	ITEM	POST. REF.	DEBIT	CREDIT	CREDIT BALANCE

12-3 WORK TOGETHER (concluded)

3., 4., 5.

CUSTOMER   CUSTOMER NO.

DATE	ITEM	POST. REF.	DEBIT	CREDIT	DEBIT BALANCE

CUSTOMER Alfredo Lopez   CUSTOMER NO. 130

DATE		ITEM	POST. REF.	DEBIT	CREDIT	DEBIT BALANCE
Oct.	1	Balance	✔			2 5 4 40
	12		15	1 2 7 2 00		1 5 2 6 40

9., 10., 11.

ACCOUNT Cash   ACCOUNT NO. 1110

DATE		ITEM	POST. REF.	DEBIT	CREDIT	BALANCE	
						DEBIT	CREDIT
Nov.	1	Balance	✔			18 8 4 0 00	
	30		18	29 0 0 1 60		47 8 4 1 60	

ACCOUNT   ACCOUNT NO.

DATE		ITEM	POST. REF.	DEBIT	CREDIT	BALANCE	
						DEBIT	CREDIT

12-2 ON YOUR OWN (concluded)

7., 8., 9.

VENDOR Art and Things   VENDOR NO. 210

DATE		ITEM	POST. REF.	DEBIT	CREDIT	CREDIT BALANCE
Nov.	1	Balance	✔			8 7 3 00
	10		17		2 8 6 2 00	3 7 3 5 00

VENDOR   VENDOR NO.

DATE		ITEM	POST. REF.	DEBIT	CREDIT	CREDIT BALANCE

12-3 ON YOUR OWN (concluded)

6., 7., 8.

CUSTOMER   CUSTOMER NO.

DATE		ITEM	POST. REF.	DEBIT	CREDIT	DEBIT BALANCE

CUSTOMER Brandee Sparks   CUSTOMER NO. 140

DATE		ITEM	POST. REF.	DEBIT	CREDIT	DEBIT BALANCE
Nov.	1	Balance	✔			2 8 6 20
	12		17	1 4 3 1 00		1 7 1 7 20

12-4 WORK TOGETHER, p. 294

Proving an accounts payable ledger

Proving an accounts receivable ledger

Extra form

		5				6				7			8				9				10				11			
	\multicolumn{4}{c}{SALES CREDIT}			\multicolumn{4}{c}{SALES TAX PAYABLE CREDIT}			\multicolumn{8}{c}{ACCOUNTS PAYABLE}			\multicolumn{4}{c}{PURCHASES DEBIT}			\multicolumn{8}{c}{CASH}	
										\multicolumn{4}{c}{DEBIT}		\multicolumn{4}{c}{CREDIT}							\multicolumn{4}{c}{DEBIT}		\multicolumn{4}{c}{CREDIT}	

Row																													Row
1																													1
2																													2
3																													3
4																													4
5																													5
6																													6
7																													7
8																													8
9																													9
10																													10
11																													11
12																													12
13																													13
14																													14
15																													15
16																													16
17																													17
18																													18
19																													19
20																													20
21																													21
22																													22
23																													23
24																													24
25																													25
26																													26
27																													27
28																													28
29																													29
30																													30
31																													31
32																													32
33																													33

12-1 APPLICATION PROBLEM, p. 296

Posting to a general ledger

2., 3.

PAGE 9

JOURNAL

	DATE	ACCOUNT TITLE	DOC. NO.	POST. REF.	GENERAL DEBIT	GENERAL CREDIT	ACCOUNTS RECEIVABLE DEBIT	ACCOUNTS RECEIVABLE CREDIT	
1	Aug. 1	Rent Expense	C180		1 2 0 0 00				1
2	5	✔	T5	✔					2
3	9	Supplies—Office	C181		9 6 00				3
4	12	✔	T12	✔					4
5	16	Prepaid Insurance	C182		1 4 4 0 00				5
6	19	✔	T19	✔					6
7	26	Advertising Expense	C183		3 2 5 00				7
8	31	✔	T31	✔					8
9	31	Totals			3 0 6 1 00	—	—	—	9
10									10
11									11
12									12
13									13
14									14
15									15
16									16
17									17
18									18
19									19
20									20
21									21
22									22
23									23
24									24
25									25
26									26
27									27
28									28
29									29
30									30
31									31
32									32

12-1 APPLICATION PROBLEM (continued)

2., 3.

	5 SALES CREDIT	6 SALES TAX PAYABLE CREDIT	7 ACCOUNTS PAYABLE DEBIT	8 ACCOUNTS PAYABLE CREDIT	9 PURCHASES DEBIT	10 CASH DEBIT	11 CASH CREDIT	
1							1 2 0 0 00	1
2	5 6 1 6 00	3 3 6 96				5 9 5 2 96		2
3							9 6 00	3
4	4 1 0 4 00	2 4 6 24				4 3 5 0 24		4
5							1 4 4 0 00	5
6	5 6 8 8 00	3 4 1 28				6 0 2 9 28		6
7							3 2 5 00	7
8	5 1 1 2 00	3 0 6 72				5 4 1 8 72		8
9	20 5 2 0 00	1 2 3 1 20	—	—	—	21 7 5 1 20	3 0 6 1 00	9
10								10
11								11
12								12
13								13
14								14
15								15
16								16
17								17
18								18
19								19
20								20
21								21
22								22
23								23
24								24
25								25
26								26
27								27
28								28
29								29
30								30
31								31
32								32

JOURNAL

	DATE	ACCOUNT TITLE	DOC. NO.	POST. REF.	GENERAL		ACCOUNTS RECEIVABLE		
					DEBIT	CREDIT	DEBIT	CREDIT	
1									1
2									2
3									3
4									4
5									5
6									6
7									7
8									8
9									9
10									10
11									11
12									12
13									13
14									14
15									15
16									16
17									17
18									18
19									19
20									20
21									21
22									22
23									23
24									24
25									25
26									26
27									27
28									28
29									29
30									30
31									31
32									32
33									33

12-1 APPLICATION PROBLEM (continued)

1., 2., 3.   **GENERAL LEDGER**

ACCOUNT _____   ACCOUNT NO. _____

DATE	ITEM	POST. REF.	DEBIT	CREDIT	BALANCE	
					DEBIT	CREDIT

ACCOUNT _____   ACCOUNT NO. _____

DATE	ITEM	POST. REF.	DEBIT	CREDIT	BALANCE	
					DEBIT	CREDIT

ACCOUNT _____   ACCOUNT NO. _____

DATE	ITEM	POST. REF.	DEBIT	CREDIT	BALANCE	
					DEBIT	CREDIT

ACCOUNT _____   ACCOUNT NO. _____

DATE	ITEM	POST. REF.	DEBIT	CREDIT	BALANCE	
					DEBIT	CREDIT

1., 2., 3.   **GENERAL LEDGER**

ACCOUNT   ACCOUNT NO.

DATE	ITEM	POST. REF.	DEBIT	CREDIT	BALANCE	
					DEBIT	CREDIT

ACCOUNT   ACCOUNT NO.

DATE	ITEM	POST. REF.	DEBIT	CREDIT	BALANCE	
					DEBIT	CREDIT

ACCOUNT   ACCOUNT NO.

DATE	ITEM	POST. REF.	DEBIT	CREDIT	BALANCE	
					DEBIT	CREDIT

ACCOUNT   ACCOUNT NO.

DATE	ITEM	POST. REF.	DEBIT	CREDIT	BALANCE	
					DEBIT	CREDIT

Extra form

	5	6	7	8	9	10	11	
	SALES CREDIT	SALES TAX PAYABLE CREDIT	ACCOUNTS PAYABLE		PURCHASES DEBIT	CASH		
			DEBIT	CREDIT		DEBIT	CREDIT	
1								1
2								2
3								3
4								4
5								5
6								6
7								7
8								8
9								9
10								10
11								11
12								12
13								13
14								14
15								15
16								16
17								17
18								18
19								19
20								20
21								21
22								22
23								23
24								24
25								25
26								26
27								27
28								28
29								29
30								30
31								31
32								32
33								33

12-2 APPLICATION PROBLEM, p. 296

Posting to an accounts payable ledger

3., 4.

PAGE 10 JOURNAL

	DATE		ACCOUNT TITLE	DOC. NO.	POST. REF.	GENERAL DEBIT	GENERAL CREDIT	ACCOUNTS RECEIVABLE DEBIT	ACCOUNTS RECEIVABLE CREDIT	
1	Sept. 20--	4	Nutrition Center	P78						1
2		8	Cornucopia, Inc.	C184						2
3		11	Healthy Foods	C185						3
4		15	Sports Nutrition	C186						4
5		20	Cornucopia, Inc.	P79						5
6		25	Sports Nutrition	P80						6
7		28	Nutrition Center	C187						7
8		30	Healthy Foods	P81						8
9		30	Totals							9
10										10
11										11
12										12
13										13
14										14
15										15
16										16
17										17
18										18
19										19
20										20
21										21
22										22
23										23
24										24
25										25
26										26
27										27
28										28
29										29
30										30
31										31

12-2 APPLICATION PROBLEM (continued)

3., 4.

		SALES CREDIT 5	SALES TAX PAYABLE CREDIT 6	ACCOUNTS PAYABLE DEBIT 7	ACCOUNTS PAYABLE CREDIT 8	PURCHASES DEBIT 9	CASH DEBIT 10	CASH CREDIT 11	
1					2 0 1 6 00	2 0 1 6 00			1
2				3 0 9 0 00				3 0 9 0 00	2
3				5 0 6 4 00				5 0 6 4 00	3
4				4 5 1 2 00				4 5 1 2 00	4
5					4 5 8 4 00	4 5 8 4 00			5
6					5 4 0 0 00	5 4 0 0 00			6
7				2 0 1 6 00				2 0 1 6 00	7
8					3 3 9 6 00	3 3 9 6 00			8
9				14 6 8 2 00	15 3 9 6 00	15 3 9 6 00		14 6 8 2 00	9
10									10
11									11
12									12
13									13
14									14
15									15
16									16
17									17
18									18
19									19
20									20
21									21
22									22
23									23
24									24
25									25
26									26
27									27
28									28
29									29
30									30
31									31

Extra form

JOURNAL

	DATE		ACCOUNT TITLE	DOC. NO.	POST. REF.	GENERAL		ACCOUNTS RECEIVABLE		
						1 DEBIT	2 CREDIT	3 DEBIT	4 CREDIT	
1										1
2										2
3										3
4										4
5										5
6										6
7										7
8										8
9										9
10										10
11										11
12										12
13										13
14										14
15										15
16										16
17										17
18										18
19										19
20										20
21										21
22										22
23										23
24										24
25										25
26										26
27										27
28										28
29										29
30										30
31										31
32										32
33										33

12-2 APPLICATION PROBLEM (continued)

1., 4.   **GENERAL LEDGER**

ACCOUNT _____   ACCOUNT NO. _____

DATE	ITEM	POST. REF.	DEBIT	CREDIT	BALANCE	
					DEBIT	CREDIT

ACCOUNT _____   ACCOUNT NO. _____

DATE	ITEM	POST. REF.	DEBIT	CREDIT	BALANCE	
					DEBIT	CREDIT

ACCOUNT _____   ACCOUNT NO. _____

DATE	ITEM	POST. REF.	DEBIT	CREDIT	BALANCE	
					DEBIT	CREDIT

ACCOUNT _____   ACCOUNT NO. _____

DATE	ITEM	POST. REF.	DEBIT	CREDIT	BALANCE	
					DEBIT	CREDIT

2., 3.   **ACCOUNTS PAYABLE LEDGER**

VENDOR   VENDOR NO.

DATE	ITEM	POST. REF.	DEBIT	CREDIT	CREDIT BALANCE

VENDOR   VENDOR NO.

DATE	ITEM	POST. REF.	DEBIT	CREDIT	CREDIT BALANCE

VENDOR   VENDOR NO.

DATE	ITEM	POST. REF.	DEBIT	CREDIT	CREDIT BALANCE

VENDOR   VENDOR NO.

DATE	ITEM	POST. REF.	DEBIT	CREDIT	CREDIT BALANCE

Extra form

	5 SALES CREDIT	6 SALES TAX PAYABLE CREDIT	7 ACCOUNTS PAYABLE DEBIT	8 CREDIT	9 PURCHASES DEBIT	10 CASH DEBIT	11 CREDIT	
1								1
2								2
3								3
4								4
5								5
6								6
7								7
8								8
9								9
10								10
11								11
12								12
13								13
14								14
15								15
16								16
17								17
18								18
19								19
20								20
21								21
22								22
23								23
24								24
25								25
26								26
27								27
28								28
29								29
30								30
31								31
32								32
33								33

12-3 APPLICATION PROBLEM, p. 297

Posting to an accounts receivable ledger

3., 4.

JOURNAL

	DATE	ACCOUNT TITLE	DOC. NO.	POST. REF.	GENERAL DEBIT	GENERAL CREDIT	ACCOUNTS RECEIVABLE DEBIT	ACCOUNTS RECEIVABLE CREDIT	
1	Oct. 5	Children's Center	R170					4 4 1 6 00	1
2	10	Southwest Community Club	S69				3 0 0 1 92		2
3	14	Eastman Sports Arena	R171					2 2 2 0 00	3
4	20	Children's Center	S70				1 7 5 5 36		4
5	24	Maple Tree Club	R172					3 5 2 8 00	5
6	27	Eastman Sports Arena	S71				1 1 1 9 36		6
7	30	Maple Tree Club	S72				2 5 4 4 00		7
8	31	Totals					8 4 2 0 64	10 1 6 4 00	8
9									9
10									10
11									11
12									12
13									13
14									14
15									15
16									16
17									17
18									18
19									19
20									20
21									21
22									22
23									23
24									24
25									25
26									26
27									27
28									28
29									29
30									30
31									31

12-3 APPLICATION PROBLEM (continued)

3., 4.

	SALES CREDIT	SALES TAX PAYABLE CREDIT	ACCOUNTS PAYABLE DEBIT	ACCOUNTS PAYABLE CREDIT	PURCHASES DEBIT	CASH DEBIT	CASH CREDIT	
1						4 4 1 6 00		1
2	2 8 3 2 00	1 6 9 92						2
3						2 2 2 0 00		3
4	1 6 5 6 00	9 9 36						4
5						3 5 2 8 00		5
6	1 0 5 6 00	6 3 36						6
7	2 4 0 0 00	1 4 4 00						7
8	7 9 4 4 00	4 7 6 64	—	—	—	10 1 6 4 00	—	8
9								9
10								10
11								11
12								12
13								13
14								14
15								15
16								16
17								17
18								18
19								19
20								20
21								21
22								22
23								23
24								24
25								25
26								26
27								27
28								28
29								29
30								30
31								31

Extra form

JOURNAL

	DATE		ACCOUNT TITLE	DOC. NO.	POST. REF.	GENERAL		ACCOUNTS RECEIVABLE	
						1 DEBIT	**2** CREDIT	**3** DEBIT	**4** CREDIT
1									
2									
3									
4									
5									
6									
7									
8									
9									
10									
11									
12									
13									
14									
15									
16									
17									
18									
19									
20									
21									
22									
23									
24									
25									
26									
27									
28									
29									
30									
31									
32									
33									

12-3 APPLICATION PROBLEM (continued)

1., 4.   **GENERAL LEDGER**

ACCOUNT _____   ACCOUNT NO. _____

DATE	ITEM	POST. REF.	DEBIT	CREDIT	BALANCE	
					DEBIT	CREDIT

ACCOUNT _____   ACCOUNT NO. _____

DATE	ITEM	POST. REF.	DEBIT	CREDIT	BALANCE	
					DEBIT	CREDIT

ACCOUNT _____   ACCOUNT NO. _____

DATE	ITEM	POST. REF.	DEBIT	CREDIT	BALANCE	
					DEBIT	CREDIT

ACCOUNT _____   ACCOUNT NO. _____

DATE	ITEM	POST. REF.	DEBIT	CREDIT	BALANCE	
					DEBIT	CREDIT

2., 3.   **ACCOUNTS RECEIVABLE LEDGER**

CUSTOMER   CUSTOMER NO.

DATE	ITEM	POST. REF.	DEBIT	CREDIT	DEBIT BALANCE

CUSTOMER   CUSTOMER NO.

DATE	ITEM	POST. REF.	DEBIT	CREDIT	DEBIT BALANCE

CUSTOMER   CUSTOMER NO.

DATE	ITEM	POST. REF.	DEBIT	CREDIT	DEBIT BALANCE

CUSTOMER   CUSTOMER NO.

DATE	ITEM	POST. REF.	DEBIT	CREDIT	DEBIT BALANCE

12-4   APPLICATION PROBLEM, p. 297

Proving subsidiary ledgers

1.

2.

Extra form

12-5 MASTERY PROBLEM, p. 298

Posting to ledgers from a journal

1., 2.

PAGE 20   JOURNAL

	DATE	ACCOUNT TITLE	DOC. NO.	POST. REF.	GENERAL DEBIT	GENERAL CREDIT	ACCOUNTS RECEIVABLE DEBIT	ACCOUNTS RECEIVABLE CREDIT	
1	Nov. 2	Rent Expense	C231		1 5 0 0 00				1
2	2	Utilities Expense	C232		2 0 7 60				2
3	3	Aquacare	P73						3
4	4	Custom Pool Supply	C233						4
5	5	Cheryl Blackman	R96					5 4 6 96	5
6	6	John Falk	S72				9 1 5 84		6
7	6	Aquacare	C234						7
8	7	✔	T7	✔					8
9	9	Malibu Pools	C235						9
10	10	Linda Karagin	R97					1 0 6 8 48	10
11	13	Sun-Brite Pool Supplies	C236						11
12	13	Aquacare	C237						12
13	14	Sun-Brite Pool Supplies	P74						13
14	14	✔	T14	✔					14
15	16	Karl Jantzen, Drawing	C238		1 2 0 0 00				15
16	16	Jeff Rutherford, Drawing	C239		1 2 0 0 00				16
17	17	Miscellaneous Expense	C240		9 6 00				17
18	17	Allen Stewart	S73				8 6 4 96		18
19	20	Advertising Expense	C241		3 2 0 40				19
20	21	Malibu Pools	P75						20
21	21	✔	T21	✔					21
22	23	John Falk	R98					1 7 2 3 56	22
23	24	Karl Jantzen, Drawing	M38		1 6 5 60				23
24		Purchases				1 6 5 60			24
25	26	Supplies—Office	C242		9 9 60				25
26	27	Custom Pool Supply	P76						26
27	28	✔	T28	✔					27
28	28	Supplies—Store	C243		1 2 7 20				28
29	30	Linda Karagin	S74				7 5 6 84		29
30	30	✔	T30	✔					30
31	30	Totals			4 9 1 6 40	1 6 5 60	2 5 3 7 64	3 3 3 9 00	31
32									32

1., 2.

PAGE 20

	SALES CREDIT	SALES TAX PAYABLE CREDIT	ACCOUNTS PAYABLE DEBIT	ACCOUNTS PAYABLE CREDIT	PURCHASES DEBIT	CASH DEBIT	CASH CREDIT	
1							1500 00	1
2							207 60	2
3			1363 20	1363 20				3
4			2382 00				2382 00	4
5						546 96		5
6	864 00	51 84						6
7			3816 00				3816 00	7
8	4368 00	262 08				4630 08		8
9			3468 00				3468 00	9
10						1068 48		10
11			2832 00				2832 00	11
12			1363 20				1363 20	12
13				3228 00	3228 00			13
14	4956 00	297 36				5253 36		14
15							1200 00	15
16							1200 00	16
17							96 00	17
18	816 00	48 96						18
19							320 40	19
20				4464 00	4464 00			20
21	4752 00	285 12				5037 12		21
22						1723 56		22
23								23
24								24
25							99 60	25
26				3516 00	3516 00			26
27	5136 00	308 16				5444 16		27
28							127 20	28
29	714 00	42 84						29
30	1008 00	60 48				1068 48		30
31	22614 00	1356 84	13861 20	12571 20	12571 20	24772 20	18612 00	31
32								32

3.

12-5 **MASTERY PROBLEM (continued)**

1., 2. **GENERAL LEDGER**

ACCOUNT Cash

ACCOUNT NO. 1110

DATE		ITEM	POST. REF.	DEBIT	CREDIT	BALANCE	
						DEBIT	CREDIT
Nov.	1	Balance	✔			20 3 1 6 00	

ACCOUNT Accounts Receivable

ACCOUNT NO. 1130

DATE		ITEM	POST. REF.	DEBIT	CREDIT	BALANCE	
						DEBIT	CREDIT
Nov.	1	Balance	✔			3 3 3 9 00	

ACCOUNT Supplies—Office

ACCOUNT NO. 1150

DATE		ITEM	POST. REF.	DEBIT	CREDIT	BALANCE	
						DEBIT	CREDIT
Nov.	1	Balance	✔			3 5 5 2 00	

ACCOUNT Supplies—Store

ACCOUNT NO. 1160

DATE		ITEM	POST. REF.	DEBIT	CREDIT	BALANCE	
						DEBIT	CREDIT
Nov.	1	Balance	✔			4 1 0 4 00	

ACCOUNT Accounts Payable

ACCOUNT NO. 2110

DATE		ITEM	POST. REF.	DEBIT	CREDIT	BALANCE	
						DEBIT	CREDIT
Nov.	1	Balance	✔				12 4 9 8 00

ACCOUNT Sales Tax Payable

ACCOUNT NO. 2120

DATE		ITEM	POST. REF.	DEBIT	CREDIT	BALANCE	
						DEBIT	CREDIT
Nov.	1	Balance	✔				1 3 3 2 00

1., 2.   **GENERAL LEDGER**

ACCOUNT Karl Jantzen, Drawing   ACCOUNT NO. 3120

DATE		ITEM	POST. REF.	DEBIT	CREDIT	BALANCE DEBIT	BALANCE CREDIT
Nov. 20--	1	Balance	✔			15 2 8 8 00	

ACCOUNT Jeff Rutherford, Drawing   ACCOUNT NO. 3140

DATE		ITEM	POST. REF.	DEBIT	CREDIT	BALANCE DEBIT	BALANCE CREDIT
Nov. 20--	1	Balance	✔			14 8 3 2 00	

ACCOUNT Sales   ACCOUNT NO. 4110

DATE		ITEM	POST. REF.	DEBIT	CREDIT	BALANCE DEBIT	BALANCE CREDIT
Nov. 20--	1	Balance	✔				220 5 1 2 00

ACCOUNT Purchases   ACCOUNT NO. 5110

DATE		ITEM	POST. REF.	DEBIT	CREDIT	BALANCE DEBIT	BALANCE CREDIT
Nov. 20--	1	Balance	✔			113 7 9 6 00	

ACCOUNT Advertising Expense   ACCOUNT NO. 6110

DATE		ITEM	POST. REF.	DEBIT	CREDIT	BALANCE DEBIT	BALANCE CREDIT
Nov. 20--	1	Balance	✔			2 3 5 8 00	

ACCOUNT Miscellaneous Expense   ACCOUNT NO. 6140

DATE		ITEM	POST. REF.	DEBIT	CREDIT	BALANCE DEBIT	BALANCE CREDIT
Nov. 20--	1	Balance	✔			1 3 6 5 60	

12-5 **MASTERY PROBLEM (continued)**

1., 2. **GENERAL LEDGER**

ACCOUNT Rent Expense   ACCOUNT NO. 6160

DATE		ITEM	POST. REF.	DEBIT	CREDIT	BALANCE	
						DEBIT	CREDIT
20-- Nov.	1	Balance	✔			15 0 0 0 00	

ACCOUNT Utilities Expense   ACCOUNT NO. 6190

DATE		ITEM	POST. REF.	DEBIT	CREDIT	BALANCE	
						DEBIT	CREDIT
20-- Nov.	1	Balance	✔			2 0 7 6 00	

1., 3. **ACCOUNTS PAYABLE LEDGER**

VENDOR Aquacare   VENDOR NO. 210

DATE		ITEM	POST. REF.	DEBIT	CREDIT	CREDIT BALANCE
20-- Nov.	1	Balance	✔			3 8 1 6 00

VENDOR Custom Pool Supply   VENDOR NO. 220

DATE		ITEM	POST. REF.	DEBIT	CREDIT	CREDIT BALANCE
20-- Nov.	1	Balance	✔			2 3 8 2 00

VENDOR Malibu Pools   VENDOR NO. 230

DATE		ITEM	POST. REF.	DEBIT	CREDIT	CREDIT BALANCE
20-- Nov.	1	Balance	✔			3 4 6 8 00

VENDOR Sun-Brite Pool Supplies   VENDOR NO. 240

DATE		ITEM	POST. REF.	DEBIT	CREDIT	CREDIT BALANCE
20-- Nov.	1	Balance	✔			2 8 3 2 00

1., 3.   **ACCOUNTS RECEIVABLE LEDGER**

CUSTOMER Cheryl Blackman   CUSTOMER NO. 110

DATE		ITEM	POST. REF.	DEBIT	CREDIT	DEBIT BALANCE
20-- Nov.	1	Balance	✔			5 4 6 96

CUSTOMER John Falk   CUSTOMER NO. 120

DATE		ITEM	POST. REF.	DEBIT	CREDIT	DEBIT BALANCE
20-- Nov.	1	Balance	✔			1 7 2 3 56

CUSTOMER Linda Karagin   CUSTOMER NO. 130

DATE		ITEM	POST. REF.	DEBIT	CREDIT	DEBIT BALANCE
20-- Nov.	1	Balance	✔			1 0 6 8 48

CUSTOMER Allen Stewart   CUSTOMER NO. 140

DATE		ITEM	POST. REF.	DEBIT	CREDIT	DEBIT BALANCE

Extra form

12-6 CHALLENGE PROBLEM, p. 298

Journalizing and posting business transactions

1., 2., 4., 5.

PAGE _____

JOURNAL

	DATE	ACCOUNT TITLE	DOC. NO.	POST. REF.	GENERAL DEBIT	GENERAL CREDIT	ACCOUNTS RECEIVABLE DEBIT	ACCOUNTS RECEIVABLE CREDIT	
1									1
2									2
3									3
4									4
5									5
6									6
7									7
8									8
9									9
10									10
11									11
12									12
13									13
14									14
15									15
16									16
17									17
18									18
19									19
20									20
21									21
22									22
23									23
24									24
25									25
26									26
27									27
28									28
29									29
30									30
31									31
32									32

12-6 CHALLENGE PROBLEM (continued)

1., 2., 4., 5.

	SALES CREDIT	SALES TAX PAYABLE CREDIT	ACCOUNTS PAYABLE DEBIT	ACCOUNTS PAYABLE CREDIT	PURCHASES DEBIT	CASH DEBIT	CASH CREDIT	
	5	6	7	8	9	10	11	
1								1
2								2
3								3
4								4
5								5
6								6
7								7
8								8
9								9
10								10
11								11
12								12
13								13
14								14
15								15
16								16
17								17
18								18
19								19
20								20
21								21
22								22
23								23
24								24
25								25
26								26
27								27
28								28
29								29
30								30
31								31
32								32

6.

12-6 CHALLENGE PROBLEM (continued)

1., 5.   **GENERAL LEDGER**

ACCOUNT Cash   ACCOUNT NO. 1110

DATE	ITEM	POST. REF.	DEBIT	CREDIT	BALANCE DEBIT	BALANCE CREDIT
20-- Oct. 1	Balance	✔			20 2 2 0 00	

ACCOUNT Accounts Receivable   ACCOUNT NO. 1130

DATE	ITEM	POST. REF.	DEBIT	CREDIT	BALANCE DEBIT	BALANCE CREDIT
20-- Oct. 1	Balance	✔			3 4 7 9 40	

ACCOUNT Supplies—Office   ACCOUNT NO. 1150

DATE	ITEM	POST. REF.	DEBIT	CREDIT	BALANCE DEBIT	BALANCE CREDIT
20-- Oct. 1	Balance	✔			3 1 6 2 00	

ACCOUNT Supplies—Store   ACCOUNT NO. 1160

DATE	ITEM	POST. REF.	DEBIT	CREDIT	BALANCE DEBIT	BALANCE CREDIT
20-- Oct. 1	Balance	✔			2 5 9 2 00	

ACCOUNT Accounts Payable   ACCOUNT NO. 2110

DATE	ITEM	POST. REF.	DEBIT	CREDIT	BALANCE DEBIT	BALANCE CREDIT
20-- Oct. 1	Balance	✔				9 6 2 7 60

ACCOUNT Sales Tax Payable   ACCOUNT NO. 2120

DATE	ITEM	POST. REF.	DEBIT	CREDIT	BALANCE DEBIT	BALANCE CREDIT
20-- Oct. 1	Balance	✔				1 5 7 4 40

1., 5.   **GENERAL LEDGER**

ACCOUNT Julie Freed, Drawing   ACCOUNT NO. 3120

DATE	ITEM	POST. REF.	DEBIT	CREDIT	BALANCE DEBIT	BALANCE CREDIT
Oct. 1	Balance	✔			14 3 0 0 00	

ACCOUNT Troy Nordstrom, Drawing   ACCOUNT NO. 3140

DATE	ITEM	POST. REF.	DEBIT	CREDIT	BALANCE DEBIT	BALANCE CREDIT
Oct. 1	Balance	✔			14 0 4 0 00	

ACCOUNT Sales   ACCOUNT NO. 4110

DATE	ITEM	POST. REF.	DEBIT	CREDIT	BALANCE DEBIT	BALANCE CREDIT
Oct. 1	Balance	✔				262 4 9 8 80

ACCOUNT Purchases   ACCOUNT NO. 5110

DATE	ITEM	POST. REF.	DEBIT	CREDIT	BALANCE DEBIT	BALANCE CREDIT
Oct. 1	Balance	✔			135 0 0 0 00	

ACCOUNT Advertising Expense   ACCOUNT NO. 6110

DATE	ITEM	POST. REF.	DEBIT	CREDIT	BALANCE DEBIT	BALANCE CREDIT
Oct. 1	Balance	✔			3 5 2 8 00	

ACCOUNT Miscellaneous Expense   ACCOUNT NO. 6140

DATE	ITEM	POST. REF.	DEBIT	CREDIT	BALANCE DEBIT	BALANCE CREDIT
Oct. 1	Balance	✔			1 6 9 2 00	

12-6 **CHALLENGE PROBLEM (continued)**

1., 5. GENERAL LEDGER

ACCOUNT Rent Expense   ACCOUNT NO. 6160

DATE		ITEM	POST. REF.	DEBIT	CREDIT	BALANCE	
						DEBIT	CREDIT
Oct.	1	Balance	✓			10 3 5 0 00	

ACCOUNT Utilities Expense   ACCOUNT NO. 6190

DATE		ITEM	POST. REF.	DEBIT	CREDIT	BALANCE	
						DEBIT	CREDIT
Oct.	1	Balance	✓			2 1 4 2 00	

1., 6. ACCOUNTS PAYABLE LEDGER

VENDOR Design Golf   VENDOR NO. 210

DATE		ITEM	POST. REF.	DEBIT	CREDIT	CREDIT BALANCE
Oct.	1	Balance	✓			2 9 1 6 00

VENDOR Eagle Golf Equipment   VENDOR NO. 220

DATE		ITEM	POST. REF.	DEBIT	CREDIT	CREDIT BALANCE
Oct.	1	Balance	✓			2 3 5 8 00

VENDOR Golf Source   VENDOR NO. 230

DATE		ITEM	POST. REF.	DEBIT	CREDIT	CREDIT BALANCE

VENDOR Pro Golf Supply   VENDOR NO. 240

DATE		ITEM	POST. REF.	DEBIT	CREDIT	CREDIT BALANCE
Oct.	1	Balance	✓			1 1 3 7 60

1., 6.

ACCOUNTS PAYABLE LEDGER

VENDOR Vista Golf Co.   VENDOR NO. 250

DATE		ITEM	POST. REF.	DEBIT	CREDIT	CREDIT BALANCE
Oct.	1	Balance	✔			3 2 1 6 00

ACCOUNTS RECEIVABLE LEDGER

CUSTOMER David Bench   CUSTOMER NO. 110

DATE		ITEM	POST. REF.	DEBIT	CREDIT	DEBIT BALANCE
Oct.	1	Balance	✔			9 7 2 00

CUSTOMER Viola Davis   CUSTOMER NO. 120

DATE		ITEM	POST. REF.	DEBIT	CREDIT	DEBIT BALANCE
Oct.	1	Balance	✔			8 2 9 44

CUSTOMER Barry Fuller   CUSTOMER NO. 130

DATE		ITEM	POST. REF.	DEBIT	CREDIT	DEBIT BALANCE

CUSTOMER Doris McCarley   CUSTOMER NO. 140

DATE		ITEM	POST. REF.	DEBIT	CREDIT	DEBIT BALANCE
Oct.	1	Balance	✔			1 3 9 2 84

CUSTOMER Leona Silva   CUSTOMER NO. 150

DATE		ITEM	POST. REF.	DEBIT	CREDIT	DEBIT BALANCE
Oct.	1	Balance	✔			2 8 5 12

12-6 CHALLENGE PROBLEM (continued)

2.

Col. No.	Column Title	Debit Totals	Credit Totals
1	General Debit	_____	
2	General Credit		_____
3	Accounts Receivable Debit	_____	
4	Accounts Receivable Credit		_____
5	Sales Credit		_____
6	Sales Tax Payable Credit		_____
7	Accounts Payable Debit	_____	
8	Accounts Payable Credit		_____
9	Purchases Debit	_____	
10	Cash Debit	_____	
11	Cash Credit		_____
	Totals	══════	══════

3.

CASH PROOF

Cash on hand at the beginning of the month .... _____

Plus total cash received during the month .... _____

Equals total .... _____

Less total cash paid during the month .... _____

Equals cash balance on hand at end of the month .... ══════

Checkbook balance on the next unused check stub .... ══════

Approaches to Collecting and Paying Sales Taxes

_____

_____

_____

_____

_____

_____

_____

_____

_____

_____

_____

_____

_____

_____

_____

_____

_____

_____

_____

_____

_____

_____

_____

_____

_____

_____

_____

_____

_____

_____

_____

_____

_____

_____

_____

_____

_____

_____

_____

_____

_____

13-1 WORK TOGETHER, p. 307

Preparing payroll time cards

Employee Number	Hours Worked		Regular Rate	Earnings		Total Earnings
	Regular	Overtime		Regular	Overtime	
1	40	5	$ 9.00	_____	_____	_____
2	40	3	12.50	_____	_____	_____
3	30	0	9.75	_____	_____	_____
4	40	2	11.00	_____	_____	_____

Extra form

Employee Number	Hours Worked		Regular Rate	Earnings		Total Earnings
	Regular	Overtime		Regular	Overtime	

Preparing payroll time cards

Employee Number	Hours Worked		Regular Rate	Earnings		Total Earnings
	Regular	Overtime		Regular	Overtime	
1	40	6	$ 9.80	_____	_____	_____
2	25	0	7.00	_____	_____	_____
3	40	4	12.00	_____	_____	_____
4	40	3	10.50	_____	_____	_____

Extra form

Employee Number	Hours Worked		Regular Rate	Earnings		Total Earnings
	Regular	Overtime		Regular	Overtime	

13-2 WORK TOGETHER, p. 313

Determining payroll tax withholding

Employee		Marital Status	Number of Withholding Allowances	Total Earnings	Federal Income Tax Withholding	Social Security Tax Withholding	Medicare Tax Withholding
No.	Name						
3	Bates, Eric C.	M	2	$1,090.00	——	——	——
4	Cohen, Jason K.	S	1	840.00	——	——	——
1	Grimes, Christi L.	M	3	1,020.00	——	——	——
6	Key, Sharon C.	S	2	980.00	——	——	——

Extra form

Employee		Marital Status	Number of Withholding Allowances	Total Earnings	Federal Income Tax Withholding	Social Security Tax Withholding	Medicare Tax Withholding
No.	Name						

Determining payroll tax withholding

Employee		Marital Status	Number of Withholding Allowances	Total Earnings	Federal Income Tax Withholding	Social Security Tax Withholding	Medicare Tax Withholding
No.	Name						
2	Marquez, Lola S.	S	1	$ 925.00	_____	_____	_____
5	Norris, John F.	M	4	1,250.00	_____	_____	_____
7	Rice, James H.	S	2	1,000.00	_____	_____	_____
9	Vale, Ann M.	M	0	1,050.00	_____	_____	_____

Extra form

Employee		Marital Status	Number of Withholding Allowances	Total Earnings	Federal Income Tax Withholding	Social Security Tax Withholding	Medicare Tax Withholding
No.	Name						

13-3 WORK TOGETHER, p. 318

Preparing payroll records

4., 5.

PAYROLL REGISTER

SEMIMONTHLY PERIOD ENDED _____ DATE OF PAYMENT _____

| EMPL. NO. | EMPLOYEE'S NAME | MARI-TAL STATUS | NO. OF ALLOW-ANCES | EARNINGS | | | DEDUCTIONS | | | | | | NET PAY | CHECK NO. |
				REGULAR	OVERTIME	TOTAL	FEDERAL INCOME TAX	SOC. SEC. TAX	MEDICARE TAX	HEALTH INSURANCE	OTHER	TOTAL		
				1	2	3	4	5	6	7	8	9	10	
1	5 Hensley, Judy	M	2	1040 00	39 00									1
2	9 McCune, Mike	S	1	920 00	51 75									2
3														3
22														22

OTHER DEDUCTIONS: B—U.S. SAVINGS BONDS; UW—UNITED WAY

6.

EARNINGS RECORD FOR QUARTER ENDED _____

EMPLOYEE NO. _____ LAST NAME _____ FIRST _____ MIDDLE INITIAL _____ MARITAL STATUS _____ WITHHOLDING ALLOWANCES _____

RATE OF PAY _____ PER HR. _____ SOCIAL SECURITY NO. _____ POSITION _____

| PAY PERIOD | | EARNINGS | | | DEDUCTIONS | | | | | | NET PAY | ACCUMULATED EARNINGS |
NO.	ENDED	REGULAR	OVERTIME	TOTAL	FEDERAL INCOME TAX	SOC. SEC. TAX	MEDICARE TAX	HEALTH INSURANCE	OTHER	TOTAL		
		1	2	3	4	5	6	7	8	9	10	11
1												
7	QUARTERLY TOTALS											

OTHER DEDUCTIONS: B—U.S. SAVINGS BONDS; UW—UNITED WAY

Preparing payroll records

7., 8.

PAYROLL REGISTER

SEMIMONTHLY PERIOD ENDED _____ DATE OF PAYMENT _____

EMPL. NO.	EMPLOYEE'S NAME	MARI-TAL STATUS	NO. OF ALLOW-ANCES	EARNINGS			DEDUCTIONS							NET PAY	CHECK NO.
				REGULAR	OVERTIME	TOTAL	FEDERAL INCOME TAX	SOC. SEC. TAX	MEDICARE TAX	HEALTH INSURANCE	OTHER	TOTAL			
				1	2	3	4	5	6	7	8	9	10		
1	8 Eubanks, Gary	M	3	1024 00	76 80										1
2	15 Park, Ellen	S	2	920 00	138 00										2
3															3
22															22

OTHER DEDUCTIONS: B—U.S. SAVINGS BONDS; UW—UNITED WAY

9.

EARNINGS RECORD FOR QUARTER ENDED _____

EMPLOYEE NO. _____ LAST NAME _____ FIRST _____ MIDDLE INITIAL _____ MARITAL STATUS _____ WITHHOLDING ALLOWANCES _____

RATE OF PAY _____ PER HR. _____ SOCIAL SECURITY NO. _____ POSITION _____

PAY PERIOD		EARNINGS			DEDUCTIONS						NET PAY	ACCUMULATED EARNINGS
NO.	ENDED	REGULAR	OVERTIME	TOTAL	FEDERAL INCOME TAX	SOC. SEC. TAX	MEDICARE TAX	HEALTH INSURANCE	OTHER	TOTAL		
		1	2	3	4	5	6	7	8	9	10	11
1												
7												
QUARTERLY TOTALS												

OTHER DEDUCTIONS: B—U.S. SAVINGS BONDS; UW—UNITED WAY

13-4 WORK TOGETHER, p. 321

Preparing payroll checks

4., 5.

NO. **599**

Date: _____ 20 ___ $ _____

To: _____

_____

For: _____

_____

BAL. BRO'T. FOR'D

AMT. DEPOSITED

TOTAL

AMT. THIS CHECK

BAL. CAR'D. FOR'D

GENERAL ACCOUNT   NO. **599**   66-877/530

ANTIQUE SHOP   _____ 20 _____

PAY TO THE ORDER OF _____ $ _____

_____ DOLLARS

For Classroom Use Only

Peoples Bank and Trust
Charlotte, NC 28206-8444

⑈053008774⑈ 196⑈2236⑈421⑈

CHECK NO. **186**

PERIOD ENDING

EARNINGS $

REG. $

O.T. $

DEDUCTIONS $

INC. TAX $

SOC. SEC. TAX $

MED. TAX $

HEALTH INS. $

OTHER $

NET PAY $

PAYROLL ACCOUNT   66-877/530

_____ 20 _____

NO. **186**

PAY TO THE ORDER OF _____ $ _____

_____ DOLLARS

For Classroom Use Only

ANTIQUE SHOP

Peoples Bank and Trust
Charlotte, NC 28206-8444

⑈053008774⑈ 196⑈2236⑈44⑈

CHECK NO. **187**

PERIOD ENDING

EARNINGS $

REG. $

O.T. $

DEDUCTIONS $

INC. TAX $

SOC. SEC. TAX $

MED. TAX $

HEALTH INS. $

OTHER $

NET PAY $

PAYROLL ACCOUNT   66-877/530

_____ 20 _____

NO. **187**

PAY TO THE ORDER OF _____ $ _____

_____ DOLLARS

For Classroom Use Only

ANTIQUE SHOP

Peoples Bank and Trust
Charlotte, NC 28206-8444

⑈053008774⑈ 196⑈2236⑈44⑈

Preparing payroll checks

6., 7.

NO. **651**

Date: _____ 20___ $_____

To: _____

For: _____

_____

BAL. BRO'T. FOR'D		
AMT. DEPOSITED		
TOTAL		
AMT. THIS CHECK		
BAL. CAR'D. FOR'D		

GENERAL ACCOUNT NO. **651** 66-877/530

THE SIGN SHOP

_____ 20 _____

PAY TO THE ORDER OF _____ $ _____

_____ DOLLARS

For Classroom Use Only

Peoples Bank and Trust

Charlotte, NC 28206-8444

⑆053008774⑆ 196‖2236‖42‖

CHECK NO. **211**

PERIOD ENDING		
EARNINGS	$	
REG.	$	
O.T.	$	
DEDUCTIONS	$	
INC. TAX	$	
SOC. SEC. TAX	$	
MED. TAX	$	
HEALTH INS.	$	
OTHER	$	
NET PAY	$	

PAYROLL ACCOUNT 66-877/530

_____ 20 _____   NO. **211**

PAY TO THE ORDER OF _____ $ _____

_____ DOLLARS

For Classroom Use Only

THE SIGN SHOP

Peoples Bank and Trust

Charlotte, NC 28206-8444

⑆053008774⑆ 196‖2236‖44‖

CHECK NO. **212**

PERIOD ENDING		
EARNINGS	$	
REG.	$	
O.T.	$	
DEDUCTIONS	$	
INC. TAX	$	
SOC. SEC. TAX	$	
MED. TAX	$	
HEALTH INS.	$	
OTHER	$	
NET PAY	$	

PAYROLL ACCOUNT 66-877/530

_____ 20 _____   NO. **212**

PAY TO THE ORDER OF _____ $ _____

_____ DOLLARS

For Classroom Use Only

THE SIGN SHOP

Peoples Bank and Trust

Charlotte, NC 28206-8444

⑆053008774⑆ 196‖2236‖44‖

13-1 APPLICATION PROBLEM, p. 323

Preparing payroll time cards

1., 2.

Card 1 — EMPLOYEE NO. 14 — NAME Marie L. Kerns — PERIOD ENDING April 15, 20 --

	MORNING		AFTERNOON		OVERTIME		HOURS	
	IN	OUT	IN	OUT	IN	OUT	REG	OT
2	759	1201	1256	501				
3	757	1202	1257	502				
4	756	1201	1258	504	701	802		
5	802	1204	101	506				
6	756	1203	1259	500				
9	759	1200	1259	459	559	731		
10	800	1200	1258	501				
11	759	1202	1257	506				
12	756	1159	1256	502	558	732		
13	757	1203	1257	501				

	HOURS	RATE	AMOUNT
REGULAR		11.80	
OVERTIME			
TOTAL HOURS		TOTAL EARNINGS	

Card 2 — EMPLOYEE NO. 11 — NAME Henry F. Miller — PERIOD ENDING April 15, 20 --

	MORNING		AFTERNOON		OVERTIME		HOURS	
	IN	OUT	IN	OUT	IN	OUT	REG	OT
2	757	1201	1259	502				
3	757	1202	1258	501	556	659		
4	756	1204	100	501				
5	757	1205	1259	500				
6	759	1205	100	502				
9	757	1204	1259	505				
10	758	1205	1256	504	600	731		
11	756	1202	1257	502				
12	756	1201	1259	501	700	932		
13	757	1200	101	500				

	HOURS	RATE	AMOUNT
REGULAR		9.80	
OVERTIME			
TOTAL HOURS		TOTAL EARNINGS	

Card 3 — EMPLOYEE NO. 16 — NAME Sylvia A. Rodriguez — PERIOD ENDING April 15, 20 --

	MORNING		AFTERNOON		OVERTIME		HOURS	
	IN	OUT	IN	OUT	IN	OUT	REG	OT
2	758	1202	1259	503				
3	757	1203	100	500	702	832		
4	800	1200	1259	500				
5	759	1201	1258	504				
6	759	1202	1255	503				
9	758	1201	1256	502				
10	756	1200	1257	501				
11	757	1202	1257	458				
12	758	1200	1259	501				
13	759	1204	1259	500				

	HOURS	RATE	AMOUNT
REGULAR		9.20	
OVERTIME			
TOTAL HOURS		TOTAL EARNINGS	

EMPLOYEE NO. ____

NAME ____

PERIOD ENDING ____

MORNING		AFTERNOON		OVERTIME		HOURS	
IN	OUT	IN	OUT	IN	OUT	REG	OT

	HOURS	RATE	AMOUNT
REGULAR			
OVERTIME			
TOTAL HOURS		TOTAL EARNINGS	

EMPLOYEE NO. ____

NAME ____

PERIOD ENDING ____

MORNING		AFTERNOON		OVERTIME		HOURS	
IN	OUT	IN	OUT	IN	OUT	REG	OT

	HOURS	RATE	AMOUNT
REGULAR			
OVERTIME			
TOTAL HOURS		TOTAL EARNINGS	

EMPLOYEE NO. ____

NAME ____

PERIOD ENDING ____

MORNING		AFTERNOON		OVERTIME		HOURS	
IN	OUT	IN	OUT	IN	OUT	REG	OT

	HOURS	RATE	AMOUNT
REGULAR			
OVERTIME			
TOTAL HOURS		TOTAL EARNINGS	

13-2 APPLICATION PROBLEM, p. 323

Determining payroll tax withholding

1., 2.

No.	Name	Marital Status	Number of Withholding Allowances	Total Earnings	Federal Income Tax Withholding	Social Security Tax Withholding	Medicare Tax Withholding
2	Baird, Tony W.	M	2	$1,220.00	___	___	___
6	Delgado, Rudy C.	M	3	1,090.00	___	___	___
3	Garza, Kay H.	S	1	940.00	___	___	___
1	Hess, Monica T.	M	5	1,060.00	___	___	___
8	Levy, Irving S.	S	1	910.00	___	___	___
7	Minick, Esther A.	S	2	990.00	___	___	___
4	Pharr, Angela S.	S	1	900.00	___	___	___
5	Reiner, Greg R.	M	3	1,250.00	___	___	___

Extra form

No.	Name	Marital Status	Number of Withholding Allowances	Total Earnings	Federal Income Tax Withholding	Social Security Tax Withholding	Medicare Tax Withholding

Extra forms

Employee		Marital Status	Number of Withholding Allowances	Total Earnings	Federal Income Tax Withholding	Social Security Tax Withholding	Medicare Tax Withholding
No.	Name						

Employee		Marital Status	Number of Withholding Allowances	Total Earnings	Federal Income Tax Withholding	Social Security Tax Withholding	Medicare Tax Withholding
No.	Name						

13-3 APPLICATION PROBLEM, p. 323

Preparing a payroll register

PAYROLL REGISTER

SEMIMONTHLY PERIOD ENDED _____ DATE OF PAYMENT _____

EMPL. NO.	EMPLOYEE'S NAME	MARI-TAL STATUS	NO. OF ALLOW-ANCES	EARNINGS REGULAR (1)	EARNINGS OVERTIME (2)	EARNINGS TOTAL (3)	FEDERAL INCOME TAX (4)	SOC. SEC. TAX (5)	MEDICARE TAX (6)	HEALTH INSURANCE (7)	OTHER (8)	TOTAL (9)	NET PAY (10)	CHECK NO.
2	Askew, Celia R.	S	1	9840 00	18 45					40 00	B 20 00			
10	Bates, James C.	M	3	7040 00						65 00				
9	Cates, Paula M.	M	2	7440 00	83 70					50 00	B 10 00			
3	Day, Stacy L.	M	2	7840 00						50 00	B 10 00			
6	Fox, Lisa M.	S	1	6800 00	51 00					40 00				
11	Jantz, Glen F.	S	1	8240 00						40 00				
1	Miller, Martin L.	S	2	10560 00	99 00					50 00				
5	Picard, Angela S.	M	4	11200 00						65 00	B 50 00			
4	Sanchez, Juan M.	M	3	9600 00	36 00					65 00				
7	Todd, Jennifer N.	S	1	11200 00	63 00					40 00	B 20 00			
8	Vargas, Frank M.	M	2	8400 00						50 00				
12	Wyatt, Scott A.	S	1	8000 00	30 00					40 00	B 10 00			

OTHER DEDUCTIONS: B—U.S. SAVINGS BONDS; UW—UNITED WAY

Extra form

PAYROLL REGISTER

SEMIMONTHLY PERIOD ENDED _____ DATE OF PAYMENT _____

EMPL. NO.	EMPLOYEE'S NAME	MARITAL STATUS	NO. OF ALLOWANCES	EARNINGS			DEDUCTIONS						NET PAY	CHECK NO.
				REGULAR	OVERTIME	TOTAL	FEDERAL INCOME TAX	SOC. SEC. TAX	MEDICARE TAX	HEALTH INSURANCE	OTHER	TOTAL		
				1	2	3	4	5	6	7	8	9	10	
1														1
2														2
3														3
4														4
5														5
6														6
7														7
8														8
9														9
10														10
11														11
12														12
13														13
14														14
15														15
16														16
17														17
18														18
19														19
20														20
21														21
22														22
23														23
24														24
25														25

OTHER DEDUCTIONS: B—U.S. SAVINGS BONDS: UW—UNITED WAY

13-4 APPLICATION PROBLEM, p. 324

Preparing an employee earnings record
1., 2., 3., 4.

EARNINGS RECORD FOR QUARTER ENDED _____

EMPLOYEE NO. _____ LAST NAME _____ FIRST _____ MIDDLE INITIAL _____ SOCIAL SECURITY NO. _____

RATE OF PAY _____ PER HR. _____ MARITAL STATUS _____ WITHHOLDING ALLOWANCES _____ POSITION _____

PAY PERIOD		EARNINGS			DEDUCTIONS						NET PAY	ACCUMULATED EARNINGS
		1	2	3	4	5	6	7	8	9	10	11
NO.	ENDED	REGULAR	OVERTIME	TOTAL	FEDERAL INCOME TAX	SOC. SEC. TAX	MEDICARE TAX	HEALTH INSURANCE	OTHER	TOTAL		
1	7/15	1320 00	135 00	1455 00	144 00	94 58	21 83	60 00	10 00 B	330 41	1124 59	
2	7/31	1200 00	90 00	1290 00	120 00	83 85	19 35	60 00	10 00 B	293 20	996 80	
3	8/15	1320 00		1320 00	126 00	85 80	19 80	60 00	10 00 B	301 60	1018 40	
4	8/31	1020 00		1020 00	81 00	66 30	15 30	60 00	10 00 B	232 60	787 40	
5	9/15	1320 00	135 00	1455 00								
6	9/30	1200 00		1200 00								
7	QUARTERLY TOTALS											

OTHER DEDUCTIONS: B—U.S. SAVINGS BONDS; UW—UNITED WAY

EARNINGS RECORD FOR QUARTER ENDED

EMPLOYEE NO.

LAST NAME

FIRST

MIDDLE INITIAL

MARITAL STATUS

WITHHOLDING ALLOWANCES

RATE OF PAY

PER HR.

SOCIAL SECURITY NO.

POSITION

PAY PERIOD		EARNINGS			DEDUCTIONS						NET PAY	ACCUMULATED EARNINGS
NO.	ENDED	REGULAR	OVERTIME	TOTAL	FEDERAL INCOME TAX	SOC. SEC. TAX	MEDICARE TAX	HEALTH INSURANCE	OTHER	TOTAL		
		1	2	3	4	5	6	7	8	9	10	11
1												
2												
3												
4												
5												
6												
7												
QUARTERLY TOTALS												

OTHER DEDUCTIONS: B—U.S. SAVINGS BONDS; UW—UNITED WAY

13-5 APPLICATION PROBLEM, p. 324

Preparing payroll checks

1., 2.

NO. **630**

Date: _____ 20___ $_____

To: _____

For: _____

_____

BAL. BRO'T. FOR'D		
AMT. DEPOSITED		
TOTAL		
AMT. THIS CHECK		
BAL. CAR'D. FOR'D		

GENERAL ACCOUNT   NO. **630**   66-877 / 530

ROYAL APPLIANCES   _____ 20 _____

PAY TO THE
ORDER OF _____ $ _____

_____ DOLLARS

For Classroom Use Only

Peoples Bank and Trust
Charlotte, NC 28206-8444   _____

⑆053008774⑆ 196ꞏ2236ꞏ4 2⑈

CHECK NO. **823**

PERIOD ENDING		
EARNINGS	$	
REG.	$	
O.T.	$	
DEDUCTIONS	$	
INC. TAX	$	
SOC. SEC. TAX	$	
MEDICARE TAX	$	
HEALTH INS.	$	
OTHER	$	
NET PAY	$	

PAYROLL ACCOUNT   66-877 / 530

_____ 20 _____   NO. **823**

PAY TO THE
ORDER OF _____ $ _____

_____ DOLLARS

For Classroom Use Only   ROYAL APPLIANCES

Peoples Bank and Trust
Charlotte, NC 28206-8444   _____

⑆053008774⑆ 196ꞏ2236ꞏ44⑈

CHECK NO. **827**

PERIOD ENDING		
EARNINGS	$	
REG.	$	
O.T.	$	
DEDUCTIONS	$	
INC. TAX	$	
SOC. SEC. TAX	$	
MEDICARE TAX	$	
HEALTH INS.	$	
OTHER	$	
NET PAY	$	

PAYROLL ACCOUNT   66-877 / 530

_____ 20 _____   NO. **827**

PAY TO THE
ORDER OF _____ $ _____

_____ DOLLARS

For Classroom Use Only   ROYAL APPLIANCES

Peoples Bank and Trust
Charlotte, NC 28206-8444   _____

⑆053008774⑆ 196ꞏ2236ꞏ44⑈

NO.

Date: _____ 20___ $ _____

To: _____

For: _____

BAL. BRO'T. FOR'D			
AMT. DEPOSITED			
TOTAL			
AMT. THIS CHECK			
BAL. CAR'D. FOR'D			

GENERAL ACCOUNT   NO.   66-877/530

_____ 20 ____

PAY TO THE ORDER OF _____ $ _____

_____ DOLLARS

For Classroom Use Only

Peoples Bank and Trust
Charlotte, NC 28206-8444   _____

⑆053008774⑆ 196 2236 42

	CHECK NO.
PERIOD ENDING	
EARNINGS	$
REG.	$
O.T.	$
DEDUCTIONS	$
INC. TAX	$
SOC. SEC. TAX	$
MEDICARE TAX	$
HEALTH INS.	$
OTHER	$
NET PAY	$

PAYROLL ACCOUNT   66-877/530

_____ 20 ____   NO.

PAY TO THE ORDER OF _____ $ _____

_____ DOLLARS

For Classroom Use Only

Peoples Bank and Trust
Charlotte, NC 28206-8444   _____

⑆053008774⑆ 196 2236 44

	CHECK NO.
PERIOD ENDING	
EARNINGS	$
REG.	$
O.T.	$
DEDUCTIONS	$
INC. TAX	$
SOC. SEC. TAX	$
MEDICARE TAX	$
HEALTH INS.	$
OTHER	$
NET PAY	$

PAYROLL ACCOUNT   66-877/530

_____ 20 ____   NO.

PAY TO THE ORDER OF _____ $ _____

_____ DOLLARS

For Classroom Use Only

Peoples Bank and Trust
Charlotte, NC 28206-8444   _____

⑆053008774⑆ 196 2236 44

13-6 MASTERY PROBLEM, p. 325

Preparing a semimonthly payroll

1.

PAYROLL REGISTER

EMPL. NO.	EMPLOYEE'S NAME	MARI- TAL STATUS	NO. OF ALLOW- ANCES	EARNINGS			DEDUCTIONS						DATE OF PAYMENT		CHECK NO.
				REGULAR	OVERTIME	TOTAL	FEDERAL INCOME TAX	SOC. SEC. TAX	MEDICARE TAX	HEALTH INSURANCE	OTHER	TOTAL	NET PAY		
				1	2	3	4	5	6	7	8	9	10		
1															1
2															2
3															3
4															4
5															5
6															6
7															7
8															8
9															9
10															10
11															11
12															12
13															13
14															14
15															15
16															16
17															17
18															18
19															19
20															20
21															21
22															22
23															23
24															24
25															25

SEMIMONTHLY PERIOD ENDED

OTHER DEDUCTIONS: B—U.S. SAVINGS BONDS; UW—UNITED WAY

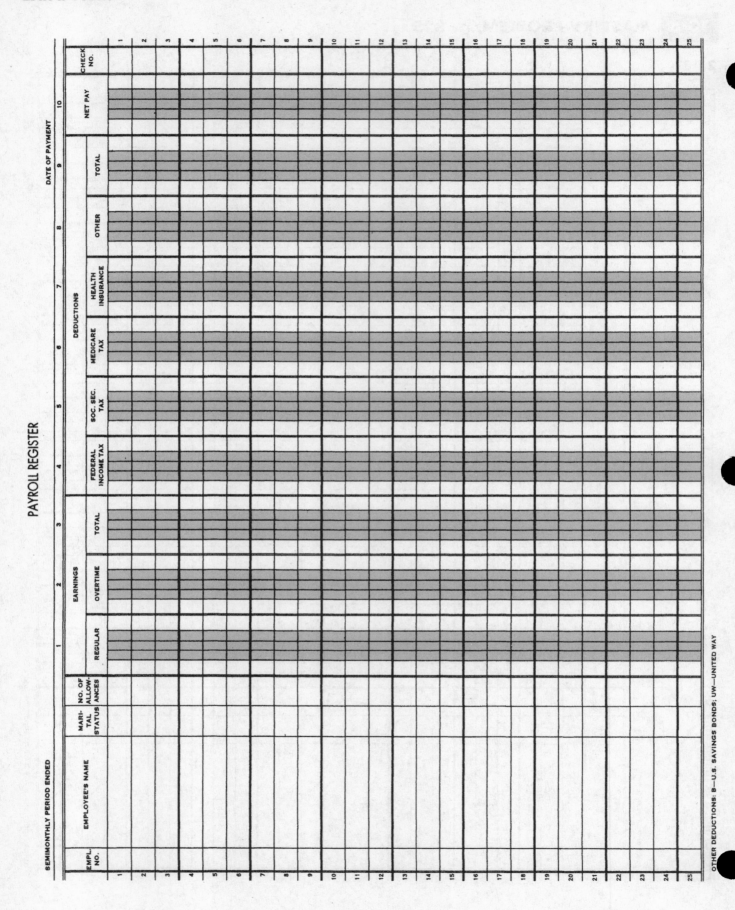

PAYROLL REGISTER

13-6 MASTERY PROBLEM (concluded)

2., 3.

NO. **872**

Date: _____ 20 ___ $_____

To: _____

_____

For: _____

_____

BAL. BRO'T. FOR'D		
AMT. DEPOSITED		
TOTAL		
AMT. THIS CHECK		
BAL. CAR'D. FOR'D		

GENERAL ACCOUNT NO. **872** 8-8335/430

RAINBO COMPANY _____ 20 _____

PAY TO THE
ORDER OF _____ $ _____

_____ DOLLARS

For Classroom Use Only

First Security Bank of Pittsburgh
Pittsburgh, PA 15210-3402

⑈043083356⑈ 005972164⑈

CHECK NO. **528**

PERIOD ENDING			
EARNINGS	$		
REG.	$		
O.T.	$		
DEDUCTIONS	$		
INC. TAX	$		
SOC. SEC. TAX	$		
MED. TAX	$		
HEALTH INS.	$		
OTHER	$		
NET PAY	$		

PAYROLL ACCOUNT 8-8335/430

_____ 20 _____ NO. **528**

PAY TO THE
ORDER OF _____ $ _____

_____ DOLLARS

For Classroom Use Only RAINBO COMPANY

First Security Bank of Pittsburgh
Pittsburgh, PA 15210-3402

⑈043083356⑈ 005972165⑈

CHECK NO. **533**

PERIOD ENDING			
EARNINGS	$		
REG.	$		
O.T.	$		
DEDUCTIONS	$		
INC. TAX	$		
SOC. SEC. TAX	$		
MED. TAX	$		
HEALTH INS.	$		
OTHER	$		
NET PAY	$		

PAYROLL ACCOUNT 8-8335/430

_____ 20 _____ NO. **533**

PAY TO THE
ORDER OF _____ $ _____

_____ DOLLARS

For Classroom Use Only RAINBO COMPANY

First Security Bank of Pittsburgh
Pittsburgh, PA 15210-3402

⑈043083356⑈ 005972165⑈

Extra forms

NO.

Date: _____ 20___ $ _____

To: _____

_____

For: _____

BAL. BRO'T. FOR'D			
AMT. DEPOSITED			
TOTAL			
AMT. THIS CHECK			
BAL. CAR'D. FOR'D			

GENERAL ACCOUNT   NO. _____   8-8335/430

_____ 20 _____

PAY TO THE
ORDER OF _____ $ _____

_____ DOLLARS

For Classroom Use Only

First Security Bank of Pittsburgh
Pittsburgh, PA 15210-3402

⑈043083356⑈ 005972164⑈

	CHECK NO.		
PERIOD ENDING			
EARNINGS	$		
REG.	$		
O.T.	$		
DEDUCTIONS	$		
INC. TAX	$		
SOC. SEC. TAX	$		
MED. TAX	$		
HEALTH INS.	$		
OTHER	$		
NET PAY	$		

PAYROLL ACCOUNT   8-8335/430

_____ 20 _____   NO.

PAY TO THE
ORDER OF _____ $ _____

_____ DOLLARS

For Classroom Use Only

First Security Bank of Pittsburgh
Pittsburgh, PA 15210-3402

⑈043083356⑈ 005972165⑈

	CHECK NO.		
PERIOD ENDING			
EARNINGS	$		
REG.	$		
O.T.	$		
DEDUCTIONS	$		
INC. TAX	$		
SOC. SEC. TAX	$		
MED. TAX	$		
HEALTH INS.	$		
OTHER	$		
NET PAY	$		

PAYROLL ACCOUNT   8-8335/430

_____ 20 _____   NO.

PAY TO THE
ORDER OF _____ $ _____

_____ DOLLARS

For Classroom Use Only

First Security Bank of Pittsburgh
Pittsburgh, PA 15210-3402

⑈043083356⑈ 005972165⑈

13-7 CHALLENGE PROBLEM, p. 326

Calculating piecework wages

PAYROLL REGISTER

SEMIMONTHLY PERIOD ENDED _____

DATE OF PAYMENT _____

EMPL. NO.	EMPLOYEE'S NAME	MARI-TAL STATUS	NO. OF ALLOW-ANCES	EARNINGS REGULAR (1)	EARNINGS INCENTIVE (2)	EARNINGS TOTAL (3)	FEDERAL INCOME TAX (4)	SOC. SEC. TAX (5)	MEDICARE TAX (6)	HEALTH INSURANCE (7)	OTHER (8)	TOTAL (9)	NET PAY (10)	CHECK NO.
1	C2 Martinez, Luis L.	S	1											1
2	C4 Price, Nancy C.	M	1											2
3	C8 King, Debra S.	M	2											3
4	A1 Heath, Scott R.	S	1											4
5	A6 Nowlin, Daniel W.	M	3											5
6	A7 Scofield, Martha A.	S	1											6
7	F5 Isaacs, Julie M.	M	2											7
8	F3 Stewart, Gary W.	M	2											8
9														9
10														10
11														11
12														12
13														13
14														14
15														15
16														16
17														17
18														18
19														19
20														20
21														21
22														22
23														23
24														24
25														25

DEDUCTIONS

OTHER DEDUCTIONS: B—U.S. SAVINGS BONDS; UW—UNITED WAY

Extra form

PAYROLL REGISTER

SEMIMONTHLY PERIOD ENDED _____ DATE OF PAYMENT _____

EMPL. NO.	EMPLOYEE'S NAME	MARI-TAL STATUS	NO. OF ALLOW-ANCES	EARNINGS			DEDUCTIONS							NET PAY	CHECK NO.
				REGULAR	INCENTIVE	TOTAL	FEDERAL INCOME TAX	SOC. SEC. TAX	MEDICARE TAX	HEALTH INSURANCE	OTHER	TOTAL			
				1	2	3	4	5	6	7	8	9		10	
1															1
2															2
3															3
4															4
5															5
6															6
7															7
8															8
9															9
10															10
11															11
12															12
13															13
14															14
15															15
16															16
17															17
18															18
19															19
20															20
21															21
22															22
23															23
24															24
25															25

OTHER DEDUCTIONS: B—U.S. SAVINGS BONDS; UW—UNITED WAY

14-1 WORK TOGETHER, p. 335

Recording a payroll

5.   **Extra forms**

Cash
_____|_____

Employee Income Tax Payable
_____|_____

Social Security Tax Payable
_____|_____

Medicare Tax Payable
_____|_____

Salary Expense
_____|_____

6.

JOURNAL

PAGE					GENERAL		PAGE		CASH	
					1	2	10		11	
	DATE	ACCOUNT TITLE	DOC. NO.	POST. REF.	DEBIT	CREDIT	DEBIT		CREDIT	
1										1
2										2
3										3
4										4
5										5
6										6
7										7
8										8
9										9
10										10

Recording a payroll

7.

Cash
_____|_____

Employee Income Tax Payable
_____|_____

Social Security Tax Payable
_____|_____

Medicare Tax Payable
_____|_____

Salary Expense
_____|_____

Extra forms

_____|_____

_____|_____

_____|_____

_____|_____

8.

PAGE

JOURNAL

PAGE

	DATE	ACCOUNT TITLE	DOC. NO.	POST. REF.	GENERAL DEBIT	GENERAL CREDIT	CASH DEBIT	CASH CREDIT	
1									1
2									2
3									3
4									4
5									5
6									6
7									7
8									8
9									9
10									10

14-2 WORK TOGETHER, p. 340

Recording employer payroll taxes

3., 4.

Employee Name	Accumulated Earnings, April 30	Total Earnings for May 1–15 Pay Period	Unemployment Taxable Earnings
Beltran, Tamela C.	$5,100.00	$637.50	_____
Cintron, Irma V.	7,350.00	920.00	_____
	Totals	_____	_____
Social Security Tax Payable		_____	
Medicare Tax Payable		_____	
Unemployment Tax Payable—Federal		_____	
Unemployment Tax Payable—State		_____	
Total Payroll Taxes		_____	

5.

PAGE

JOURNAL

	DATE	ACCOUNT TITLE	DOC. NO.	POST. REF.	GENERAL DEBIT	GENERAL CREDIT	ACCOUNTS RECEIVABLE DEBIT	ACCOUNTS RECEIVABLE CREDIT	
1									1
2									2
3									3
4									4
5									5
6									6
7									7
8									8
9									9
10									10

Recording employer payroll taxes

6., 7.

Employee Name	Accumulated Earnings, May 31	Total Earnings for June 1–15 Pay Period	Unemployment Taxable Earnings
Cowaski, Renee Y.	$ 5,730.00	$ 720.00	_____
LeCrone, Mark J.	10,500.00	1,320.00	_____
Totals		_____	_____

Social Security Tax Payable	_____
Medicare Tax Payable	_____
Unemployment Tax Payable—Federal	_____
Unemployment Tax Payable—State	_____
Total Payroll Taxes	_____

8.

PAGE

JOURNAL

	DATE	ACCOUNT TITLE	DOC. NO.	POST. REF.	GENERAL DEBIT	GENERAL CREDIT	ACCOUNTS RECEIVABLE DEBIT	ACCOUNTS RECEIVABLE CREDIT	
1									1
2									2
3									3
4									4
5									5
6									6
7									7
8									8
9									9
10									10

14-3 WORK TOGETHER, p. 345

Reporting withholding and payroll taxes

Form **941**	**Employer's Quarterly Federal Tax Return**	OMB No. 1545-0029

Department of the Treasury
Internal Revenue Service

▶ See separate instructions for information on completing this return.
Please type or print.

Enter state code for state in which deposits were made ONLY if different from state in address to the right ▶ ☐ (see page 3 of instructions).

Name (as distinguished from trade name)	Date quarter ended
Trade name, if any	Employer identification number
Address (number and street)	City, state, and ZIP code

OMB No. 1545-0029

T	
FF	
FD	
FP	
I	
T	

If address is different from prior return, check here ▶ ☐

IRS Use

| 1 1 1 1 1 1 1 1 1 1 | 2 | 3 3 3 3 3 3 3 | 4 4 4 | 5 5 5 |

6   7   8 8 8 8 8 8 8   9 9 9 9   10 10 10 10 10 10 10 10 10 10

If you do not have to file returns in the future, check here ▶ ☐ and enter date final wages paid ▶
If you are a seasonal employer, see **Seasonal employers** on page 1 of the instructions and check here ▶ ☐

1	Number of employees in the pay period that includes March 12th . ▶	1		
2	Total wages and tips, plus other compensation		**2**	
3	Total income tax withheld from wages, tips, and sick pay		**3**	
4	Adjustment of withheld income tax for preceding quarters of calendar year		**4**	
5	Adjusted total of income tax withheld (line 3 as adjusted by line 4—see instructions) . .		**5**	
6	Taxable social security wages	**6a**	× 13% (.13) =	**6b**	
	Taxable social security tips	**6c**	× 13% (.13) =	**6d**	
7	Taxable Medicare wages and tips . . .	**7a**	× 3% (.03) =	**7b**	
8	Total social security and Medicare taxes (add lines 6b, 6d, and 7b). Check here if wages are not subject to social security and/or Medicare tax . . . . ▶ ☐		**8**	
9	Adjustment of social security and Medicare taxes (see instructions for required explanation) Sick Pay $ _____ ± Fractions of Cents $ _____ ± Other $ _____ =		**9**	
10	Adjusted total of social security and Medicare taxes (line 8 as adjusted by line 9—see instructions)		**10**	
11	**Total taxes** (add lines 5 and 10)		**11**	
12	Advance earned income credit (EIC) payments made to employees		**12**	
13	Net taxes (subtract line 12 from line 11). **This should equal line 17, column (d) below (or line D of Schedule B (Form 941))**		**13**	
14	Total deposits for quarter, including overpayment applied from a prior quarter		**14**	
15	**Balance due** (subtract line 14 from line 13). See instructions		**15**	

16 **Overpayment,** if line 14 is more than line 13, enter excess here ▶ $ _____
and check if to be: ☐ Applied to next return **OR** ☐ Refunded.

- **All filers:** If line 13 is less than $500, you need not complete line 17 or Schedule B (Form 941).
- **Semiweekly schedule depositors:** Complete Schedule B (Form 941) and check here . . . . ▶ ☐
- **Monthly schedule depositors:** Complete line 17, columns (a) through (d), and check here . . . . ▶ ☐

17	**Monthly Summary of Federal Tax Liability.** Do not complete if you were a semiweekly schedule depositor.

(a) First month liability	(b) Second month liability	(c) Third month liability	(d) Total liability for quarter

Sign Here

Under penalties of perjury, I declare that I have examined this return, including accompanying schedules and statements, and to the best of my knowledge and belief, it is true, correct, and complete.

Signature ▶   Print Your Name and Title ▶   Date ▶

For Privacy Act and Paperwork Reduction Act Notice, see page 4 of separate instructions.   Cat. No. 17001Z   Form **941**

Reporting withholding and payroll taxes

Form **941**

Department of the Treasury
Internal Revenue Service

Employer's Quarterly Federal Tax Return

▶ See separate instructions for information on completing this return.
Please type or print.

Enter state code for state in which deposits were made ONLY if different from state in address to the right ▶ ☐ (see page 3 of instructions).

Name (as distinguished from trade name)	Date quarter ended
Trade name, if any	Employer identification number
Address (number and street)	City, state, and ZIP code

OMB No. 1545-0029

T
FF
FD
FP
I
T

If address is different from prior return, check here ▶ ☐

IRS Use

1	1	1	1	1	1	1	1	1	1	2	3	3	3	3	3	3	3	4	4	4	5	5	5
6	7	8	8	8	8	8	8	8		9	9	9	9	9	10	10	10	10	10	10	10	10	10

If you do not have to file returns in the future, check here ▶ ☐ and enter date final wages paid ▶

If you are a seasonal employer, see **Seasonal employers** on page 1 of the instructions and check here ▶ ☐

1	Number of employees in the pay period that includes March 12th . ▶	1	
2	Total wages and tips, plus other compensation	2	
3	Total income tax withheld from wages, tips, and sick pay	3	
4	Adjustment of withheld income tax for preceding quarters of calendar year	4	
5	Adjusted total of income tax withheld (line 3 as adjusted by line 4—see instructions) . . .	5	
6	Taxable social security wages		
7	Taxable Medicare wages and tips . . .		
8	Total social security and Medicare taxes (add lines 6b, 6d, and 7b). Check here if wages are not subject to social security and/or Medicare tax . . . . ▶ ☐	8	
9	Adjustment of social security and Medicare taxes (see instructions for required explanation) Sick Pay $ _____ ± Fractions of Cents $ _____ ± Other $ _____ =	9	
10	Adjusted total of social security and Medicare taxes (line 8 as adjusted by line 9—see instructions)	10	
11	**Total taxes** (add lines 5 and 10)	11	
12	Advance earned income credit (EIC) payments made to employees	12	
13	Net taxes (subtract line 12 from line 11). **This should equal line 17, column (d) below (or line D of Schedule B (Form 941))**	13	
14	Total deposits for quarter, including overpayment applied from a prior quarter	14	
15	**Balance due** (subtract line 14 from line 13). See instructions	15	

Lines 6 and 7:

Taxable social security wages .	**6a**		× 13% (.13) =	**6b**
Taxable social security tips . .	**6c**		× 13% (.13) =	**6d**
Taxable Medicare wages and tips	**7a**		× 3% (.03) =	**7b**

16 **Overpayment,** if line 14 is more than line 13, enter excess here ▶ $ _____ and check if to be: ☐ Applied to next return **OR** ☐ Refunded.

- **All filers:** If line 13 is less than $500, you need not complete line 17 or Schedule B (Form 941).
- **Semiweekly schedule depositors:** Complete Schedule B (Form 941) and check here . . . . ▶ ☐
- **Monthly schedule depositors:** Complete line 17, columns (a) through (d), and check here . . . . ▶ ☐

17	**Monthly Summary of Federal Tax Liability.** Do not complete if you were a semiweekly schedule depositor.

(a) First month liability	(b) Second month liability	(c) Third month liability	(d) Total liability for quarter

Sign Here

Under penalties of perjury, I declare that I have examined this return, including accompanying schedules and statements, and to the best of my knowledge and belief, it is true, correct, and complete.

Signature ▶

Print Your Name and Title ▶

Date ▶

For Privacy Act and Paperwork Reduction Act Notice, see page 4 of separate instructions.

Cat. No. 17001Z

Form **941**

14-4 WORK TOGETHER, p. 351

Paying withholding and payroll taxes

3., 4.

		JOURNAL					

	DATE	ACCOUNT TITLE	DOC. NO.	POST. REF.	GENERAL DEBIT	GENERAL CREDIT	CASH DEBIT	CASH CREDIT	
1									1
2									2
3									3
4									4
5									5
6									6
7									7
8									8
9									9
10									10
11									11
12									12
13									13
14									14
15									15
16									16
17									17
18									18
19									19
20									20
21									21
22									22
23									23
24									24
25									25
26									26
27									27
28									28
29									29
30									30
31									31

Paying withholding and payroll taxes

5., 6.

JOURNAL

	DATE	ACCOUNT TITLE	DOC. NO.	POST. REF.	GENERAL DEBIT	GENERAL CREDIT	CASH DEBIT	CASH CREDIT	
1									1
2									2
3									3
4									4
5									5
6									6
7									7
8									8
9									9
10									10
11									11
12									12
13									13
14									14
15									15
16									16
17									17
18									18
19									19
20									20
21									21
22									22
23									23
24									24
25									25
26									26
27									27
28									28
29									29
30									30
31									31

14-1 APPLICATION PROBLEM, p. 353

Recording a payroll

JOURNAL

					GENERAL		CASH	
	DATE	ACCOUNT TITLE	DOC. NO.	POST. REF.	DEBIT	CREDIT	DEBIT	CREDIT
1								
2								
3								
4								
5								
6								
7								
8								
9								
10								
11								
12								
13								
14								
15								
16								
17								
18								
19								
20								
21								
22								
23								
24								
25								
26								
27								
28								
29								
30								
31								
32								

Extra form

JOURNAL

	DATE	ACCOUNT TITLE	DOC. NO.	POST. REF.	GENERAL		CASH		
					1 DEBIT	2 CREDIT	10 DEBIT	11 CREDIT	
1									1
2									2
3									3
4									4
5									5
6									6
7									7
8									8
9									9
10									10
11									11
12									12
13									13
14									14
15									15
16									16
17									17
18									18
19									19
20									20
21									21
22									22
23									23
24									24
25									25
26									26
27									27
28									28
29									29
30									30
31									31
32									32

14-2 APPLICATION PROBLEM, p. 353

Recording employer payroll taxes

1., 2., 4.

Employee Name	Accumulated Earnings, March 31	Total Earnings for April 1–15 Pay Period	Unemployment Taxable Earnings, April 15	Accumulated Earnings, April 15	Total Earnings for April 16–30 Pay Period	Unemployment Taxable Earnings, April 30
Bolser, Frank T.	$4,860.00	$ 810.00	_____	_____	$ 795.00	_____
Denham, Beth R.	5,670.00	945.00	_____	_____	980.00	_____
Harjo, Teresa S.	7,500.00	1,250.00	–	_____	1,250.00	_____
Knutzen, John L.	3,720.00	620.00	_____	_____	635.00	_____
Prescott, Laura F.	4,560.00	760.00	_____	_____	740.00	_____
Schmidt, Ian T.	6,900.00	1,150.00	_____	_____	1,125.00	_____
	Totals	_____	_____	Totals	_____	_____

Social Security Tax Payable	_____		Social Security Tax Payable	_____
Medicare Tax Payable	_____		Medicare Tax Payable	_____
Unemployment Tax Payable—Federal	_____		Unemployment Tax Payable—Federal	_____
Unemployment Tax Payable—State	_____		Unemployment Tax Payable—State	_____

3., 5.

JOURNAL

	DATE	ACCOUNT TITLE	DOC. NO.	POST. REF.	GENERAL DEBIT	GENERAL CREDIT	CASH DEBIT	CASH CREDIT	
1									1
2									2
3									3
4									4
5									5
6									6
7									7
8									8
9									9
10									10
11									11
12									12

PAGE

JOURNAL

PAGE

	DATE		ACCOUNT TITLE	DOC. NO.	POST. REF.	GENERAL		CASH	
						DEBIT (1)	CREDIT (2)	DEBIT (10)	CREDIT (11)
1									
2									
3									
4									
5									
6									
7									
8									
9									
10									
11									
12									
13									
14									
15									
16									
17									
18									
19									
20									
21									
22									
23									
24									
25									
26									
27									
28									
29									
30									
31									
32									

14-3 APPLICATION PROBLEM, p. 354

Reporting withholding and payroll taxes

Form 941

Department of the Treasury
Internal Revenue Service

Employer's Quarterly Federal Tax Return

▶ See separate instructions for information on completing this return.
Please type or print.

Enter state
code for state
in which
deposits were
made ONLY if
different from
state in
address to
the right ▶ ☐
(see page
3 of
instructions).

Name (as distinguished from trade name)	Date quarter ended
Trade name, if any	Employer identification number
Address (number and street)	City, state, and ZIP code

OMB No. 1545-0029

| T |
| FF |
| FD |
| FP |
| I |
| T |

If address is
different
from prior
return, check
here ▶ ☐

IRS Use

| 1 1 1 1 1 1 1 1 1 1 | 2 | 3 3 3 3 3 3 3 | 4 4 4 | 5 5 5 |

| 6 | 7 | 8 8 8 8 8 8 8 | 9 9 9 9 | 10 10 10 10 10 10 10 10 10 10 |

If you do not have to file returns in the future, check here ▶ ☐ and enter date final wages paid ▶
If you are a seasonal employer, see **Seasonal employers** on page 1 of the instructions and check here ▶ ☐

1	Number of employees in the pay period that includes March 12th . ▶	1		
2	Total wages and tips, plus other compensation		**2**	
3	Total income tax withheld from wages, tips, and sick pay		**3**	
4	Adjustment of withheld income tax for preceding quarters of calendar year . . .		**4**	
5	Adjusted total of income tax withheld (line 3 as adjusted by line 4—see instructions) . . .		**5**	

6	Taxable social security wages	**6a**		× 13% (.13) =	**6b**	
	Taxable social security tips	**6c**		× 13% (.13) =	**6d**	
7	Taxable Medicare wages and tips . . .	**7a**		× 3% (.03) =	**7b**	

8	Total social security and Medicare taxes (add lines 6b, 6d, and 7b). Check here if wages are not subject to social security and/or Medicare tax . . . . ▶ ☐	**8**	
9	Adjustment of social security and Medicare taxes (see instructions for required explanation) Sick Pay $ _____ ± Fractions of Cents $ _____ ± Other $ _____ =	**9**	
10	Adjusted total of social security and Medicare taxes (line 8 as adjusted by line 9—see instructions)	**10**	
11	**Total taxes** (add lines 5 and 10)	**11**	
12	Advance earned income credit (EIC) payments made to employees	**12**	
13	Net taxes (subtract line 12 from line 11). **This should equal line 17, column (d) below (or line D of Schedule B (Form 941))**	**13**	
14	Total deposits for quarter, including overpayment applied from a prior quarter . . .	**14**	
15	**Balance due** (subtract line 14 from line 13). See instructions	**15**	
16	**Overpayment,** if line 14 is more than line 13, enter excess here ▶ $ _____ and check if to be: ☐ Applied to next return **OR** ☐ Refunded.		

• **All filers:** If line 13 is less than $500, you need not complete line 17 or Schedule B (Form 941).
• **Semiweekly schedule depositors:** Complete Schedule B (Form 941) and check here . . . . ▶ ☐
• **Monthly schedule depositors:** Complete line 17, columns (a) through (d), and check here . . . . ▶ ☐

17	**Monthly Summary of Federal Tax Liability.** Do not complete if you were a semiweekly schedule depositor.			
	(a) First month liability	(b) Second month liability	(c) Third month liability	(d) Total liability for quarter

Sign Here

Under penalties of perjury, I declare that I have examined this return, including accompanying schedules and statements, and to the best of my knowledge and belief, it is true, correct, and complete.

Signature ▶   Print Your Name and Title ▶   Date ▶

For Privacy Act and Paperwork Reduction Act Notice, see page 4 of separate instructions.   Cat. No. 17001Z   Form **941**

Form **941**

Department of the Treasury
Internal Revenue Service

Employer's Quarterly Federal Tax Return

▶ See separate instructions for information on completing this return.
Please type or print.

Enter state code for state in which deposits were made ONLY if different from state in address to the right ▶ [:]
(see page 3 of instructions).

Name (as distinguished from trade name)	Date quarter ended
Trade name, if any	Employer identification number
Address (number and street)	City, state, and ZIP code

OMB No. 1545-0029

| T |
| FF |
| FD |
| FP |
| I |
| T |

If address is different from prior return, check here ▶ [ ]

IRS Use

| 1 | 1 | 1 | 1 | 1 | 1 | 1 | 1 | 1 | 1 | 2 | 3 | 3 | 3 | 3 | 3 | 3 | 3 | 4 | 4 | 4 | 5 | 5 | 5 |

| 6 | 7 | 8 | 8 | 8 | 8 | 8 | 8 | 8 | 9 | 9 | 9 | 9 | 10 | 10 | 10 | 10 | 10 | 10 | 10 | 10 | 10 | 10 |

If you do not have to file returns in the future, check here ▶ [ ] and enter date final wages paid ▶
If you are a seasonal employer, see **Seasonal employers** on page 1 of the instructions and check here ▶ [ ]

1	Number of employees in the pay period that includes March 12th . ▶	1
2	Total wages and tips, plus other compensation	**2**
3	Total income tax withheld from wages, tips, and sick pay	**3**
4	Adjustment of withheld income tax for preceding quarters of calendar year	**4**
5	Adjusted total of income tax withheld (line 3 as adjusted by line 4—see instructions) . . .	**5**
6	Taxable social security wages	**6a**	× 13% (.13) =	**6b**
	Taxable social security tips	**6c**	× 13% (.13) =	**6d**
7	Taxable Medicare wages and tips . . .	**7a**	× 3% (.03) =	**7b**
8	Total social security and Medicare taxes (add lines 6b, 6d, and 7b). Check here if wages are not subject to social security and/or Medicare tax . . . . ▶ [ ]	**8**
9	Adjustment of social security and Medicare taxes (see instructions for required explanation) Sick Pay $ _____ ± Fractions of Cents $ _____ ± Other $ _____ =	**9**
10	Adjusted total of social security and Medicare taxes (line 8 as adjusted by line 9—see instructions)	**10**
11	**Total taxes** (add lines 5 and 10)	**11**
12	Advance earned income credit (EIC) payments made to employees	**12**
13	Net taxes (subtract line 12 from line 11). **This should equal line 17, column (d) below (or line D of Schedule B (Form 941))**	**13**
14	Total deposits for quarter, including overpayment applied from a prior quarter	**14**
15	**Balance due** (subtract line 14 from line 13). See instructions	**15**
16	**Overpayment,** if line 14 is more than line 13, enter excess here ▶ $ _____	

and check if to be: [ ] Applied to next return **OR** [ ] Refunded.

- **All filers:** If line 13 is less than $500, you need not complete line 17 or Schedule B (Form 941).
- **Semiweekly schedule depositors:** Complete Schedule B (Form 941) and check here . . . . ▶ [ ]
- **Monthly schedule depositors:** Complete line 17, columns (a) through (d), and check here . . . . . . ▶ [ ]

17	**Monthly Summary of Federal Tax Liability.** Do not complete if you were a semiweekly schedule depositor.
(a) First month liability	**(b)** Second month liability	**(c)** Third month liability	**(d)** Total liability for quarter

Sign Here

Under penalties of perjury, I declare that I have examined this return, including accompanying schedules and statements, and to the best of my knowledge and belief, it is true, correct, and complete.

Signature ▶

Print Your Name and Title ▶

Date ▶

For Privacy Act and Paperwork Reduction Act Notice, see page 4 of separate instructions.　　Cat. No. 17001Z　　Form **941**

14-4 APPLICATION PROBLEM, p. 354

Paying withholding and payroll taxes

1., 2., 3.

JOURNAL

		DATE	ACCOUNT TITLE	DOC. NO.	POST. REF.	GENERAL DEBIT	GENERAL CREDIT	CASH DEBIT	CASH CREDIT	
1										1
2										2
3										3
4										4
5										5
6										6
7										7
8										8
9										9
10										10
11										11
12										12
13										13
14										14
15										15
16										16
17										17
18										18
19										19
20										20
21										21
22										22
23										23
24										24
25										25
26										26
27										27
28										28
29										29
30										30
31										31

Extra form

JOURNAL

	DATE		ACCOUNT TITLE	DOC. NO.	POST. REF.	GENERAL			CASH		
						DEBIT 1	CREDIT 2		DEBIT 10	CREDIT 11	
1											1
2											2
3											3
4											4
5											5
6											6
7											7
8											8
9											9
10											10
11											11
12											12
13											13
14											14
15											15
16											16
17											17
18											18
19											19
20											20
21											21
22											22
23											23
24											24
25											25
26											26
27											27
28											28
29											29
30											30
31											31
32											32

14-5 MASTERY PROBLEM, p. 354

Journalizing payroll transactions

1., 2.

JOURNAL

					GENERAL		CASH	
	DATE	ACCOUNT TITLE	DOC. NO.	POST. REF.	DEBIT	CREDIT	DEBIT	CREDIT
1								
2								
3								
4								
5								
6								
7								
8								
9								
10								
11								
12								
13								
14								
15								
16								
17								
18								
19								
20								
21								
22								
23								
24								
25								
26								
27								
28								
29								
30								
31								
32								
33								

3., 4.

JOURNAL

	DATE	ACCOUNT TITLE	DOC. NO.	POST. REF.	GENERAL DEBIT	GENERAL CREDIT	CASH DEBIT	CASH CREDIT	
1									1
2									2
3									3
4									4
5									5
6									6
7									7
8									8
9									9
10									10
11									11
12									12
13									13
14									14
15									15
16									16
17									17
18									18
19									19
20									20
21									21
22									22
23									23
24									24
25									25
26									26
27									27
28									28
29									29
30									30

14-6 CHALLENGE PROBLEM, p. 355

Journalizing and posting payroll transactions

1., 2.

JOURNAL

PAGE

	DATE	ACCOUNT TITLE	DOC. NO.	POST. REF.	GENERAL DEBIT	GENERAL CREDIT	CASH DEBIT	CASH CREDIT	
1									1
2									2
3									3
4									4
5									5
6									6
7									7
8									8
9									9
10									10
11									11
12									12
13									13
14									14
15									15
16									16
17									17
18									18
19									19
20									20
21									21
22									22
23									23
24									24
25									25
26									26
27									27
28									28
29									29
30									30

2., 3., 4.

JOURNAL

PAGE

	DATE	ACCOUNT TITLE	DOC. NO.	POST. REF.	GENERAL DEBIT	GENERAL CREDIT	CASH DEBIT	CASH CREDIT	
1									1
2									2
3									3
4									4
5									5
6									6
7									7
8									8
9									9
10									10
11									11
12									12
13									13
14									14
15									15
16									16
17									17
18									18
19									19
20									20
21									21
22									22
23									23
24									24
25									25
26									26
27									27
28									28
29									29
30									30

14-6 CHALLENGE PROBLEM (continued)

1., 3.

GENERAL LEDGER

ACCOUNT Employee Income Tax Payable   ACCOUNT NO. 2120

DATE	ITEM	POST. REF.	DEBIT	CREDIT	BALANCE DEBIT	BALANCE CREDIT
Jan. 1	Balance	✔				1 2 9 2 00

ACCOUNT Social Security Tax Payable   ACCOUNT NO. 2130

DATE	ITEM	POST. REF.	DEBIT	CREDIT	BALANCE DEBIT	BALANCE CREDIT
Jan. 1	Balance	✔				1 5 2 7 50

ACCOUNT Medicare Tax Payable   ACCOUNT NO. 2140

DATE	ITEM	POST. REF.	DEBIT	CREDIT	BALANCE DEBIT	BALANCE CREDIT
Jan. 1	Balance	✔				1 7 6 25

1., 3.   GENERAL LEDGER

ACCOUNT Unemployment Tax Payable—Federal   ACCOUNT NO. 2150

DATE	ITEM	POST. REF.	DEBIT	CREDIT	BALANCE DEBIT	BALANCE CREDIT
20-- Jan. 1	Balance	✔				2 6 4 00

ACCOUNT Unemployment Tax Payable—State   ACCOUNT NO. 2160

DATE	ITEM	POST. REF.	DEBIT	CREDIT	BALANCE DEBIT	BALANCE CREDIT
20-- Jan. 1	Balance	✔				1 7 8 2 00

ACCOUNT U.S. Savings Bonds Payable   ACCOUNT NO. 2180

DATE	ITEM	POST. REF.	DEBIT	CREDIT	BALANCE DEBIT	BALANCE CREDIT
20-- Jan. 1	Balance	✔				3 0 0 00

ACCOUNT Payroll Taxes Expense   ACCOUNT NO. 6150

DATE	ITEM	POST. REF.	DEBIT	CREDIT	BALANCE DEBIT	BALANCE CREDIT

ACCOUNT Salary Expense   ACCOUNT NO. 6170

DATE	ITEM	POST. REF.	DEBIT	CREDIT	BALANCE DEBIT	BALANCE CREDIT

Extra form

JOURNAL

	DATE	ACCOUNT TITLE	DOC. NO.	POST. REF.	GENERAL		ACCOUNTS RECEIVABLE		
					DEBIT	CREDIT	DEBIT	CREDIT	
1									1
2									2
3									3
4									4
5									5
6									6
7									7
8									8
9									9
10									10
11									11
12									12
13									13
14									14
15									15
16									16
17									17
18									18
19									19
20									20
21									21
22									22
23									23
24									24
25									25
26									26
27									27
28									28
29									29
30									30
31									31
32									32
33									33

REINFORCEMENT ACTIVITY 2 PART A, p. 360

An Accounting Cycle for a Partnership: Journalizing and Posting Transactions

1., 2.

PAGE 23   JOURNAL

	DATE	ACCOUNT TITLE	DOC. NO.	POST. REF.	GENERAL DEBIT	GENERAL CREDIT	ACCOUNTS RECEIVABLE DEBIT	ACCOUNTS RECEIVABLE CREDIT	
1									1
2									2
3									3
4									4
5									5
6									6
7									7
8									8
9									9
10									10
11									11
12									12
13									13
14									14
15									15
16									16
17									17
18									18
19									19
20									20
21									21
22									22
23									23
24									24
25									25
26									26
27									27
28									28
29									29
30									30
31									31
32									32
33									33
34									34
35									35

REINFORCEMENT ACTIVITY 2   PART A (continued)

1., 2.

	5 SALES CREDIT	6 SALES TAX PAYABLE CREDIT	7 ACCOUNTS PAYABLE DEBIT	8 ACCOUNTS PAYABLE CREDIT	9 PURCHASES DEBIT	10 CASH DEBIT	11 CASH CREDIT	
1								1
2								2
3								3
4								4
5								5
6								6
7								7
8								8
9								9
10								10
11								11
12								12
13								13
14								14
15								15
16								16
17								17
18								18
19								19
20								20
21								21
22								22
23								23
24								24
25								25
26								26
27								27
28								28
29								29
30								30
31								31
32								32
33								33
34								34
35								35

3., 4., 5., 7., 8.

PAGE 24   JOURNAL

	DATE	ACCOUNT TITLE	DOC. NO.	POST. REF.	GENERAL		ACCOUNTS RECEIVABLE		
					DEBIT	**CREDIT**	**DEBIT**	**CREDIT**	
1									1
2									2
3									3
4									4
5									5
6									6
7									7
8									8
9									9
10									10
11									11
12									12
13									13
14									14
15									15
16									16
17									17
18									18
19									19
20									20
21									21
22									22
23									23
24									24
25									25
26									26
27									27
28									28
29									29
30									30
31									31
32									32
33									33
34									34
35									35
36									36
37									37

REINFORCEMENT ACTIVITY 2 PART A (continued)

3., 4., 5., 7., 8.

PAGE 24

		SALES CREDIT	SALES TAX PAYABLE CREDIT	ACCOUNTS PAYABLE		PURCHASES DEBIT	CASH		
		5	6	7 DEBIT	8 CREDIT	9	10 DEBIT	11 CREDIT	
1									1
2									2
3									3
4									4
5									5
6									6
7									7
8									8
9									9
10									10
11									11
12									12
13									13
14									14
15									15
16									16
17									17
18									18
19									19
20									20
21									21
22									22
23									23
24									24
25									25
26									26
27									27
28									28
29									29
30									30
31									31
32									32
33									33
34									34
35									35
36									36
37									37

Extra form

		5	6		ACCOUNTS PAYABLE 7		8		9		CASH 10		11		
		SALES CREDIT	SALES TAX PAYABLE CREDIT		DEBIT		CREDIT		PURCHASES DEBIT		DEBIT		CREDIT		
1															1
2															2
3															3
4															4
5															5
6															6
7															7
8															8
9															9
10															10
11															11
12															12
13															13
14															14
15															15
16															16
17															17
18															18
19															19
20															20
21															21
22															22
23															23
24															24
25															25
26															26
27															27
28															28
29															29
30															30
31															31
32															32
33															33

REINFORCEMENT ACTIVITY 2 PART A (continued)

The general ledger used in Reinforcement Activity 2, Part A, will be needed to complete Part B.
1., 4., 6., 8., 10., 16., 17., 18.   **GENERAL LEDGER**

ACCOUNT Cash   ACCOUNT NO. 1110

DATE		ITEM	POST. REF.	DEBIT	CREDIT	BALANCE DEBIT	BALANCE CREDIT
Dec.	1	Balance	✔			23 3 4 0 00	

ACCOUNT Petty Cash   ACCOUNT NO. 1120

DATE		ITEM	POST. REF.	DEBIT	CREDIT	BALANCE DEBIT	BALANCE CREDIT
Jan.	1	Balance	✔			5 0 0 00	

ACCOUNT Accounts Receivable   ACCOUNT NO. 1130

DATE		ITEM	POST. REF.	DEBIT	CREDIT	BALANCE DEBIT	BALANCE CREDIT
Dec.	1	Balance	✔			1 6 6 7 38	

ACCOUNT Merchandise Inventory   ACCOUNT NO. 1140

DATE		ITEM	POST. REF.	DEBIT	CREDIT	BALANCE DEBIT	BALANCE CREDIT
Jan.	1	Balance	✔			258 7 0 0 00	

ACCOUNT Supplies—Office   ACCOUNT NO. 1145

DATE		ITEM	POST. REF.	DEBIT	CREDIT	BALANCE DEBIT	BALANCE CREDIT
Dec.	1	Balance	✔			4 4 3 0 00	

ACCOUNT Supplies—Store   ACCOUNT NO. 1150

DATE		ITEM	POST. REF.	DEBIT	CREDIT	BALANCE DEBIT	BALANCE CREDIT
Dec.	1	Balance	✔			5 2 6 0 00	

1., 4., 6., 8., 10., 16., 17., 18.   GENERAL LEDGER

ACCOUNT Prepaid Insurance   ACCOUNT NO. 1160

DATE	ITEM	POST. REF.	DEBIT	CREDIT	BALANCE DEBIT	BALANCE CREDIT
20-- Dec. 1	Balance	✔			2 1 8 0 00	

ACCOUNT Accounts Payable   ACCOUNT NO. 2110

DATE	ITEM	POST. REF.	DEBIT	CREDIT	BALANCE DEBIT	BALANCE CREDIT
20-- Dec. 1	Balance	✔				5 2 2 2 00

ACCOUNT Employee Income Tax Payable   ACCOUNT NO. 2120

DATE	ITEM	POST. REF.	DEBIT	CREDIT	BALANCE DEBIT	BALANCE CREDIT
20-- Dec. 1	Balance	✔				3 4 2 00

ACCOUNT Social Security Tax Payable   ACCOUNT NO. 2130

DATE	ITEM	POST. REF.	DEBIT	CREDIT	BALANCE DEBIT	BALANCE CREDIT
20-- Dec. 1	Balance	✔				7 6 7 00

ACCOUNT Medicare Tax Payable   ACCOUNT NO. 2135

DATE	ITEM	POST. REF.	DEBIT	CREDIT	BALANCE DEBIT	BALANCE CREDIT
20-- Dec. 1	Balance	✔				1 7 7 00

ACCOUNT Sales Tax Payable   ACCOUNT NO. 2140

DATE	ITEM	POST. REF.	DEBIT	CREDIT	BALANCE DEBIT	BALANCE CREDIT
20-- Dec. 1	Balance	✔				1 9 4 5 00

REINFORCEMENT ACTIVITY 2   PART A (continued)

1., 4., 6., 8., 10., 16., 17., 18.   **GENERAL LEDGER**

ACCOUNT Unemployment Tax Payable—Federal   ACCOUNT NO. 2150

DATE	ITEM	POST. REF.	DEBIT	CREDIT	BALANCE DEBIT	BALANCE CREDIT
20-- Dec. 1	Balance	✔				1 1 60

ACCOUNT Unemployment Tax Payable—State   ACCOUNT NO. 2160

DATE	ITEM	POST. REF.	DEBIT	CREDIT	BALANCE DEBIT	BALANCE CREDIT
20-- Dec. 1	Balance	✔				7 8 30

ACCOUNT Health Insurance Premiums Payable   ACCOUNT NO. 2170

DATE	ITEM	POST. REF.	DEBIT	CREDIT	BALANCE DEBIT	BALANCE CREDIT
20-- Dec. 1	Balance	✔				3 4 0 00

ACCOUNT U.S. Savings Bonds Payable   ACCOUNT NO. 2180

DATE	ITEM	POST. REF.	DEBIT	CREDIT	BALANCE DEBIT	BALANCE CREDIT
20-- Dec. 1	Balance	✔				6 0 00

ACCOUNT United Way Donations Payable   ACCOUNT NO. 2190

DATE	ITEM	POST. REF.	DEBIT	CREDIT	BALANCE DEBIT	BALANCE CREDIT
20-- Dec. 1	Balance	✔				1 2 0 00

ACCOUNT Ester Burks, Capital   ACCOUNT NO. 3110

DATE	ITEM	POST. REF.	DEBIT	CREDIT	BALANCE DEBIT	BALANCE CREDIT
20-- Jan. 1	Balance	✔				112 5 8 5 50

1., 4., 6., 8., 10., 16., 17., 18.   **GENERAL LEDGER**

ACCOUNT Ester Burks, Drawing   ACCOUNT NO. 3120

DATE		ITEM	POST. REF.	DEBIT	CREDIT	BALANCE DEBIT	BALANCE CREDIT
Dec. 20--	1	Balance	✔			16 500 00	

ACCOUNT Juan Ortiz, Capital   ACCOUNT NO. 3130

DATE		ITEM	POST. REF.	DEBIT	CREDIT	BALANCE DEBIT	BALANCE CREDIT
Jan. 20--	1	Balance	✔				111 703 58

ACCOUNT Juan Ortiz, Drawing   ACCOUNT NO. 3140

DATE		ITEM	POST. REF.	DEBIT	CREDIT	BALANCE DEBIT	BALANCE CREDIT
Dec. 20--	1	Balance	✔			16 500 00	

ACCOUNT Income Summary   ACCOUNT NO. 3150

DATE		ITEM	POST. REF.	DEBIT	CREDIT	BALANCE DEBIT	BALANCE CREDIT

ACCOUNT Sales   ACCOUNT NO. 4110

DATE		ITEM	POST. REF.	DEBIT	CREDIT	BALANCE DEBIT	BALANCE CREDIT
Dec. 20--	1	Balance	✔				330 700 00

ACCOUNT Purchases   ACCOUNT NO. 5110

DATE		ITEM	POST. REF.	DEBIT	CREDIT	BALANCE DEBIT	BALANCE CREDIT
Dec. 20--	1	Balance	✔			138 910 00	

REINFORCEMENT ACTIVITY 2　PART A (continued)

1., 4., 6., 8., 10., 16., 17., 18.　　GENERAL LEDGER

ACCOUNT Advertising Expense　　　　　　　　　　　　　　ACCOUNT NO. 6110

DATE	ITEM	POST. REF.	DEBIT	CREDIT	BALANCE DEBIT	BALANCE CREDIT
Dec. 1	Balance	✔			5 0 7 5 00	

ACCOUNT Credit Card Fee Expense　　　　　　　　　　　ACCOUNT NO. 6120

DATE	ITEM	POST. REF.	DEBIT	CREDIT	BALANCE DEBIT	BALANCE CREDIT
Dec. 1	Balance	✔			3 4 9 0 00	

ACCOUNT Insurance Expense　　　　　　　　　　　　　　ACCOUNT NO. 6130

DATE	ITEM	POST. REF.	DEBIT	CREDIT	BALANCE DEBIT	BALANCE CREDIT

ACCOUNT Miscellaneous Expense　　　　　　　　　　　ACCOUNT NO. 6140

DATE	ITEM	POST. REF.	DEBIT	CREDIT	BALANCE DEBIT	BALANCE CREDIT
Dec. 1	Balance	✔			2 0 2 0 00	

ACCOUNT Payroll Taxes Expense　　　　　　　　　　　ACCOUNT NO. 6150

DATE	ITEM	POST. REF.	DEBIT	CREDIT	BALANCE DEBIT	BALANCE CREDIT
Dec. 1	Balance	✔			6 8 1 9 60	

ACCOUNT Rent Expense   ACCOUNT NO. 6160

DATE	ITEM	POST. REF.	DEBIT	CREDIT	BALANCE DEBIT	BALANCE CREDIT
20-- Dec. 1	Balance	✔			13 2 0 0 00	

ACCOUNT Salary Expense   ACCOUNT NO. 6170

DATE	ITEM	POST. REF.	DEBIT	CREDIT	BALANCE DEBIT	BALANCE CREDIT
20-- Dec. 1	Balance	✔			62 1 5 0 00	

ACCOUNT Supplies Expense—Office   ACCOUNT NO. 6175

DATE	ITEM	POST. REF.	DEBIT	CREDIT	BALANCE DEBIT	BALANCE CREDIT

ACCOUNT Supplies Expense—Store   ACCOUNT NO. 6180

DATE	ITEM	POST. REF.	DEBIT	CREDIT	BALANCE DEBIT	BALANCE CREDIT

ACCOUNT Utilities Expense   ACCOUNT NO. 6190

DATE	ITEM	POST. REF.	DEBIT	CREDIT	BALANCE DEBIT	BALANCE CREDIT
20-- Dec. 1	Balance	✔			3 3 1 0 00	

REINFORCEMENT ACTIVITY 2 PART A (continued)

1., 4., 9.   **ACCOUNTS PAYABLE LEDGER**

VENDOR ABC Optical Co.   VENDOR NO. 210

DATE		ITEM	POST. REF.	DEBIT	CREDIT	CREDIT BALANCE
Dec.	1	Balance	✔			1 2 7 2 00

VENDOR Central Office Supply   VENDOR NO. 220

DATE		ITEM	POST. REF.	DEBIT	CREDIT	CREDIT BALANCE

VENDOR Eyecare Optical   VENDOR NO. 230

DATE		ITEM	POST. REF.	DEBIT	CREDIT	CREDIT BALANCE
Dec.	1	Balance	✔			1 1 7 0 00

VENDOR Optical Mart   VENDOR NO. 240

DATE		ITEM	POST. REF.	DEBIT	CREDIT	CREDIT BALANCE
Dec.	1	Balance	✔			2 2 0 0 00

VENDOR Solar Optical   VENDOR NO. 250

DATE		ITEM	POST. REF.	DEBIT	CREDIT	CREDIT BALANCE
Dec.	1	Balance	✔			5 8 0 00

VENDOR Zen Supply   VENDOR NO. 260

DATE		ITEM	POST. REF.	DEBIT	CREDIT	CREDIT BALANCE

1., 9.

ACCOUNTS RECEIVABLE LEDGER

CUSTOMER Doritha Busch   CUSTOMER NO. 110

DATE	ITEM	POST. REF.	DEBIT	CREDIT	DEBIT BALANCE

CUSTOMER Linda Cortez   CUSTOMER NO. 120

DATE		ITEM	POST. REF.	DEBIT	CREDIT	DEBIT BALANCE
Dec.	1	Balance	✔			4 1 3 40

CUSTOMER Dallas Giles   CUSTOMER NO. 130

DATE	ITEM	POST. REF.	DEBIT	CREDIT	DEBIT BALANCE

CUSTOMER Kristin Jung   CUSTOMER NO. 140

DATE		ITEM	POST. REF.	DEBIT	CREDIT	DEBIT BALANCE
Dec.	1	Balance	✔			8 2 1 50

CUSTOMER Jack O'Brien   CUSTOMER NO. 150

DATE	ITEM	POST. REF.	DEBIT	CREDIT	DEBIT BALANCE

CUSTOMER Don Teal   CUSTOMER NO. 160

DATE		ITEM	POST. REF.	DEBIT	CREDIT	DEBIT BALANCE
Dec.	1	Balance	✔			4 3 2 48

REINFORCEMENT ACTIVITY 2 **PART A (concluded)**

9.

Extra form

15-1, 15-2, and 15-3 WORK TOGETHER, pp. 371, 377, 384

15-1 Beginning an 8-column work sheet, 15-2 Analyzing and recording adjustments on a work sheet, 15-3 Completing an 8-column work sheet

Paradise Company

Work Sheet

For Year Ended December 31, 20 – –

	ACCOUNT TITLE	TRIAL BALANCE		ADJUSTMENTS		INCOME STATEMENT		BALANCE SHEET	
		DEBIT	CREDIT	DEBIT	CREDIT	DEBIT	CREDIT	DEBIT	CREDIT
1	Cash								
2	Petty Cash								
3	Accounts Receivable								
4	Merchandise Inventory								
5	Supplies—Office								
6	Supplies—Store								
7	Prepaid Insurance								
8	Accounts Payable								
9	Sales Tax Payable								
10	Jean Brower, Capital								
11	Jean Brower, Drawing								
12	Dale Edson, Capital								
13	Dale Edson, Drawing								
14	Income Summary								
15	Sales								
16	Purchases								
17	Advertising Expense								
18	Credit Card Fee Expense								
19	Insurance Expense								
20	Miscellaneous Expense								
21	Rent Expense								
22	Supplies Expense—Office								
23	Supplies Expense—Store								
24	Utilities Expense								
25									
26									
27									

15-1 Beginning an 8-column work sheet, 15-2 Analyzing and recording adjustments on a work sheet, 15-3 Completing an 8-column work sheet

Mueller Company

Work Sheet

For Year Ended December 31, 20 – –

ACCOUNT TITLE	TRIAL BALANCE		ADJUSTMENTS		INCOME STATEMENT		BALANCE SHEET	
	DEBIT	CREDIT	DEBIT	CREDIT	DEBIT	CREDIT	DEBIT	CREDIT
Cash								
Petty Cash								
Accounts Receivable								
Merchandise Inventory								
Supplies—Office								
Supplies—Store								
Prepaid Insurance								
Accounts Payable								
Sales Tax Payable								
Harry Glover, Capital								
Harry Glover, Drawing								
Laura Montez, Capital								
Laura Montez, Drawing								
Income Summary								
Sales								
Purchases								
Advertising Expense								
Credit Card Fee Expense								
Insurance Expense								
Miscellaneous Expense								
Rent Expense								
Supplies Expense—Office								
Supplies Expense—Store								
Utilities Expense								

15-1 and 15-2 WORK TOGETHER (concluded)

ANALYSIS FOR ADJUSTMENTS

1. What is the balance of Merchandise Inventory? _____

2. What should the balance be for this account? _____

3. What must be done to correct the account balance?
   _____ _____

4. What adjustment is made? _____

   _____ _____

   _____ _____

1. What is the balance of Supplies—Office? _____

2. What should the balance be for this account? _____

3. What must be done to correct the account balance?
   _____

4. What adjustment is made? _____

   _____ _____

   _____ _____

1. What is the balance of Supplies—Store? _____

2. What should the balance be for this account? _____

3. What must be done to correct the account balance?
   _____

4. What adjustment is made? _____

   _____ _____

   _____ _____

1. What is the balance of Prepaid Insurance? _____

2. What should the balance be for this account? _____

3. What must be done to correct the account balance?
   _____

4. What adjustment is made? _____

   _____ _____

   _____ _____

ANALYSIS FOR ADJUSTMENTS

1. What is the balance of Merchandise Inventory? _____
2. What should the balance be for this account? _____
3. What must be done to correct the account balance?

   _____ _____
4. What adjustment is made?

   _____ _____

   _____ _____

1. What is the balance of Supplies—Office? _____
2. What should the balance be for this account? _____
3. What must be done to correct the account balance?

   _____ _____
4. What adjustment is made?

   _____ _____

   _____ _____

1. What is the balance of Supplies—Store? _____
2. What should the balance be for this account? _____
3. What must be done to correct the account balance?

   _____ _____
4. What adjustment is made?

   _____ _____

   _____ _____

1. What is the balance of Prepaid Insurance? _____
2. What should the balance be for this account? _____
3. What must be done to correct the account balance?

   _____ _____
4. What adjustment is made?

   _____ _____

   _____ _____

15-1 APPLICATION PROBLEM, p. 386

Beginning an 8-column work sheet for a merchandising business

1., 2., 3.

Drake Park Supply Company

Work Sheet

For Year Ended December 31, 20 - -

ACCOUNT TITLE	TRIAL BALANCE		ADJUSTMENTS		INCOME STATEMENT		BALANCE SHEET	
	DEBIT	CREDIT	DEBIT	CREDIT	DEBIT	CREDIT	DEBIT	CREDIT
	1	2	3	4	5	6	7	8

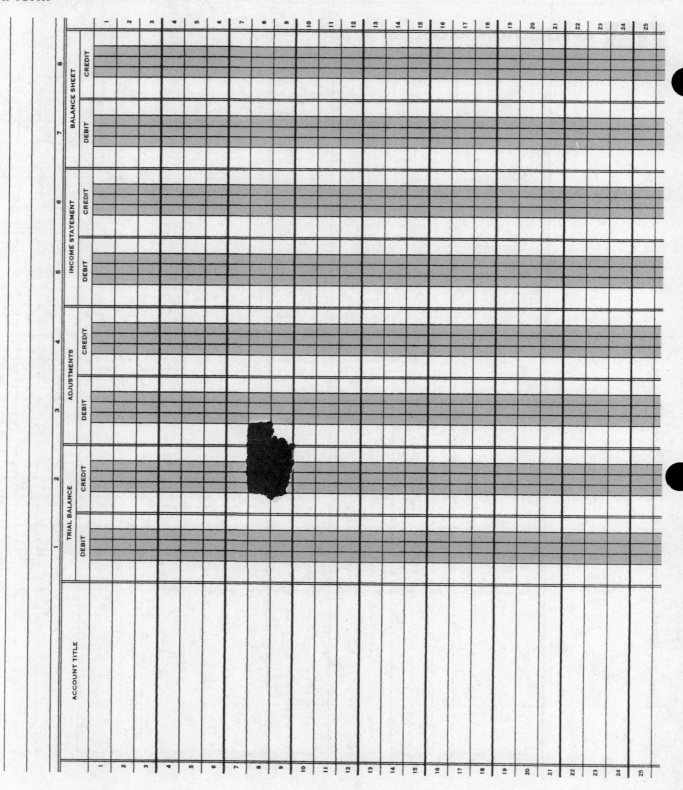

15-2 APPLICATION PROBLEM, p. 386

Analyzing and recording adjustments on a work sheet

1	2	3	4	5
Business	Adjustment Number	Accounts Affected	Adjustment Column Debit	Credit
A	1.	Income Summary	$16,800.00	
		Merchandise Inventory		$16,800.00
	2.			
	3.			
	4.			
B	1.			
	2.			
	3.			
	4.			
C	1.			
	2.			
	3.			
	4.			

Extra form

1	2	3	4	5
			Adjustment Column	
Business	Adjustment Number	Accounts Affected	Debit	Credit

15-3 APPLICATION PROBLEM, p. 387

Completing an 8-column work sheet for a merchandising business

1., 2., 3., 4., 5., 6.

Lotus Gallery

Work Sheet

For Year Ended December 31, 20 --

#	ACCOUNT TITLE	TRIAL BALANCE DEBIT	TRIAL BALANCE CREDIT	ADJUSTMENTS DEBIT	ADJUSTMENTS CREDIT	INCOME STATEMENT DEBIT	INCOME STATEMENT CREDIT	BALANCE SHEET DEBIT	BALANCE SHEET CREDIT
1	Cash	26320 00							
2	Petty Cash	300 00							
3	Accounts Receivable	10690 00							
4	Merchandise Inventory	254245 00			(a) 14890 00				
5	Supplies—Office	6091 00			(b) 4445 00				
6	Supplies—Store	6516 00			(c) 3678 00				
7	Prepaid Insurance	5540 00			(d) 3020 00				
8	Accounts Payable		10740 00						
9	Sales Tax Payable		1985 00						
10	Debbie Craig, Capital		117880 00						
11	Debbie Craig, Drawing	20530 00							
12	Kara Lee, Capital		118520 00						
13	Kara Lee, Drawing	20980 00							
14	Income Summary			(a) 14890 00					
15	Sales		316440 00						
16	Purchases	178560 00							
17	Advertising Expense	6204 00							
18	Credit Card Fee Expense	3264 00							
19	Insurance Expense			(d) 3020 00					
20	Miscellaneous Expense	2577 00							
21	Rent Expense	20160 00							
22	Supplies Expense—Office			(b) 4445 00					
23	Supplies Expense—Store			(c) 3678 00					
24	Utilities Expense	3588 00							
25		565565 00	565565 00	26033 00	26033 00				
26									
27									

Extra form

ACCOUNT TITLE	TRIAL BALANCE		ADJUSTMENTS		INCOME STATEMENT		BALANCE SHEET	
	DEBIT	CREDIT	DEBIT	CREDIT	DEBIT	CREDIT	DEBIT	CREDIT
	1	2	3	4	5	6	7	8
1								
2								
3								
4								
5								
6								
7								
8								
9								
10								
11								
12								
13								
14								
15								
16								
17								
18								
19								
20								
21								
22								
23								
24								
25								
26								
27								

Extra form

ACCOUNT TITLE		TRIAL BALANCE		ADJUSTMENTS		INCOME STATEMENT		BALANCE SHEET	
		DEBIT	CREDIT	DEBIT	CREDIT	DEBIT	CREDIT	DEBIT	CREDIT
		1	2	3	4	5	6	7	8
25									
26									
27									
28									
29									
30									
31									
32									
33									
34									
35									
36									
37									
38									
39									
40									
41									
42									
43									
44									
45									
46									
47									
48									
49									
50									

15-4 MASTERY PROBLEM, p. 387

(Note: This Work Sheet is concluded on page 383.)

Preparing an 8-column work sheet for a merchandising business

1., 2.

Seidler Supply

Work Sheet

For Year Ended December 31, 20 --

	ACCOUNT TITLE	TRIAL BALANCE DEBIT	TRIAL BALANCE CREDIT	ADJUSTMENTS DEBIT	ADJUSTMENTS CREDIT	INCOME STATEMENT DEBIT	INCOME STATEMENT CREDIT	BALANCE SHEET DEBIT	BALANCE SHEET CREDIT
1	Cash	28488 00							
2	Petty Cash	600 00							
3	Accounts Receivable	12240 00							
4	Merchandise Inventory	222360 00							
5	Supplies—Office	6702 00							
6	Supplies—Store	6882 00							
7	Prepaid Insurance	5130 00							
8	Accounts Payable		11616 00						
9	Employ. Inc. Tax Payable		5722 00						
10	Social Security Tax Payable		676 00						
11	Medicare Tax Payable		156 00						
12	Sales Tax Payable		1651 00						
13	Unemploy. Tax Pay.—Fed.		128 00						
14	Unemploy. Tax Pay.—State		864 00						
15	Health Ins. Prem. Payable		100 00						
16	U.S. Savings Bonds Payable		100 00						
17	United Way Don. Payable		75 00						
18	Rex Flanery, Capital		128990 00						
19	Rex Flanery, Drawing	22000 00							
20	David Stein, Capital		129850 00						
21	David Stein, Drawing	22300 00							
22	Income Summary								
23	Sales		350360 00						
24	Purchases	193550 00							

15-4 MASTERY PROBLEM, p. 387 (concluded)

Seidler Supply

Work Sheet (continued)

For Year Ended December 31, 20 – –

	ACCOUNT TITLE	TRIAL BALANCE		ADJUSTMENTS		INCOME STATEMENT		BALANCE SHEET	
		1 DEBIT	2 CREDIT	3 DEBIT	4 CREDIT	5 DEBIT	6 CREDIT	7 DEBIT	8 CREDIT
25	Advertising Expense	7 1 0 0 00							
26	Credit Card Fee Expense	3 2 8 2 00							
27	Insurance Expense								
28	Miscellaneous Expense	2 8 0 6 00							
29	Payroll Taxes Expense	6 2 9 4 00							
30	Rent Expense	20 1 6 0 00							
31	Salary Expense	62 4 0 0 00							
32	Supplies Expense—Office								
33	Supplies Expense—Store								
34	Utilities Expense	3 7 4 4 00							
35		626 0 3 8 00	626 0 3 8 00						
36									
37									
38									
39									
40									
41									
42									
43									
44									
45									
46									
47									
48									
49									
50									

ACCOUNT TITLE	TRIAL BALANCE		ADJUSTMENTS		INCOME STATEMENT		BALANCE SHEET	
	DEBIT	CREDIT	DEBIT	CREDIT	DEBIT	CREDIT	DEBIT	CREDIT
	1	2	3	4	5	6	7	8
1								
2								
3								
4								
5								
6								
7								
8								
9								
10								
11								
12								
13								
14								
15								
16								
17								
18								
19								
20								
21								
22								
23								
24								

Extra form

Forms	Advantages	Disadvantages
8-column work sheet		
10-column work sheet		

15-5 CHALLENGE PROBLEM, p. 388

Preparing a 10-column work sheet for a merchandising business

1.

K. B. Cycle Shop

Work Sheet

For Year Ended December 31, 20 – –

	ACCOUNT TITLE	TRIAL BALANCE		ADJUSTMENTS		
		DEBIT	CREDIT	DEBIT	CREDIT	
1	Cash	38 0 1 0 00				1
2	Petty Cash	5 0 0 00				2
3	Accounts Receivable	14 2 3 0 00				3
4	Merchandise Inventory	323 8 0 5 00				4
5	Supplies—Office	7 6 9 5 00				5
6	Supplies—Store	8 0 0 0 00				6
7	Prepaid Insurance	5 9 4 0 00				7
8	Accounts Payable		15 4 8 0 00			8
9	Sales Tax Payable		1 2 1 5 00			9
10	Kevin Bolin, Capital		170 1 6 0 00			10
11	Kevin Bolin, Drawing	24 0 0 0 00				11
12	Barbara May, Capital		170 0 0 0 00			12
13	Barbara May, Drawing	24 8 0 0 00				13
14	Income Summary					14
15	Sales		269 3 3 0 00			15
16	Purchases	129 8 5 5 00				16
17	Advertising Expense	9 2 1 0 00				17
18	Credit Card Fee Expense	3 5 7 5 00				18
19	Insurance Expense					19
20	Miscellaneous Expense	3 7 9 5 00				20
21	Rent Expense	27 9 0 0 00				21
22	Supplies Expense—Office					22
23	Supplies Expense—Store					23
24	Utilities Expense	4 8 7 0 00				24
25		626 1 8 5 00	626 1 8 5 00			25
26						26
27						27
28						28
29						29

15-5 CHALLENGE PROBLEM (continued)

1.

	ADJUSTED TRIAL BALANCE		INCOME STATEMENT		BALANCE SHEET		
	5 DEBIT	6 CREDIT	7 DEBIT	8 CREDIT	9 DEBIT	10 CREDIT	
1							1
2							2
3							3
4							4
5							5
6							6
7							7
8							8
9							9
10							10
11							11
12							12
13							13
14							14
15							15
16							16
17							17
18							18
19							19
20							20
21							21
22							22
23							23
24							24
25							25
26							26
27							27
28							28
29							29

2.

Forms	Advantages	Disadvantages
8-column work sheet		
10-column work sheet		

16-1 WORK TOGETHER, p. 396

Preparing an income statement for a merchandising business

A to Z Auto Parts
Work Sheet
For Year Ended December 31, 20 - -

	ACCOUNT TITLE	TRIAL BALANCE DEBIT	TRIAL BALANCE CREDIT	ADJUSTMENTS DEBIT	ADJUSTMENTS CREDIT	INCOME STATEMENT DEBIT	INCOME STATEMENT CREDIT	BALANCE SHEET DEBIT	BALANCE SHEET CREDIT
1	Cash	23780 00						23780 00	
2	Petty Cash	300 00						300 00	
3	Accounts Receivable	9624 00						9624 00	
4	Merchandise Inventory	228820 00			(a)13400 00			215420 00	
5	Supplies—Office	5480 00			(b)4000 00			1480 00	
6	Supplies—Store	5864 00			(c)3310 00			2554 00	
7	Prepaid Insurance	4986 00			(d)2700 00			2286 00	
8	Accounts Payable		9666 00						9666 00
9	Sales Tax Payable		17886 00						17886 00
10	Mack Cruz, Capital		106100 00						106100 00
11	Mack Cruz, Drawing	18450 00						18450 00	
12	Rose Hurst, Capital		106700 00						106700 00
13	Rose Hurst, Drawing	18900 00						18900 00	
14	Income Summary			(a)13400 00		13400 00			
15	Sales		284800 00				284800 00		
16	Purchases	160700 00				160700 00			
17	Advertising Expense	5580 00				5580 00			
18	Credit Card Fee Expense	2940 00				2940 00			
19	Insurance Expense			(d)2700 00		2700 00			
20	Miscellaneous Expense	2398 00				2398 00			
21	Rent Expense	18000 00				18000 00			
22	Supplies Expense—Office			(b)4000 00		4000 00			
23	Supplies Expense—Store			(c)3310 00		3310 00			
24	Utilities Expense	3230 00				3230 00			
25		509052 00	509052 00	23410 00	23410 00	216258 00	284800 00	292794 00	224252 00
26	Net Income					68542 00			68542 00
27						284800 00	284800 00	292794 00	292794 00

Preparing an income statement for a merchandising business

Electron Games

Work Sheet

For Year Ended December 31, 20--

	ACCOUNT TITLE	TRIAL BALANCE DEBIT	CREDIT	ADJUSTMENTS DEBIT	CREDIT	INCOME STATEMENT DEBIT	CREDIT	BALANCE SHEET DEBIT	CREDIT
1	Cash	24490 00						24490 00	
2	Petty Cash	500 00						500 00	
3	Accounts Receivable	11230 00						11230 00	
4	Merchandise Inventory	266960 00			(a)15640 00			251320 00	
5	Supplies—Office	6390 00			(b)4670 00			1720 00	
6	Supplies—Store	6840 00			(c)3860 00			2980 00	
7	Prepaid Insurance	5830 00			(d)3190 00			2640 00	
8	Accounts Payable		11280 00						11280 00
9	Sales Tax Payable		2080 00						2080 00
10	Caren Grant, Capital		121100 00						121100 00
11	Caren Grant, Drawing	21550 00						21550 00	
12	Craig Payne, Capital		124440 00						124440 00
13	Craig Payne, Drawing	22000 00						22000 00	
14	Income Summary			(a)15640 00		15640 00			
15	Sales		332260 00				332260 00		
16	Purchases	187500 00				187500 00			
17	Advertising Expense	6520 00				6520 00			
18	Credit Card Fee Expense	3430 00				3430 00			
19	Insurance Expense			(d)3190 00		3190 00			
20	Miscellaneous Expense	2550 00				2550 00			
21	Rent Expense	21600 00				21600 00			
22	Supplies Expense—Office			(b)4670 00		4670 00			
23	Supplies Expense—Store			(c)3860 00		3860 00			
24	Utilities Expense	3770 00				3770 00			
25		591160 00	591160 00	27360 00	27360 00	252730 00	332260 00	338430 00	258900 00
26	Net Income					79530 00			79530 00
27						332260 00	332260 00	338430 00	338430 00

16-1 WORK TOGETHER (concluded)

4., 5.

					% OF SALES

6., 7.

							% OF SALES

16-2 WORK TOGETHER, p. 401

Analyzing component percentages

4., 5.

Component	Acceptable Percentage	Actual Percentage	Acceptable Result		Recommended Action if Needed
			Yes	No	
Cost of merchandise sold	No more than 63.0%				
Gross profit on sales	No less than 37.0%				

Extra form

Component	Acceptable Percentage	Actual Percentage	Acceptable Result		Recommended Action if Needed
			Yes	No	

Analyzing component percentages

6., 7.

Component	Acceptable Percentage	Actual Percentage	Acceptable Result		Recommended Action if Needed
			Yes	No	
Total expenses	No more than 13.0%				
Net income	No less than 25.0%				

Extra form

Component	Acceptable Percentage	Actual Percentage	Acceptable Result		Recommended Action if Needed
			Yes	No	

16-3 WORK TOGETHER, p. 407

Preparing distribution of net income and owners' equity statements

4.

5.

Preparing distribution of net income and owners' equity statements

6.

7.

16-4 WORK TOGETHER, p. 412

Preparing a balance sheet for a partnership

Preparing a balance sheet for a partnership

16-1 APPLICATION PROBLEM, p. 414

Preparing an income statement for a merchandising business

Flower Mart

Work Sheet

For Year Ended December 31, 20 – –

	ACCOUNT TITLE	TRIAL BALANCE DEBIT (1)	TRIAL BALANCE CREDIT (2)	ADJUSTMENTS DEBIT (3)	ADJUSTMENTS CREDIT (4)	INCOME STATEMENT DEBIT (5)	INCOME STATEMENT CREDIT (6)	BALANCE SHEET DEBIT (7)	BALANCE SHEET CREDIT (8)
4	Merchandise Inventory	179900 00			(a) 6820 00			173080 00	
15	Sales		162300 00				162300 00		
16	Purchases	73000 00				73000 00			
17	Advertising Expense	4130 00				4130 00			
18	Credit Card Fee Expense	1640 00				1640 00			
19	Insurance Expense			(d) 2160 00		2160 00			
20	Miscellaneous Expense	1990 00				1990 00			
21	Rent Expense	12480 00				12480 00			
22	Supplies Expense—Office			(b) 2490 00		2490 00			
23	Supplies Expense—Store			(c) 2180 00		2180 00			
24	Utilities Expense	2140 00				2140 00			
25		333510 00	333510 00	13650 00	13650 00	109030 00	162300 00	224700 00	171430 00
26	Net Income					53270 00			53270 00
27						162300 00	162300 00	224700 00	224700 00
28									
29									
30									
31									
32									

					% OF SALES

16-1 APPLICATION PROBLEM (concluded)

1., 2.

					% OF SALES

			% OF SALES

16-2 APPLICATION PROBLEM, p. 414

Analyzing component percentages

Historic Door Supply Co.

Income Statement

For Year Ended December 31, 20 – –

			% OF SALES
Revenue:			
Sales		352 600 00	100.0
Cost of Merchandise Sold:			
Merchandise Inventory, January 1, 20 – –	225 400 00		
Purchases	158 300 00		
Total Cost of Merchandise Available for Sale	383 700 00		
Less Merchandise Inventory, December 31, 20 – –	212 200 00		
Cost of Merchandise Sold		171 500 00	48.6
Gross Profit on Sales		181 100 00	51.4
Expenses:			
Advertising Expense	5 500 00		
Credit Card Fee Expense	2 890 00		
Insurance Expense	2 640 00		
Miscellaneous Expense	2 182 15		
Payroll Taxes Expense	7 299 75		
Rent Expense	18 000 00		
Salary Expense	60 153 00		
Supplies Expense—Office	3 940 00		
Supplies Expense—Store	3 260 00		
Utilities Expense	3 180 00		
Total Expenses		109 044 90	30.9
Net Income		72 055 10	20.4

Extra form

			% OF SALES

16-2 APPLICATION PROBLEM (concluded)

1., 2., 3., 4.

Component	Acceptable Percentage	Actual Percentage	Acceptable Result		Recommended Action If Needed
			Yes	No	
Cost of merchandise sold	No more than 47.5%				
Gross profit on sales	No less than 52.5%				
Total expenses	No more than 29.0%				
Net income	No less than 23.5%				

Component	Acceptable Percentage	Actual Percentage	Acceptable Result		Recommended Action If Needed
			Yes	No	

16-3 APPLICATION PROBLEM, p. 415

Preparing distribution of net income and owners' equity statements (net income)

1.

2.

16-4 APPLICATION PROBLEM, p. 415

Preparing an owners' equity statement (net loss)

16-5 APPLICATION PROBLEM, p. 415

Preparing a balance sheet for a partnership

Athletic Supply

Work Sheet

For Year Ended December 31, 20 - -

	TRIAL BALANCE		ADJUSTMENTS		INCOME STATEMENT		BALANCE SHEET	
ACCOUNT TITLE	DEBIT 1	CREDIT 2	DEBIT 3	CREDIT 4	DEBIT 5	CREDIT 6	DEBIT 7	CREDIT 8
1 Cash	22738 00						22738 00	
2 Petty Cash	350 00						350 00	
3 Accounts Receivable	11622 00						11622 00	
4 Merchandise Inventory	269832 00			(a)10236 00			259596 00	
5 Supplies—Office	5922 00			(b)3732 00			2190 00	
6 Supplies—Store	6252 00			(c)3288 00			2964 00	
7 Prepaid Insurance	5130 00			(d)3240 00			1890 00	
8 Accounts Payable		10596 00						10596 00
9 Sales Tax Payable		1014 00						1014 00
10								
11								
12								
13								
14								
15								
16								
17								
18								
19								
20								
21								

16-5 **APPLICATION PROBLEM (concluded)**

Extra form

16-6 **MASTERY PROBLEM, p. 416**

Preparing financial statements

1.

					% OF SALES

2.

16-6 MASTERY PROBLEM (continued)

3.

4.

16-7 CHALLENGE PROBLEM, p. 417

Preparing financial statements (unequal distribution of net income; additional investment)

1.

2.

17-1 WORK TOGETHER, p. 425

Journalizing adjusting entries

PAGE 12

JOURNAL

	DATE	ACCOUNT TITLE	DOC. NO.	POST. REF.	GENERAL DEBIT	GENERAL CREDIT	ACCOUNTS RECEIVABLE DEBIT	ACCOUNTS RECEIVABLE CREDIT	
1									1
2									2
3									3
4									4
5									5
6									6
7									7
8									8
9									9
10									10
11									11
12									12
13									13
14									14
15									15
16									16
17									17
18									18
19									19
20									20
21									21
22									22
23									23
24									24
25									25
26									26
27									27
28									28
29									29
30									30
31									31
32									32

Journalizing adjusting entries

PAGE 15

JOURNAL

	DATE	ACCOUNT TITLE	DOC. NO.	POST. REF.	GENERAL		ACCOUNTS RECEIVABLE		
					DEBIT	CREDIT	DEBIT	CREDIT	
1									1
2									2
3									3
4									4
5									5
6									6
7									7
8									8
9									9
10									10
11									11
12									12
13									13
14									14
15									15
16									16
17									17
18									18
19									19
20									20
21									21
22									22
23									23
24									24
25									25
26									26
27									27
28									28
29									29
30									30
31									31
32									32
33									33

17-2 and 17-3 WORK TOGETHER, pp. 430, 434

17-2 Journalizing closing entries for income statement accounts
17-3 Journalizing additional closing entries

PAGE 12

JOURNAL

						1 GENERAL DEBIT	2 GENERAL CREDIT	3 ACCOUNTS RECEIVABLE DEBIT	4 ACCOUNTS RECEIVABLE CREDIT	
	DATE	ACCOUNT TITLE	DOC. NO.	POST. REF.						
1										1
2										2
3										3
4										4
5										5
6										6
7										7
8										8
9										9
10										10
11										11
12										12
13										13
14										14
15										15
16										16
17										17
18										18
19										19
20										20
21										21
22										22
23										23
24										24
25										25
26										26
27										27
28										28
29										29
30										30
31										31
32										32

17-2 Journalizing closing entries for income statement accounts
17-3 Journalizing additional closing entries

PAGE 15

JOURNAL

	DATE	ACCOUNT TITLE	DOC. NO.	POST. REF.	GENERAL DEBIT	GENERAL CREDIT	ACCOUNTS RECEIVABLE DEBIT	ACCOUNTS RECEIVABLE CREDIT	
1									1
2									2
3									3
4									4
5									5
6									6
7									7
8									8
9									9
10									10
11									11
12									12
13									13
14									14
15									15
16									16
17									17
18									18
19									19
20									20
21									21
22									22
23									23
24									24
25									25
26									26
27									27
28									28
29									29
30									30
31									31
32									32

	5	6	7	8	
	INCOME STATEMENT		BALANCE SHEET		
ACCOUNT TITLE	DEBIT	CREDIT	DEBIT	CREDIT	
11 Beth Fairbanks, Drawing			31 0 0 0 00		11
13 Chris Gilder, Drawing			29 9 0 0 00		13
15 Sales		260 0 0 0 00			15
16 Purchases	118 0 0 0 00				16
17 Advertising Expense	4 0 6 0 00				17
18 Credit Card Fee Expense	2 6 7 0 00				18
19 Insurance Expense	3 1 5 0 00				19
20 Miscellaneous Expense	1 7 2 0 00				20
21 Rent Expense	18 0 0 0 00				21
22 Supplies Expense—Office	3 7 3 0 00				22
23 Supplies Expense—Store	3 9 0 0 00				23
24 Utilities Expense	3 6 7 0 00				24
25					25
26					26
27					27
28					28
29					29

Fairbanks Auto Supply

Distribution of Net Income Statement

For Year Ended December 31, 20 – –

Beth Fairbanks	
50% of Net Income	43 0 5 0 00
Chris Gilder	
50% of Net Income	43 0 5 0 00
Net Income	86 1 0 0 00

	ACCOUNT TITLE	INCOME STATEMENT		BALANCE SHEET		
		DEBIT	CREDIT	DEBIT	CREDIT	
11	Orrin Harrod, Drawing			28 0 0 0 00		11
13	Lisa Klaus, Drawing			28 7 0 0 00		13
15	Sales		271 4 0 0 00			15
16	Purchases	132 1 6 0 00				16
17	Advertising Expense	4 5 5 0 00				17
18	Credit Card Fee Expense	2 9 8 0 00				18
19	Insurance Expense	3 5 3 0 00				19
20	Miscellaneous Expense	1 9 3 0 00				20
21	Rent Expense	20 1 6 0 00				21
22	Supplies Expense—Office	4 1 7 0 00				22
23	Supplies Expense—Store	4 3 7 0 00				23
24	Utilities Expense	4 1 2 0 00				24
25						25
26						26
27						27
28						28

Custom Aquarium

Distribution of Net Income Statement

For Year Ended December 31, 20 – –

Orrin Harrod	
50% of Net Income	38 3 1 5 00
Lisa Klaus	
50% of Net Income	38 3 1 5 00
Net Income	76 6 3 0 00

17-4 WORK TOGETHER, p. 439

Preparing a post-closing trial balance

ACCOUNT TITLE	DEBIT	CREDIT

Preparing a post-closing trial balance

ACCOUNT TITLE	DEBIT	CREDIT

17-1 APPLICATION PROBLEM, p. 441

Journalizing adjusting entries

PAGE 12

JOURNAL

	DATE	ACCOUNT TITLE	DOC. NO.	POST. REF.	GENERAL DEBIT	GENERAL CREDIT	ACCOUNTS RECEIVABLE DEBIT	ACCOUNTS RECEIVABLE CREDIT	
1									1
2									2
3									3
4									4
5									5
6									6
7									7
8									8
9									9
10									10
11									11
12									12
13									13
14									14
15									15
16									16
17									17
18									18
19									19
20									20
21									21
22									22
23									23
24									24
25									25
26									26
27									27
28									28
29									29
30									30
31									31
32									32
33									33

JOURNAL

	DATE	ACCOUNT TITLE	DOC. NO.	POST. REF.	GENERAL		ACCOUNTS RECEIVABLE	
					1 DEBIT	2 CREDIT	3 DEBIT	4 CREDIT
1								
2								
3								
4								
5								
6								
7								
8								
9								
10								
11								
12								
13								
14								
15								
16								
17								
18								
19								
20								
21								
22								
23								
24								
25								
26								
27								
28								
29								
30								
31								
32								
33								

17-2 and 17-3 APPLICATION PROBLEMS, pp. 441, 442

17-2 Journalizing closing entries for income statement accounts
17-3 Journalizing additional closing entries

PAGE 14

JOURNAL

	DATE	ACCOUNT TITLE	DOC. NO.	POST. REF.	GENERAL DEBIT	GENERAL CREDIT	ACCOUNTS RECEIVABLE DEBIT	ACCOUNTS RECEIVABLE CREDIT	
1									1
2									2
3									3
4									4
5									5
6									6
7									7
8									8
9									9
10									10
11									11
12									12
13									13
14									14
15									15
16									16
17									17
18									18
19									19
20									20
21									21
22									22
23									23
24									24
25									25
26									26
27									27
28									28
29									29
30									30
31									31
32									32

JOURNAL

	DATE	ACCOUNT TITLE	DOC. NO.	POST. REF.	GENERAL		ACCOUNTS RECEIVABLE		
					DEBIT	CREDIT	DEBIT	CREDIT	
1									1
2									2
3									3
4									4
5									5
6									6
7									7
8									8
9									9
10									10
11									11
12									12
13									13
14									14
15									15
16									16
17									17
18									18
19									19
20									20
21									21
22									22
23									23
24									24
25									25
26									26
27									27
28									28
29									29
30									30
31									31
32									32
33									33

17-4 APPLICATION PROBLEM, p. 442

Preparing a post-closing trial balance

_____
_____
_____

ACCOUNT TITLE	DEBIT	CREDIT

Extra form

ACCOUNT TITLE	DEBIT	CREDIT

17-5 APPLICATION PROBLEM, p. 443

Journalizing and posting adjusting and closing entries; preparing a post-closing trial balance

1., 2., 3., 4.

PAGE 24   JOURNAL

| | DATE | ACCOUNT TITLE | DOC. NO. | POST. REF. | GENERAL | | ACCOUNTS RECEIVABLE | | |
					DEBIT	CREDIT	DEBIT	CREDIT	
1									1
2									2
3									3
4									4
5									5
6									6
7									7
8									8
9									9
10									10
11									11
12									12
13									13
14									14
15									15
16									16
17									17
18									18
19									19
20									20
21									21
22									22
23									23
24									24
25									25
26									26
27									27
28									28
29									29
30									30
31									31
32									32

5.

ACCOUNT TITLE	DEBIT	CREDIT

17-5 **APPLICATION PROBLEM (continued)**

2., 4., 5. **GENERAL LEDGER**

ACCOUNT Cash   ACCOUNT NO. 1110

DATE	ITEM	POST. REF.	DEBIT	CREDIT	BALANCE DEBIT	BALANCE CREDIT
20-- Dec. 31	Balance	✔			22 3 7 9 00	

ACCOUNT Petty Cash   ACCOUNT NO. 1120

DATE	ITEM	POST. REF.	DEBIT	CREDIT	BALANCE DEBIT	BALANCE CREDIT
20-- Dec. 31	Balance	✔			4 0 0 00	

ACCOUNT Accounts Receivable   ACCOUNT NO. 1130

DATE	ITEM	POST. REF.	DEBIT	CREDIT	BALANCE DEBIT	BALANCE CREDIT
20-- Dec. 31	Balance	✔			10 1 8 9 00	

ACCOUNT Merchandise Inventory   ACCOUNT NO. 1140

DATE	ITEM	POST. REF.	DEBIT	CREDIT	BALANCE DEBIT	BALANCE CREDIT
20-- Jan. 1	Balance	✔			253 0 1 4 00	

ACCOUNT Supplies—Office   ACCOUNT NO. 1145

DATE	ITEM	POST. REF.	DEBIT	CREDIT	BALANCE DEBIT	BALANCE CREDIT
20-- Dec. 31	Balance	✔			5 4 1 6 00	

ACCOUNT Supplies—Store   ACCOUNT NO. 1150

DATE	ITEM	POST. REF.	DEBIT	CREDIT	BALANCE DEBIT	BALANCE CREDIT
20-- Dec. 31	Balance	✔			5 2 6 7 00	

ACCOUNT Prepaid Insurance   ACCOUNT NO. 1160

DATE	ITEM	POST. REF.	DEBIT	CREDIT	BALANCE DEBIT	BALANCE CREDIT
20-- Dec. 31	Balance	✔			4 3 0 0 00	

ACCOUNT Accounts Payable   ACCOUNT NO. 2110

DATE	ITEM	POST. REF.	DEBIT	CREDIT	BALANCE DEBIT	BALANCE CREDIT
20-- Dec. 31	Balance	✔				10 6 1 5 00

2., 4., 5.   **GENERAL LEDGER**

ACCOUNT Employee Income Tax Payable   ACCOUNT NO. 2120

DATE		ITEM	POST. REF.	DEBIT	CREDIT	BALANCE	
						DEBIT	CREDIT
20-- Dec.	31	Balance	✔				4 5 4 00

ACCOUNT Social Security Tax Payable   ACCOUNT NO. 2130

DATE		ITEM	POST. REF.	DEBIT	CREDIT	BALANCE	
						DEBIT	CREDIT
20-- Dec.	31	Balance	✔				7 0 4 20

ACCOUNT Medicare Tax Payable   ACCOUNT NO. 2135

DATE		ITEM	POST. REF.	DEBIT	CREDIT	BALANCE	
						DEBIT	CREDIT
20-- Dec.	31	Balance	✔				1 6 4 70

ACCOUNT Sales Tax Payable   ACCOUNT NO. 2140

DATE		ITEM	POST. REF.	DEBIT	CREDIT	BALANCE	
						DEBIT	CREDIT
20-- Dec.	31	Balance	✔				1 8 1 7 00

ACCOUNT Unemployment Tax Payable—Federal   ACCOUNT NO. 2150

DATE		ITEM	POST. REF.	DEBIT	CREDIT	BALANCE	
						DEBIT	CREDIT
20-- Dec.	31	Balance	✔				1 3 60

ACCOUNT Unemployment Tax Payable—State   ACCOUNT NO. 2160

DATE		ITEM	POST. REF.	DEBIT	CREDIT	BALANCE	
						DEBIT	CREDIT
20-- Dec.	31	Balance	✔				9 1 80

ACCOUNT Emma Bose, Capital   ACCOUNT NO. 3110

DATE		ITEM	POST. REF.	DEBIT	CREDIT	BALANCE	
						DEBIT	CREDIT
20-- Dec.	31	Balance	✔				156 2 6 7 00

ACCOUNT Emma Bose, Drawing   ACCOUNT NO. 3120

DATE		ITEM	POST. REF.	DEBIT	CREDIT	BALANCE	
						DEBIT	CREDIT
20-- Dec.	31	Balance	✔			18 2 2 5 00	

2., 4., 5.   **GENERAL LEDGER**

ACCOUNT Kris Manuel, Capital   ACCOUNT NO. 3130

DATE		ITEM	POST. REF.	DEBIT	CREDIT	BALANCE DEBIT	BALANCE CREDIT
20-- Dec.	31	Balance	✔				153 3 4 9 70

ACCOUNT Kris Manuel, Drawing   ACCOUNT NO. 3140

DATE		ITEM	POST. REF.	DEBIT	CREDIT	BALANCE DEBIT	BALANCE CREDIT
20-- Dec.	31	Balance	✔			18 4 0 0 00	

ACCOUNT Income Summary   ACCOUNT NO. 3150

DATE		ITEM	POST. REF.	DEBIT	CREDIT	BALANCE DEBIT	BALANCE CREDIT

ACCOUNT Sales   ACCOUNT NO. 4110

DATE		ITEM	POST. REF.	DEBIT	CREDIT	BALANCE DEBIT	BALANCE CREDIT
20-- Dec.	31	Balance	✔				275 0 6 0 00

ACCOUNT Purchases   ACCOUNT NO. 5110

DATE		ITEM	POST. REF.	DEBIT	CREDIT	BALANCE DEBIT	BALANCE CREDIT
20-- Dec.	31	Balance	✔			151 7 4 0 00	

ACCOUNT Advertising Expense   ACCOUNT NO. 6110

DATE		ITEM	POST. REF.	DEBIT	CREDIT	BALANCE DEBIT	BALANCE CREDIT
20-- Dec.	31	Balance	✔			5 6 6 4 00	

ACCOUNT Credit Card Fee Expense   ACCOUNT NO. 6120

DATE		ITEM	POST. REF.	DEBIT	CREDIT	BALANCE DEBIT	BALANCE CREDIT
20-- Dec.	31	Balance	✔			3 9 1 2 00	

2., 4., 5.

GENERAL LEDGER

ACCOUNT Insurance Expense   ACCOUNT NO. 6130

DATE	ITEM	POST. REF.	DEBIT	CREDIT	BALANCE DEBIT	BALANCE CREDIT

ACCOUNT Miscellaneous Expense   ACCOUNT NO. 6140

DATE	ITEM	POST. REF.	DEBIT	CREDIT	BALANCE DEBIT	BALANCE CREDIT
Dec. 31	Balance	✔			2 3 1 6 00	

ACCOUNT Payroll Taxes Expense   ACCOUNT NO. 6150

DATE	ITEM	POST. REF.	DEBIT	CREDIT	BALANCE DEBIT	BALANCE CREDIT
Dec. 31	Balance	✔			6 9 1 7 00	

ACCOUNT Rent Expense   ACCOUNT NO. 6160

DATE	ITEM	POST. REF.	DEBIT	CREDIT	BALANCE DEBIT	BALANCE CREDIT
Dec. 31	Balance	✔			18 7 2 0 00	

ACCOUNT Salary Expense   ACCOUNT NO. 6170

DATE	ITEM	POST. REF.	DEBIT	CREDIT	BALANCE DEBIT	BALANCE CREDIT
Dec. 31	Balance	✔			68 1 5 0 00	

ACCOUNT Supplies Expense—Office   ACCOUNT NO. 6175

DATE	ITEM	POST. REF.	DEBIT	CREDIT	BALANCE DEBIT	BALANCE CREDIT

ACCOUNT Supplies Expense—Store   ACCOUNT NO. 6180

DATE	ITEM	POST. REF.	DEBIT	CREDIT	BALANCE DEBIT	BALANCE CREDIT

ACCOUNT Utilities Expense   ACCOUNT NO. 6190

DATE	ITEM	POST. REF.	DEBIT	CREDIT	BALANCE DEBIT	BALANCE CREDIT
Dec. 31	Balance	✔			3 5 2 8 00	

17-6 MASTERY PROBLEM, p. 444

Journalizing and posting adjusting and closing entries; preparing a post-closing trial balance

1., 2., 3., 4.

PAGE 25

JOURNAL

	DATE	ACCOUNT TITLE	DOC. NO.	POST. REF.	GENERAL DEBIT	GENERAL CREDIT	ACCOUNTS RECEIVABLE DEBIT	ACCOUNTS RECEIVABLE CREDIT	
1									1
2									2
3									3
4									4
5									5
6									6
7									7
8									8
9									9
10									10
11									11
12									12
13									13
14									14
15									15
16									16
17									17
18									18
19									19
20									20
21									21
22									22
23									23
24									24
25									25
26									26
27									27
28									28
29									29
30									30
31									31
32									32

5.

ACCOUNT TITLE	DEBIT	CREDIT

17-6 MASTERY PROBLEM (continued)

2., 4., 5.   **GENERAL LEDGER**

ACCOUNT Cash   ACCOUNT NO. 1110

DATE	ITEM	POST. REF.	DEBIT	CREDIT	BALANCE DEBIT	BALANCE CREDIT
20-- Dec. 31	Balance	✔			25 967 00	

ACCOUNT Petty Cash   ACCOUNT NO. 1120

DATE	ITEM	POST. REF.	DEBIT	CREDIT	BALANCE DEBIT	BALANCE CREDIT
20-- Dec. 31	Balance	✔			500 00	

ACCOUNT Accounts Receivable   ACCOUNT NO. 1130

DATE	ITEM	POST. REF.	DEBIT	CREDIT	BALANCE DEBIT	BALANCE CREDIT
20-- Dec. 31	Balance	✔			9 925 00	

ACCOUNT Merchandise Inventory   ACCOUNT NO. 1140

DATE	ITEM	POST. REF.	DEBIT	CREDIT	BALANCE DEBIT	BALANCE CREDIT
20-- Jan. 1	Balance	✔			331 940 00	

ACCOUNT Supplies—Office   ACCOUNT NO. 1145

DATE	ITEM	POST. REF.	DEBIT	CREDIT	BALANCE DEBIT	BALANCE CREDIT
20-- Dec. 31	Balance	✔			5 555 00	

ACCOUNT Supplies—Store   ACCOUNT NO. 1150

DATE	ITEM	POST. REF.	DEBIT	CREDIT	BALANCE DEBIT	BALANCE CREDIT
20-- Dec. 31	Balance	✔			4 922 00	

ACCOUNT Prepaid Insurance   ACCOUNT NO. 1160

DATE	ITEM	POST. REF.	DEBIT	CREDIT	BALANCE DEBIT	BALANCE CREDIT
20-- Dec. 31	Balance	✔			3 485 00	

ACCOUNT Accounts Payable   ACCOUNT NO. 2110

DATE	ITEM	POST. REF.	DEBIT	CREDIT	BALANCE DEBIT	BALANCE CREDIT
20-- Dec. 31	Balance	✔				9 005 00

2., 4., 5. GENERAL LEDGER

ACCOUNT Employee Income Tax Payable   ACCOUNT NO. 2120

DATE	ITEM	POST. REF.	DEBIT	CREDIT	BALANCE DEBIT	BALANCE CREDIT
Dec. 31	Balance	✔				4 7 5 00

ACCOUNT Social Security Tax Payable   ACCOUNT NO. 2130

DATE	ITEM	POST. REF.	DEBIT	CREDIT	BALANCE DEBIT	BALANCE CREDIT
Dec. 31	Balance	✔				7 3 6 56

ACCOUNT Medicare Tax Payable   ACCOUNT NO. 2135

DATE	ITEM	POST. REF.	DEBIT	CREDIT	BALANCE DEBIT	BALANCE CREDIT
Dec. 31	Balance	✔				1 7 2 26

ACCOUNT Sales Tax Payable   ACCOUNT NO. 2140

DATE	ITEM	POST. REF.	DEBIT	CREDIT	BALANCE DEBIT	BALANCE CREDIT
Dec. 31	Balance	✔				2 3 4 0 00

ACCOUNT Unemployment Tax Payable—Federal   ACCOUNT NO. 2150

DATE	ITEM	POST. REF.	DEBIT	CREDIT	BALANCE DEBIT	BALANCE CREDIT
Dec. 31	Balance	✔				1 4 24

ACCOUNT Unemployment Tax Payable—State   ACCOUNT NO. 2160

DATE	ITEM	POST. REF.	DEBIT	CREDIT	BALANCE DEBIT	BALANCE CREDIT
Dec. 31	Balance	✔				9 6 12

ACCOUNT Anna Cao, Capital   ACCOUNT NO. 3110

DATE	ITEM	POST. REF.	DEBIT	CREDIT	BALANCE DEBIT	BALANCE CREDIT
Dec. 31	Balance	✔				156 4 5 0 00

ACCOUNT Anna Cao, Drawing   ACCOUNT NO. 3120

DATE	ITEM	POST. REF.	DEBIT	CREDIT	BALANCE DEBIT	BALANCE CREDIT
Dec. 31	Balance	✔			22 8 0 0 00	

17-6 MASTERY PROBLEM (continued)

2., 4., 5.   **GENERAL LEDGER**

ACCOUNT Inez O'Neal, Capital   ACCOUNT NO. 3130

DATE	ITEM	POST. REF.	DEBIT	CREDIT	BALANCE DEBIT	BALANCE CREDIT
20-- Dec. 31	Balance	✔				153 9 6 2 82

ACCOUNT Inez O'Neal, Drawing   ACCOUNT NO. 3140

DATE	ITEM	POST. REF.	DEBIT	CREDIT	BALANCE DEBIT	BALANCE CREDIT
20-- Dec. 31	Balance	✔			23 4 0 0 00	

ACCOUNT Income Summary   ACCOUNT NO. 3150

DATE	ITEM	POST. REF.	DEBIT	CREDIT	BALANCE DEBIT	BALANCE CREDIT

ACCOUNT Sales   ACCOUNT NO. 4110

DATE	ITEM	POST. REF.	DEBIT	CREDIT	BALANCE DEBIT	BALANCE CREDIT
20-- Dec. 31	Balance	✔				374 5 0 0 00

ACCOUNT Purchases   ACCOUNT NO. 5110

DATE	ITEM	POST. REF.	DEBIT	CREDIT	BALANCE DEBIT	BALANCE CREDIT
20-- Dec. 31	Balance	✔			156 5 4 0 00	

ACCOUNT Advertising Expense   ACCOUNT NO. 6110

DATE	ITEM	POST. REF.	DEBIT	CREDIT	BALANCE DEBIT	BALANCE CREDIT
20-- Dec. 31	Balance	✔			6 2 1 6 00	

ACCOUNT Credit Card Fee Expense   ACCOUNT NO. 6120

DATE	ITEM	POST. REF.	DEBIT	CREDIT	BALANCE DEBIT	BALANCE CREDIT
20-- Dec. 31	Balance	✔			4 1 0 4 00	

2., 4., 5.　　　　　　　　　　　　　　**GENERAL LEDGER**

ACCOUNT Insurance Expense　　　　　　　　　　　　ACCOUNT NO. 6130

DATE	ITEM	POST. REF.	DEBIT	CREDIT	BALANCE DEBIT	BALANCE CREDIT

ACCOUNT Miscellaneous Expense　　　　　　　　　　ACCOUNT NO. 6140

DATE	ITEM	POST. REF.	DEBIT	CREDIT	BALANCE DEBIT	BALANCE CREDIT
Dec. 20-- 31	Balance	✔			2 4 7 2 00	

ACCOUNT Payroll Taxes Expense　　　　　　　　　　ACCOUNT NO. 6150

DATE	ITEM	POST. REF.	DEBIT	CREDIT	BALANCE DEBIT	BALANCE CREDIT
Dec. 20-- 31	Balance	✔			7 2 3 0 00	

ACCOUNT Rent Expense　　　　　　　　　　　　　　ACCOUNT NO. 6160

DATE	ITEM	POST. REF.	DEBIT	CREDIT	BALANCE DEBIT	BALANCE CREDIT
Dec. 20-- 31	Balance	✔			18 0 0 0 00	

ACCOUNT Salary Expense　　　　　　　　　　　　　ACCOUNT NO. 6170

DATE	ITEM	POST. REF.	DEBIT	CREDIT	BALANCE DEBIT	BALANCE CREDIT
Dec. 20-- 31	Balance	✔			71 2 4 0 00	

ACCOUNT Supplies Expense—Office　　　　　　　　ACCOUNT NO. 6175

DATE	ITEM	POST. REF.	DEBIT	CREDIT	BALANCE DEBIT	BALANCE CREDIT

ACCOUNT Supplies Expense—Store　　　　　　　　ACCOUNT NO. 6180

DATE	ITEM	POST. REF.	DEBIT	CREDIT	BALANCE DEBIT	BALANCE CREDIT

ACCOUNT Utilities Expense　　　　　　　　　　　　ACCOUNT NO. 6190

DATE	ITEM	POST. REF.	DEBIT	CREDIT	BALANCE DEBIT	BALANCE CREDIT
Dec. 20-- 31	Balance	✔			3 4 5 6 00	

	5	6	7	8	9	10	
	ADJUSTED TRIAL BALANCE		INCOME STATEMENT		BALANCE SHEET		
	DEBIT	CREDIT	DEBIT	CREDIT	DEBIT	CREDIT	
1							1
2							2
3							3
4							4
5							5
6							6
7							7
8							8
9							9
10							10
11							11
12							12
13							13
14							14
15							15
16							16
17							17
18							18
19							19
20							20
21							21
22							22
23							23
24							24
25							25
26							26
27							27
28							28
29							29
30							30
31							31
32							32

17-7 CHALLENGE PROBLEM, p. 445

Completing end-of-fiscal-period work

1.

Lighting

Work

For Year Ended

	ACCOUNT TITLE	TRIAL BALANCE DEBIT	TRIAL BALANCE CREDIT	ADJUSTMENTS DEBIT	ADJUSTMENTS CREDIT	
1	Cash	24 540 00				1
2	Petty Cash	300 00				2
3	Accounts Receivable	10 298 00				3
4	Merchandise Inventory	251 068 00				4
5	Supplies—Office	5 957 00				5
6	Supplies—Store	4 916 00				6
7	Prepaid Insurance	4 554 00				7
8	Accounts Payable		10 143 00			8
9	Sales Tax Payable		1 460 00			9
10	Alan Dykes, Capital		113 122 00			10
11	Alan Dykes, Drawing	20 880 00				11
12	Dona Regan, Capital		109 298 00			12
13	Dona Regan, Drawing	20 500 00				13
14	Income Summary					14
15	Sales		293 730 00			15
16	Purchases	152 700 00				16
17	Advertising Expense	6 372 00				17
18	Credit Card Fee Expense	1 224 00				18
19	Insurance Expense					19
20	Miscellaneous Expense	2 844 00				20
21	Rent Expense	17 280 00				21
22	Supplies Expense—Office					22
23	Supplies Expense—Store					23
24	Utilities Expense	4 320 00				24
25		527 753 00	527 753 00			25
26						26
27						27
28						28
29						29

1.

Solutions
_____

Sheet
_____

December 31, 20 – –

	5	6	7	8	9	10
	ADJUSTED TRIAL BALANCE		INCOME STATEMENT		BALANCE SHEET	
	DEBIT	CREDIT	DEBIT	CREDIT	DEBIT	CREDIT
1						
2						
3						
4						
5						
6						
7						
8						
9						
10						
11						
12						
13						
14						
15						
16						
17						
18						
19						
20						
21						
22						
23						
24						
25						
26						
27						
28						
29						

Extra form

	ACCOUNT TITLE	TRIAL BALANCE		ADJUSTMENTS	
		1 DEBIT	2 CREDIT	3 DEBIT	4 CREDIT
1					
2					
3					
4					
5					
6					
7					
8					
9					
10					
11					
12					
13					
14					
15					
16					
17					
18					
19					
20					
21					
22					
23					
24					
25					
26					
27					
28					
29					
30					
31					
32					

17-7 **CHALLENGE PROBLEM (continued)**

2.

	% OF SALES

3.

4.

17-7 CHALLENGE PROBLEM (continued)

5.

6., 7., 8., 9.

PAGE 24

JOURNAL

	DATE	ACCOUNT TITLE	DOC. NO.	POST. REF.	GENERAL		ACCOUNTS RECEIVABLE		
					DEBIT	CREDIT	DEBIT	CREDIT	
1									1
2									2
3									3
4									4
5									5
6									6
7									7
8									8
9									9
10									10
11									11
12									12
13									13
14									14
15									15
16									16
17									17
18									18
19									19
20									20
21									21
22									22
23									23
24									24
25									25
26									26
27									27
28									28
29									29
30									30
31									31
32									32
33									33

17-7 CHALLENGE PROBLEM (continued)

7., 9., 10. GENERAL LEDGER

ACCOUNT Cash   ACCOUNT NO. 1110

DATE		ITEM	POST. REF.	DEBIT	CREDIT	BALANCE	
						DEBIT	CREDIT
20-- Dec.	31	Balance	✔			24 5 4 0 00	

ACCOUNT Petty Cash   ACCOUNT NO. 1120

DATE		ITEM	POST. REF.	DEBIT	CREDIT	BALANCE	
						DEBIT	CREDIT
20-- Dec.	31	Balance	✔			3 0 0 00	

ACCOUNT Accounts Receivable   ACCOUNT NO. 1130

DATE		ITEM	POST. REF.	DEBIT	CREDIT	BALANCE	
						DEBIT	CREDIT
20-- Dec.	31	Balance	✔			10 2 9 8 00	

ACCOUNT Merchandise Inventory   ACCOUNT NO. 1140

DATE		ITEM	POST. REF.	DEBIT	CREDIT	BALANCE	
						DEBIT	CREDIT
20-- Jan.	1	Balance	✔			251 0 6 8 00	

ACCOUNT Supplies—Office   ACCOUNT NO. 1145

DATE		ITEM	POST. REF.	DEBIT	CREDIT	BALANCE	
						DEBIT	CREDIT
20-- Dec.	31	Balance	✔			5 9 5 7 00	

ACCOUNT Supplies—Store   ACCOUNT NO. 1150

DATE		ITEM	POST. REF.	DEBIT	CREDIT	BALANCE	
						DEBIT	CREDIT
20-- Dec.	31	Balance	✔			4 9 1 6 00	

ACCOUNT Prepaid Insurance   ACCOUNT NO. 1160

DATE		ITEM	POST. REF.	DEBIT	CREDIT	BALANCE	
						DEBIT	CREDIT
20-- Dec.	31	Balance	✔			4 5 5 4 00	

7., 9., 10.   **GENERAL LEDGER**

ACCOUNT Accounts Payable   ACCOUNT NO. 2110

DATE	ITEM	POST. REF.	DEBIT	CREDIT	BALANCE DEBIT	BALANCE CREDIT
20-- Dec. 31	Balance	✔				10 1 4 3 00

ACCOUNT Sales Tax Payable   ACCOUNT NO. 2120

DATE	ITEM	POST. REF.	DEBIT	CREDIT	BALANCE DEBIT	BALANCE CREDIT
20-- Dec. 31	Balance	✔				1 4 6 0 00

ACCOUNT Alan Dykes, Capital   ACCOUNT NO. 3110

DATE	ITEM	POST. REF.	DEBIT	CREDIT	BALANCE DEBIT	BALANCE CREDIT
20-- Dec. 31	Balance	✔				113 1 2 2 00

ACCOUNT Alan Dykes, Drawing   ACCOUNT NO. 3120

DATE	ITEM	POST. REF.	DEBIT	CREDIT	BALANCE DEBIT	BALANCE CREDIT
20-- Dec. 31	Balance	✔			20 8 8 0 00	

ACCOUNT Dona Regan, Capital   ACCOUNT NO. 3130

DATE	ITEM	POST. REF.	DEBIT	CREDIT	BALANCE DEBIT	BALANCE CREDIT
20-- Dec. 31	Balance	✔				109 2 9 8 00

ACCOUNT Dona Regan, Drawing   ACCOUNT NO. 3140

DATE	ITEM	POST. REF.	DEBIT	CREDIT	BALANCE DEBIT	BALANCE CREDIT
20-- Dec. 31	Balance	✔			20 5 0 0 00	

17-7 CHALLENGE PROBLEM (continued)

7., 9., 10.   GENERAL LEDGER

ACCOUNT Income Summary   ACCOUNT NO. 3150

DATE	ITEM	POST. REF.	DEBIT	CREDIT	BALANCE DEBIT	BALANCE CREDIT

ACCOUNT Sales   ACCOUNT NO. 4110

DATE	ITEM	POST. REF.	DEBIT	CREDIT	BALANCE DEBIT	BALANCE CREDIT
Dec. 31	Balance	✔				293 730 00

ACCOUNT Purchases   ACCOUNT NO. 5110

DATE	ITEM	POST. REF.	DEBIT	CREDIT	BALANCE DEBIT	BALANCE CREDIT
Dec. 31	Balance	✔			152 700 00	

ACCOUNT Advertising Expense   ACCOUNT NO. 6110

DATE	ITEM	POST. REF.	DEBIT	CREDIT	BALANCE DEBIT	BALANCE CREDIT
Dec. 31	Balance	✔			6 372 00	

ACCOUNT Credit Card Fee Expense   ACCOUNT NO. 6120

DATE	ITEM	POST. REF.	DEBIT	CREDIT	BALANCE DEBIT	BALANCE CREDIT
Dec. 31	Balance	✔			1 224 00	

ACCOUNT Insurance Expense   ACCOUNT NO. 6130

DATE	ITEM	POST. REF.	DEBIT	CREDIT	BALANCE DEBIT	BALANCE CREDIT

ACCOUNT Miscellaneous Expense   ACCOUNT NO. 6140

DATE	ITEM	POST. REF.	DEBIT	CREDIT	BALANCE DEBIT	BALANCE CREDIT
Dec. 31	Balance	✔			2 844 00	

7., 9., 10.   **GENERAL LEDGER**

ACCOUNT Rent Expense   ACCOUNT NO. 6150

DATE	ITEM	POST. REF.	DEBIT	CREDIT	BALANCE DEBIT	BALANCE CREDIT
20-- Dec. 31	Balance	✔			17 28 0 00	

ACCOUNT Supplies Expense—Office   ACCOUNT NO. 6160

DATE	ITEM	POST. REF.	DEBIT	CREDIT	BALANCE DEBIT	BALANCE CREDIT

ACCOUNT Supplies Expense—Store   ACCOUNT NO. 6170

DATE	ITEM	POST. REF.	DEBIT	CREDIT	BALANCE DEBIT	BALANCE CREDIT

ACCOUNT Utilities Expense   ACCOUNT NO. 6180

DATE	ITEM	POST. REF.	DEBIT	CREDIT	BALANCE DEBIT	BALANCE CREDIT
20-- Dec. 31	Balance	✔			4 32 0 00	

ACCOUNT   ACCOUNT NO.

DATE	ITEM	POST. REF.	DEBIT	CREDIT	BALANCE DEBIT	BALANCE CREDIT

ACCOUNT   ACCOUNT NO.

DATE	ITEM	POST. REF.	DEBIT	CREDIT	BALANCE DEBIT	BALANCE CREDIT

ACCOUNT   ACCOUNT NO.

DATE	ITEM	POST. REF.	DEBIT	CREDIT	BALANCE DEBIT	BALANCE CREDIT

17-7 CHALLENGE PROBLEM (continued)

10.

ACCOUNT TITLE	DEBIT	CREDIT

11. Inventory Auditing Challenges

_____

_____

_____

_____

_____

_____

_____

_____

_____

_____

_____

_____

_____

_____

_____

_____

_____

_____

_____

_____

_____

_____

_____

_____

_____

_____

_____

_____

_____

_____

_____

_____

REINFORCEMENT ACTIVITY 2 PART B, p. 448

An Accounting Cycle for a Partnership: End-of-Fiscal-Period Work
The general ledger used in Reinforcement Activity 2, Part A, is needed to complete Part B.

10., 11.

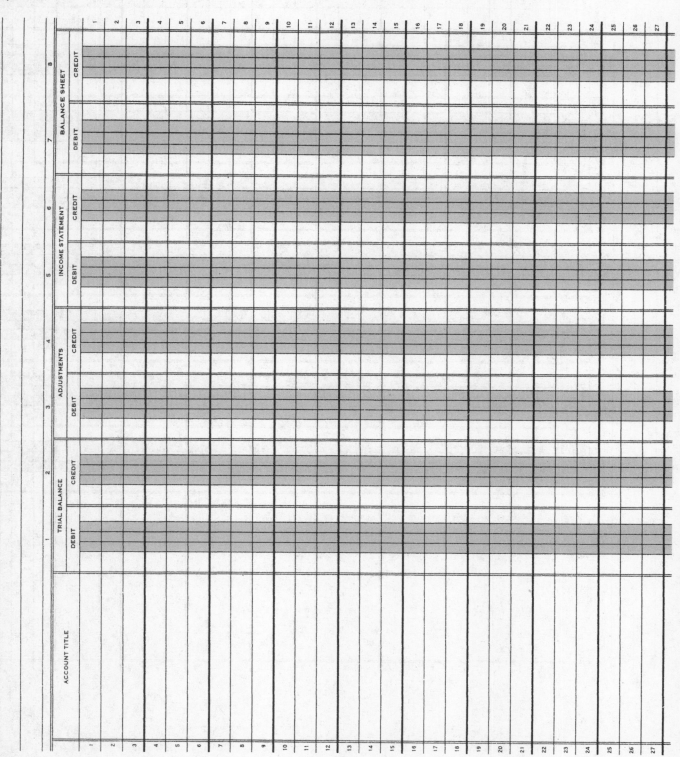

10., 11.

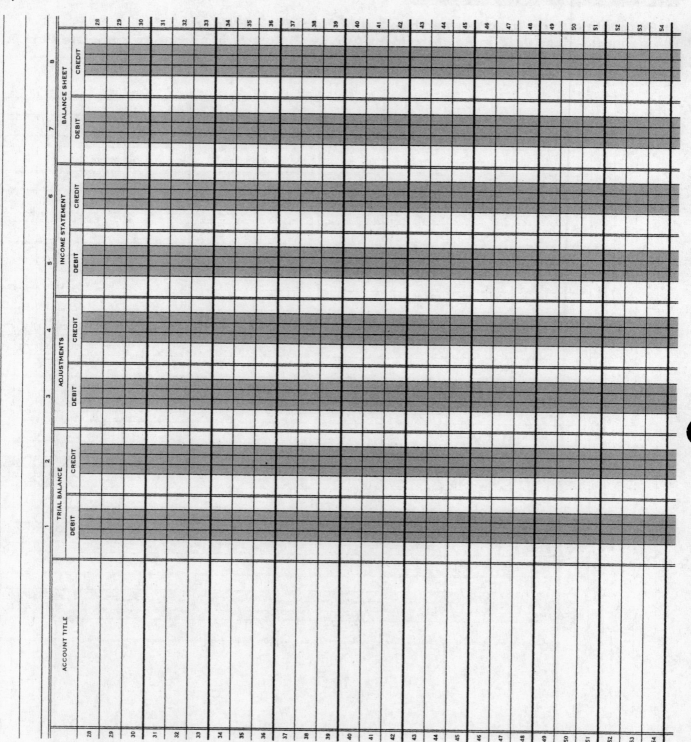

REINFORCEMENT ACTIVITY 2 PART B (continued)

12.

			% OF SALES

13.

14.

REINFORCEMENT ACTIVITY 2 PART B (continued)

15.

16., 17.

PAGE 25

JOURNAL

	DATE	ACCOUNT TITLE	DOC. NO.	POST. REF.	GENERAL DEBIT	GENERAL CREDIT	ACCOUNTS RECEIVABLE DEBIT	ACCOUNTS RECEIVABLE CREDIT	
1									1
2									2
3									3
4									4
5									5
6									6
7									7
8									8
9									9
10									10
11									11
12									12
13									13
14									14
15									15
16									16
17									17
18									18
19									19
20									20
21									21
22									22
23									23
24									24
25									25
26									26
27									27
28									28
29									29
30									30
31									31
32									32

REINFORCEMENT ACTIVITY 2 PART B (concluded)

18.

ACCOUNT TITLE	DEBIT	CREDIT

Extra form

ACCOUNT TITLE	DEBIT	CREDIT

Name _____ Date _____ Class _____

Extra form

Extra form

				% OF SALES

Extra form

		% OF SALES

Extra form

ACCOUNT TITLE	DEBIT	CREDIT

Extra form

JOURNAL

	DATE	ACCOUNT TITLE	DOC. NO.	POST. REF.	GENERAL		ACCOUNTS RECEIVABLE		
					DEBIT 1	**CREDIT** 2	**DEBIT** 3	**CREDIT** 4	
1									1
2									2
3									3
4									4
5									5
6									6
7									7
8									8
9									9
10									10
11									11
12									12
13									13
14									14
15									15
16									16
17									17
18									18
19									19
20									20
21									21
22									22
23									23
24									24
25									25
26									26
27									27
28									28
29									29
30									30
31									31
32									32

Extra form

		5		6		7 ACCOUNTS PAYABLE	8		9		10 CASH	11	PAGE	
		SALES CREDIT		SALES TAX PAYABLE CREDIT		DEBIT	CREDIT		PURCHASES DEBIT		DEBIT	CREDIT		
1														1
2														2
3														3
4														4
5														5
6														6
7														7
8														8
9														9
10														10
11														11
12														12
13														13
14														14
15														15
16														16
17														17
18														18
19														19
20														20
21														21
22														22
23														23
24														24
25														25
26														26
27														27
28														28
29														29
30														30
31														31
32														32

Extra form

ACCOUNT NO.

DATE	ITEM	POST. REF.	DEBIT	CREDIT	BALANCE	
					DEBIT	CREDIT

ACCOUNT ACCOUNT NO.

DATE	ITEM	POST. REF.	DEBIT	CREDIT	BALANCE	
					DEBIT	CREDIT

ACCOUNT ACCOUNT NO.

DATE	ITEM	POST. REF.	DEBIT	CREDIT	BALANCE	
					DEBIT	CREDIT

ACCOUNT ACCOUNT NO.

DATE	ITEM	POST. REF.	DEBIT	CREDIT	BALANCE	
					DEBIT	CREDIT

ACCOUNT ACCOUNT NO.

DATE	ITEM	POST. REF.	DEBIT	CREDIT	BALANCE	
					DEBIT	CREDIT

Extra form

ACCOUNT _____ ACCOUNT NO. _____

DATE	ITEM	POST. REF.	DEBIT	CREDIT	BALANCE	
					DEBIT	CREDIT

ACCOUNT _____ ACCOUNT NO. _____

DATE	ITEM	POST. REF.	DEBIT	CREDIT	BALANCE	
					DEBIT	CREDIT

ACCOUNT _____ ACCOUNT NO. _____

DATE	ITEM	POST. REF.	DEBIT	CREDIT	BALANCE	
					DEBIT	CREDIT

ACCOUNT _____ ACCOUNT NO. _____

DATE	ITEM	POST. REF.	DEBIT	CREDIT	BALANCE	
					DEBIT	CREDIT

ACCOUNT _____ ACCOUNT NO. _____

DATE	ITEM	POST. REF.	DEBIT	CREDIT	BALANCE	
					DEBIT	CREDIT

Extra form

Extra form

VENDOR							VENDOR NO.
DATE	ITEM	POST. REF.	DEBIT	CREDIT	CREDIT BALANCE		

ITEM	POST. REF.	DEBIT	CREDIT	DEBIT BALANCE